D0068171

NEW ENGLAND
WALKS

NEW ENGLAND
WALKS

Gary Ferguson

Illustrations and maps by Kent Humphreys
Research coordinated by Jane Ferguson

Fulcrum Publishing
Golden, Colorado

Copyright © 1995 Gary Ferguson
Illustrations and maps by Kent Humphreys
Cover photo copyright © 1995 Henryk T. Kaiser, Stock Imagery

All rights reserved. No part of this book may be reproduced or transmitted in any form or by any means, electronic or mechanical, including photocopying, recording, or by any information storage and retrieval system, without permission in writing from the publisher.

New England Walks provides safety tips about weather and travel, but good decision making and sound judgment are the responsibility of the individual.

Library of Congress Cataloging-in-Publication Data
Ferguson, Gary, 1956–
    New England walks / by Gary Ferguson.
        p.   cm.
    Includes bibliographical references and index.
    ISBN 1-55591-220-6
    1. Hiking—New England—Guidebooks. 2. New England—Description and travel. I. Title.
    GV199.42.N38F46   1995
    796.5'1'0974—dc20   94-38960
                                                             CIP

Printed in the United States of America
0   9   8   7   6   5   4   3   2   1

Fulcrum Publishing
350 Indiana Street, Suite 350
Golden, Colorado 80401-5093

*To Chuck, who taught me that the best views
come to those farthest out on the limb.
Thanks.*

ᐧ Contents ᐧ

Contents

▪ Introduction ▪

Follow any of a thousand threads in the cultural tapestry of America, and sooner or later you'll find yourself in New England. Held in the short swell of land rising from the north shore of Long Island Sound to the chilly blue waters of Passamaquoddy Bay— less than 2 percent of the nation—are the underpinnings of much of our religion, economic structure, politics, art, and literature. As historian Bernard DeVoto wrote in 1932, New England was "the first old civilization, the first permanent civilization in America."

What is perhaps less apparent is the degree to which our ideology was fueled by this landscape—the roll of the Atlantic, the hush of primeval forests, the swell of broad-shouldered mountains. Even the Puritans, whose stern, somber religion demanded that they subdue the wilderness, were dazzled by nature's abundance. John Josselyn was astounded by the great flocks of migrating passenger pigeons in colonial America, which he tells us "had neither beginning or ending, length nor breadth, and so thick that I could see no sun." In 1630 Reverend Higginson confesses that "the abundance of Sea-Fish are almost beyond believing." There were geese, ducks, and turkey too numerous to count, and deer, elk, fox, beaver, otter, martin, and moose. And even though colonial writer Thomas Morton was measuring this plenty according to how it filled basic human needs (in particular, a warm fire and a full belly), his comments were hardly uninspired. "If this land be not riche," he said, "then is the whole world poore."

As New England's struggling population stabilized, and then blossomed through the Revolution, the relationship of some of her people to their natural surroundings began to blossom as well. Ralph Waldo Emerson spent much of his life cultivating the notion that we should establish not just pragmatic, but spiritual ties to the American landscape. He was quick to embrace the transcendental essays of University of Vermont President John Marsh, and wasted no time in building from them his own credo concerning the worth of the wilds. "The lover of nature," he concluded, "is he whose inward and outward senses are still truly adjusted to each other; who has retained the spirit of infancy even into the era of manhood."

Not far away lived a friend and protégé of Emerson's, a man named Henry David Thoreau. Eccentric as Thoreau may have seemed to his neighbors, he minced no words when writing about the profound opportunity for personal satisfaction that awaited him in the forests surrounding Concord. "I went to the woods because I wished to live deliberately, to front only the essential facts of life, and see if I could not learn what it had to teach, and not, when I came to die, discover that I had not lived."

Both Emerson and Thoreau traveled widely through the natural areas of New England—to Mount Monadnock and the summits of the White Mountains, to the thick, dark forests of Maine, to the shimmering waters of Lake Champlain. But they were hardly the only ones seeking personal and creative vision from the landscape. Also making pilgrimages were Henry Wadsworth Longfellow, William Cullen Bryant, Rudyard Kipling, Thornton Wilder, Francis Parkman, Herman Melville, Robert Frost, and Mark Twain. Nathaniel Hawthorne absolutely fell in love with the mountains of New Hampshire, roaming them time and time again to glean material for such works as *The Great Stone Face, The Ambitious Guest,* and *Canterbury Pilgrims.* Appropriately, Hawthorne died at the edge of the high country in 1864, in a small inn on the banks of the Pemigewasset River.

Nor did the grandeur of New England escape the attention of the art world. It was the great work of landscape painter Thomas Cole in New Hampshire's White Mountains that launched the famous Hudson River School. After a grueling climb to the top of Mount Chocorua in 1928, Cole made a telling note in his diary: "With all its beauty the scene was too extended and maplike for the canvas," he wrote. "It was not for sketches that I ascended Chocorua but for thoughts; and for these this was truly the region." Also to the mountains came Frederick Church, Albert Bierstadt, Godfrey Frankenstein, Thomas Doughty, and Asher Durand, to name but a very few.

Introduction

Perhaps the real excitement of New England is that you can still find such rich tapestries of quiet forests, dancing rivers, and untrammeled mountain paths. The walks in this book were chosen not so much for destinations, as for the weave of life found along the way. I fully hope that at least a few of you get so sidetracked in some nook or cranny that you never do reach the turnaround points. Throw a lunch, a pair of binoculars, and a set of guidebooks into your day pack and hit the trail. What happens after that is clearly best left to chance.

To strengthen his case about the virtues of walking, Thoreau once related an anecdote about the English Romantic poet William Wordsworth, a man nearly as dedicated to rambling across the countryside by foot as was Thoreau himself. A traveler, so the story goes, stopped by Wordsworth's house when he was not at home and asked his servant if he could see the poet's study. "Here is his library," she answered, "but his study is out of doors."

As it was in Thoreau's time, the landscape of New England remains one of the finest studies in the world. Abandon the desk and the easy chair, and come see for yourself.

The Coast

The great rhythms of nature, today so dully disregarded, wounded
even, have here their spacious and primeval liberty; cloud and shadow
of cloud, wind and tide, tremor of night and day. Journeying birds alight
here and fly away again all unseen, schools of great fish move beneath
the waves, the surf flings its spray against the sun.

—*Henry Beston*
The Outermost House

Set foot in almost any New England coastal preserve, from
the windblown tip of Cananicut Island to the stark volcanic cliffs
of West Quoddy Head, and you'll discover there a timeless magic—
a spin of rhythms and mysteries unique to the edge of the sea. Here
are soft, crescent beaches and mammoth rock promontories; wave-
worn spits of glacial debris and marshes wrapped in cordgrass;
places where the tide rises 3 or 4 feet with a whisper, and others
where it comes in with a rush, burying headlands 10 times that
high. And everywhere, it seems, are birds—sanderlings, knots,
dowitchers, piping plovers, and sandpipers scurrying along the
sand and mud flats; willets, great blue herons, snowy egrets, and
clapper rails feeding in the salt marshes; and eiders—great rafts of
them—bobbing up and down in the ocean waves.

How incredible it would be to have a high-speed film of the
past 200 million years, the earth's oceans and land masses swirling
and brewing like thunderclouds in a summer storm. When the
North American continent ripped loose from its moorings with two
other continental land masses 150 million years ago, it took with it
chunks of Europe and Africa that would eventually become portions of the upper New England coast. Ever so slowly the mass
drifted westward, finally arriving at its present position 80 million
years later. Great submergences, uplifts, and erosions followed.
Long swells of mountains were created and then destroyed again,
picked apart grain after grain by the patient, probing fingers of
water and wind.

In much more recent times the coast was sculpted and
scoured by at least four periods of advancing glacial ice; the last of
these, known as the Wisconsin Ice Age, peaked about 15,000 to
20,000 years ago. In New England the Wisconsin glaciers reached
about as far south as present-day Long Island and Martha's Vineyard, where they dumped their upland cargo of rocks and gravel

into a sinewy ridge known as a terminal moraine. So big were these ice flows—many more than 5,000 feet thick—that in some places the land sank 200 to 300 feet under their weight.

In most places, the sea did not rush in to fill these newly made lowlands; the amount of water held by these gargantuan Pleistocene Popsicles meant that the ocean along much of New England would have been more than 200 feet lower than it is today. When the climate finally warmed and all that ice began to melt, tremendous rivers of water poured over the land, spreading thick layers of glacial debris and sediment. (This is precisely how the upper reaches of Cape Cod were formed.) As the melt continued, the ocean waters rose higher and higher, submerging much of the northern New England coast in the process. With the weight of all that ice off its back the land mass rebounded and then, like a rubber band stretched past its resting point, resettled once again.

The result of the great uplifts, the outpourings of molten rock, the drift of tectonic plates, and the grind of glaciers was to set the stage for what would become one of the richest braids of life anywhere along the Atlantic. Fine-tuned by climate, currents, and tidal flows, the northern offshore islands evolved into rookeries for seabirds and breeding grounds for seals. The submerged banks from Maine to Cape Cod gave rise to tremendous fish populations. The salt marshes and mudflats of Massachusetts came to sustain flock after flock of wading birds.

Though we'll be taking a closer look at many of these creatures in the walks that follow, perhaps at this point we should yield center stage to New England's most famous, and probably its most representative ocean inhabitant, the American lobster. So abundant were lobster in colonial times that they were considered a trash food, fit for little else but fertilizer and feed for dogs. Even so, beginning with a small fishery at Cape Cod established around 1800, it took less than a century for lobster to be severely depleted throughout New England waters.

Anyone trying to figure out how to eat a lobster for the first time might come to the conclusion that the creature was put together by sheer happenstance. But in fact its design makes perfect sense. The protective shell is made of chiton and lime, fashioned into plates of various shapes and sizes—from a large, single piece covering the back, to a series of flexible sheets that protect the abdomen. This outer skeleton has to be shed ("molted") as the animal grows, a process that occurs about two dozen times over five years (roughly the amount of time needed for a lobster to reach 1 pound). During these molting stages, each of which lasts about two weeks, a lobster will lay low in its ocean burrow until the new shell hardens enough to protect it from predators.

The lobster has 10 legs (its claws are considered modified legs), and moves through the water using small oarlike devices located on the underside of its body. If you look at the claws you'll notice that they are not the same size. The smaller one has sharp teeth, used to cut and rip fish into pieces, while the large one is a crushing claw, employed to smash the shells of mussels and clams. Though a large lobster has few enemies, occasionally it will lose a claw in a fight. No problem. Lost claws, as well as other legs, are replaced over a period of three to four molts.

While a 1-pound lobster is typical dinner fare, that's hardly as big as they get. Capable of living for a 100 years, they can in fact reach the kind of proportions that B-grade monster movies are made of; one specimen caught off the coast of Nova Scotia in 1977 measured 3.5 feet from claw to tail, and weighed in at over 44 pounds! By and large, though, such specimens are rarely encountered. With more than two million traps off the coast of New England alone, few have the chance to grow anywhere close to that size; today a mature adult lobster has only about a 10 percent chance of escaping the dinner table— a statistic that suggests an uncanny ability to maintain populations in the face of heavy predation.

Though most people prize lobster for its taste, James Joyce claimed that French poet and playwright Gerard de Nerval found this hearty crustacean to be an ideal pet. As the story goes, Nerval was spotted one day leading a lobster through Paris' Palais-Royal gardens at the end of a blue silk ribbon. When quizzed about this by a baffled spectator, he informed the fellow rather matter-of-factly that a lobster is no more ridiculous a pet than is a dog. They're peaceful and serious companions, explained Nerval, and they never invade your privacy or nag you by barking. "What's more," he added, "they know the secrets of the sea."

And that, most of us would agree, is something very special indeed.

The Forest

Why should not we, who have renounced the king's authority, have
our national preserves, where no villages need be destroyed, in which
the bear and panther, and some even of the hunter race, may still exist,
and not be "civilized off the face of the earth," ... not for idle sport or
food, but for inspiration and our own true recreation? or shall we, like the
villains, grub them all up, poaching on our own national domains?

—*Henry David Thoreau*
The Maine Woods

Nowhere will you find a more profound testimony to the
healing abilities of nature than in the forests of New England.
Despite nearly 300 years of hard use and abuse, today these
woodlands still weave enchantment across the land—from the
hush of pitch pine groves at Cape Cod to the flutter of sugarbush
in the windswept valleys of northern Vermont.

Long before the Pilgrims landed in Massachusetts in 1620,
explorers from wood-poor Europe stood in awe of these trees.
When Verrazzano arrived at Narragansett Bay in 1524 he found not
tangled thickets of useless, impenetrable wilderness, as is commonly believed, but an open patchwork of robust, towering oaks,
hickories, chestnuts, and scattered pines—a blend that extended
throughout eastern Massachusetts, Rhode Island, and Connecticut. Besides providing good habitat for game, there was abundant
high-grade timber for building lumber, shingles, and firewood,
with more than enough left over to export back across the Atlantic.
Indeed, the first commercial cargo the Pilgrims sent to England
was a ship full of clean, strong clapboard.

On the other hand, the forests in the more northern reaches
of New England were thicker and denser, made up primarily of
conifers, beech, birch, and maple. While these lands were less
appealing for settlement, their commercial possibilities seemed
endless. There were gargantuan white pines from which could be
fashioned one-piece masts for ships of the Royal Navy. Sassafras
was shipped to Europe not only for tea and tonic, but as a highly
touted treatment for syphilis. Sugar maples were there too, not
only for sugar, but for use in crafting tool handles and fine furniture.
Due to their high resistance to rot, cedar groves were especially
prized. Beyond wood products the forests of New England supported an abundance of beaver, fox, lynx, otter, mink, and marten,

all of which provided a strong base for the development of a European fur trade.

Unfortunately, far too often these remarkable forests were treated as if there was no end to them. Virtually all colonial building materials—even roof shingles—were fashioned from sections of only the largest trees, without a single blemish. Smaller or slightly imperfect wood was simply gathered into enormous piles and burned. Agriculture, of course, was of even more consequence, as farmers cleared every beech-maple grove they could get their hands on in order to get at the moist, rich soils that lay beneath. Together the sawmill and the plow changed the face of northern and southern New England in remarkably little time. By 1835, 75 percent of the forested lands of southern and central New England had been cleared; the majority of commercially valuable timber, even in the remote mountains of New Hampshire and Vermont, was gone by 1875. In many places, gone too was the once-plentiful beaver, the wild turkey, and the white-tailed deer. And so today it seems rather close to a miracle that New England still holds so many vital, beautiful forests.

To better understand the composition of these wood-lands, we have to turn back the pages some 12,000 to 20,000 years. This was the close of the ice age, when the mammoth glaciers that had bulldozed their way southward out of Canada, grinding down jagged mountain peaks and scooping out tremendous "U"-shaped valleys, at last began to retreat. Under the warm fingers of the sun they fell back, inch by inch, into the colder regions of the north.

For a long time the thin, cold soils left in the wake of these ice sheets supported nothing but Arctic vegetation. Indeed, had you been able to don your wool underwear and ramble around a bit, you would have found the scene to look much like the Arctic tundra looks today. But as temperatures increased, spruce and then fir began creeping northward through the valleys, slowly pushing the Arctic vegetation higher and higher until it remained only on the tops of the highest northern New England peaks, where it can still be found today. It was only later that hardwoods like aspen and birch were able to gain a roothold, again beginning in the warmer, more protected valleys, and then working their way upslope. These were followed by even warmer climate species, such as maple, oak, and white pine.

In those early days of forest "migration" there was a kind of jostling for position that took place among the various tree species; this eventually resulted in a fairly stable patchwork of oak and hickory in the south, and in the north yellow birch, beech, and sugar maple, along with large pockets of spruce, hemlock, and white pine. Of course even today the distribution of these species follows no distinct line. The rise and fall of mountains, highly variant soils, and the twisted maze of shaded valleys and ravines that cut across this landscape have created a mix of forest that defies easy categorization.

But no matter the exact blend of trees, the beauty these forests bring to the six New England states is immeasurable. This is especially true in autumn, when great clatters of birds can be seen hopscotching along the flyways, and long swells of leaf canopies begin to shimmer with splashes of color so vibrant they seem lit from within. October in New England is as much a feeling as it is a visual sensation—a time when, as the poet Humbert Wolfe once described it, "the air is wild with leaves."

Such dazzling flushes of color are triggered by the combination of shorter days and cooler temperatures. At a certain point cells are activated in the tissues connecting the leaf to the stem; gradually, the moisture and nutrients that flowed into the leaf all summer are choked off. When this happens the chlorophyll, with its overpowering green, begins to break down, revealing other hues that have been there all along. Yellows and oranges, for example, are the result of carotene and xanthophyll pigments suddenly becoming visible.

The magnificent reds, pinks, and even purples we see, however, are the result of a slightly different process. These shades are found only in trees that have large amounts of carbohydrates in their leaves. It's the breaking down of these carbohydrates in the presence of bright sunlight that forms a special red pigment known as *anthocyanin*. (That bright sunlight, incidentally, is a very important part of the equation. Overcast days just before peak color will diminish the intensity of the show.) Do a little pigment mixing, especially of anthocyanin and carotene, and maples, white oak, and sumac let loose with their deepest, most dazzling blush. Eventually, of course, the dried stem breaks loose from the branch and the leaf floats to the forest floor, where it will be broken down to provide nutrients for other plants in springs to come. How many leaves actually fall during a New England autumn? One estimate placed the number at a cool 72 billion bushels.

Fall is a time when deciduous trees shut down for the winter, but when those juices do start flowing again after the first March thaw, another event begins to draw special attention—"sugarin." When a sugar maple reaches maturity, usually in about 40 years, taps are inserted into the trunk through which sap flows drip by drip into attached buckets. This rather watery liquid is then heated to high temperatures in a large steel evaporator pan. Within this pan are a series of compartments through which the sap flows toward a special draw-off valve; at just the right moment it gets poured off as maple syrup. Unfortunately, the amount of sap you collect is hardly the amount of syrup you end up pouring off; it takes about 40 gallons of sap to make a single gallon of syrup. Today Vermont continues to lead the nation in the production of maple syrup, tapping roughly a million trees to produce about 500,000 gallons. (When the Indians showed New Englanders how to tap the sap from maple trees, the newcomers began regular harvesting of it in order to produce sugar, not syrup.)

There was a time in many Vermont villages when the annual sugaring-off was a common social event. Neighbors would gather round while a quantity of syrup was poured off and then simmered in a special pan until it formed a thick, gooey sugar. This was eaten as is, or sometimes dribbled onto pans of packed snow and then wound onto forks or wooden paddles. A tub of sour pickles was always on hand, standing by as an antidote to the incredible sweetness of the main course.

Although there's little left in New England of Longfellow's "forest primeval," the magic remains. It's scattered across the land in a thousand secret nooks and crannies, waiting to be discovered yet again by the next passerby. Certainly there could be no greater priority than the preservation of these woods—both for the sake of the life forms they nourish, as well as for the hope they spark in the human heart.

The Mountains

A people who climb the ridges and sleep under the stars in high
mountain meadows, who enter the forest and scale the peaks, who
explore glaciers and walk ridges buried deep in snow—these people will
give their country some of the indomitable spirit of the mountains.

—William O. Douglas
Of Men and Mountains

Although New England's mountains have been pared by ice,
wind, and water to roughly half their former size, they remain
among the most magnificent of New England's habitats. There are
the smooth, gentle drumlins of the Windham Hills in eastern
Connecticut, and solitary massifs rising high and lonely above the
forested plains of southern New Hampshire. There are the yawning north-south swells of the Green Mountains, the stark profiles
of the Teconics, and the complex metamorphic mishmash of the
White Mountains.

As far as pleasant destinations go, it would be hard not to be
overjoyed with any of these uplands. Visitors in the far north
regularly lose their breath at the grandeur of Maine's Mount
Katahdin; indeed, on certain days this peak takes on a face akin to
what native peoples saw—home of the fierce god Pamola, who, as
one 1880s visitor tells it, is so ferocious "that he can pick up a moose
in one of his claws." At one time trails to the summit of Katahdin
were so rugged that guides told of hikers wearing out the seats of
their pants sliding down them.

From Katahdin you can drift through a long tumble of high,
rolling lake country in southwest Maine, finally reaching the
shoulder of 6,288-foot Mount Washington, in the White Mountains. The thermometer atop this peak has plunged to 50 degrees
below zero, and during certain parts of winter the winds regularly
reach hurricane velocity. In April of 1934 gauges on the summit of
Washington pegged the wind at a phenomenal 231 miles per
hour—the biggest alpine blow recorded anywhere on earth.

Seventy miles to the west of Mount Washington is 4,303-foot
Mount Mansfield, the crowning jewel of the Green Mountains.
The Greens are among the oldest ranges in New England, having
risen from the earth nearly 450 million years ago. The forces of
wind, water, and ice have long been at work on these peaks,
removing several miles of rock since they were first formed—

rounding and sculpting them into the soft profiles you see today. Though gentler in stature, the Green Mountains still exude a striking sense of wildness. Ethan Allen, swearing to maintain the independent nation of Vermont, said he would, if necessary, "retire with the hardy Green Mountain Boys to the desolate Caverns of the [Green] Mountains, and from there wage war with human nature at large!" The Greens are also the home of the legendary French-Canadian creature "loup-garou," a man half changed into a wolf as punishment for some past evil. Though impervious to bullets and blades, some think this wolf-man may have met his demise. After all, it's been quite a few years since any hunters have come wild-eyed into Green Mountain villages, babbling strange tales of coming face to face with a werewolf.

The mountains begin to mellow as they drift toward western Massachusetts, home of the lovely Berkshires. Yet the steep, wooded faces of this range, uncut by a single river, created a formidable barrier to westward passage. (The route that did eventually cut through the Berkshires was along an old Indian path known as the Mohawk Trail; it would become the gateway through which thousands of easterners would pass on their exodus to the American West.) Many a New Englander has fallen head over heels in love with this sublime country, among them Oliver Wendell Holmes, Nathaniel Hawthorne, and Herman Melville, the latter claiming that the roll of the Berkshires sparked memories of ocean waves.

The formation of New England's mountainous regions is remarkably complex; taken together, they can send the most dedicated rock hound into a geological head spin. To give you a better sense for the depth of these tales, let's take a quick look at the development of northern Appalachians, which geologists refer to as the Acadian Mountains.

Long ago, about the time that fish were becoming fish, there was a great series of collisions between three massive continental plates located thousands of miles to the southeast. On the continental plate we call Laurentia, from which North America would be fashioned, the eastern fringes of sedimentary rock were shoved westward for 10 miles with such force that they folded upon each other, layer after layer. The heat and pressure that accompanied these movements was intense enough to change the very nature of the rocks, first melting them, and then recasting them into schist, slate, and gneiss (pronounced "nice").

As the collisions continued, those original rocks were lifted and squeezed back toward the east again. The uplifting, folding, and oozing of molten rocks marked much of the period, with great domes of semimolten gneiss rising to the surface like bubbles in a boiling pot of molasses. On and on went the great uplifts, until the northern Appalachians finally came to rest 50 million years later. Yet even as great mountains are created, they are being destroyed by the forces of erosion. Grain by grain these rugged, soaring peaks were slowly worn into a flat delta, only to be again uplifted and sliced by erosion.

Following this first great mountain-building episode, those three original land masses we mentioned earlier fused into a great supercontinent known as Pangaea, which remained intact for nearly 200 million years. Tremendous forces rose yet again within the earth and tore the continents apart, though along slightly different fracture lines. This is how parts of Europe and Africa ended up welded to our east coast. And then, ever so slowly, America began to drift to the northwest.

It stretches the imagination to think that great continents could go floating around the surface of the earth. But it becomes slightly more believable when you consider that we're standing on less than 20 miles of solid crust, which in turn rests on nearly 4,000 miles of shifting, unstable rock and magma. Proportionately, our solid footing is only half as thick as an eggshell is to the inner portion of the egg! Such movement, in fact, continues to carry us westward at a rate of about 2 inches per year.

So when geologists say that a mountain is 400 million years old, they're not implying that it was sitting where we see it today for that long, but rather that the rocks that formed the range were created at that time by certain processes within the earth. The actual shaping of the New England peaks into the profiles we see is much more the result of erosion. This ranges from tiny refinements made by falling raindrops, to great ravines carved by tumbling streams; from the chiseling of cliff faces by freezing water expanding in the cracks, to mammoth glaciers, enough rocks and gravel clutched in their bellies to gouge and scour 50,000 square miles of land.

Fresh Water

> By such a river it is impossible to believe that one will ever be tired
> or cold. Every sense applauds it. ... Watch its racing current, its steady
> renewal of force: it is transient and eternal. And listen again to its sounds:
> get far enough away so that the noise of falling tons of water does not
> stun the ears, and hear how much is going on underneath—a whole
> symphony of smaller sounds, hiss and splash and gurgle, the small talk
> of side channels, the whisper of blown and scattered spray gathering
> itself and beginning to flow again, secret and invisible, among the wet
> rocks.
>
> *—Wallace Stegner*
> Sound of Mountain Water

Coming to New England from the arid West, I was completely overwhelmed at the abundance of water here: brackish and sweet, cloudy and clear, walking and running across the landscape at every turn of the trail. There are the mammoth lakes—Moosehead, Winnipesaukee, Sebago, and Menphremagog—chopped each spring and fall by winds that stir nutrients and oxygen back into their depths. There are the wide meanderings of the Connecticut River and the wild dance of the Allagash, with 10,000 streams, brooks, and rivulets in between. There are rich, organic ponds and marshes scattered across the countryside in such quantities that it seems as if some torrential rainstorm had let loose and flooded all the lowland basins. And then there are the strange, hauntingly beautiful bogs, where mats of leatherleaf, sphagnum, laurel, and rosemary float on water as acidic as a puddle of vinegar.

This plethora of lakes, rivers, and streams suggests not only an abundance of precipitation in New England, but also serves as a clear reminder of how this landscape was sculpted into the form we see it today. It was water in the form of a 2,000-mile-long ice flow inching out of Canada 15,000 to 20,000 years ago that made sharp uplands smooth, that carved great "U"-shaped valleys and bulldozed the deep basins that would one day become lakes. Even today streams and rivers shape the land by cutting downward into the earth; the future look of these valleys depends on both the speed of the flow, as well as how easily the underlying rock is yielding to the force. Sometimes New England's water is slow and sluggish, murky with tiny particles of fields and mountainsides suspended in its depths. At other times it is fast and furious, probing weak joints and cracks in the bedrock to form cascades, waterfalls, and plunge pools lined with ferns.

For us, however, who can imagine only far shorter spans of time, such geological wizardry is little more than a vague concept, a fantasy of what might have been or will be in the millions of years yet to come. Far more appreciable is the fantastic weave of life nourished by New England waters. The great blue heron, poised on her thin black legs at the edge of a river, waiting for a fish to swim within easy reach. A mated pair of Canada geese, sharing a complicated ritual known as the greeting ceremony, bobbing their long black necks and singing a masterfully orchestrated honking song. A kingfisher perched on a dead snag, about to plunge head first into the still waters to nab a fish with his long, sharp beak. The circling osprey, also fishing, but on the wing, plucking prey with barbed talons. Elsewhere we find muskrat, chowing down on a meal of cattail tubers. And flowers almost beyond belief—the flush of violet in a clump of blue flag iris, the bright yellow of marsh marigolds, the soft ivory clusters of pepperbush.

As you explore these runs of fresh water, watch how every seep of moisture completely alters the life found there. This is, in fact, one of the most remarkable consequences of beaver activity. Not only do their flooded areas sustain them, but myriad other life—swallows, loons, sandpipers, ducks, pond lilies, rushes, sedges, lotus, fish, frogs, newts, and muskrat. Water is truly the magic elixir. And perhaps nowhere is this fact more beautifully revealed than in the folds of New England.

▪ CONNECTICUT ▪

CONNECTICUT

· · ·

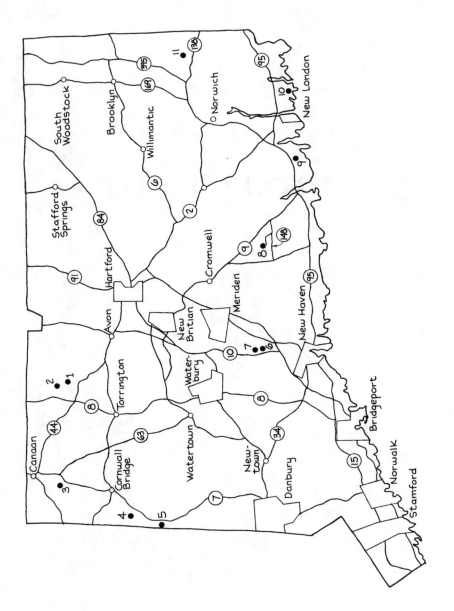

Connecticut

WALK #1—BEAVER SWAMP TRAIL

DISTANCE: 3 miles
ENVIRONMENT: Forest
LOCATION: Peoples State Forest. From the town of Winsted, head east on U.S. Route 44 for approximately 4 miles, and turn left (north) onto Connecticut Route 318. Follow this for 0.8 mile to a stop sign, at the junction of Route 318 and West River Road. Continue straight from this intersection and cross a bridge over the Farmington River; immediately after this bridge, make a left turn onto East River Road. Follow East River Road for 0.7 mile, and turn right into the Peoples State Forest at Greenwoods Road. In 1.4 miles you'll reach our path—the Charles Pack Trail—on the right side of the road; a small parking area is located a short distance past the trailhead, on the left. *Note:* At the time of this writing a new trail guide was being prepared for this walk; stop and pick up a copy from the Stone Museum, on Greenwoods Road.

I wonder if all those schoolchildren and boy scouts and civic groups who purchased and donated these lands to the state in 1924 had any real inkling what a precious gift they were giving to future generations. That this 3,000-acre slice of hardwood forest and marsh, stream and soaring promontory would still be here after some 270 years of hard use, once again rich and full of enchantment, seems nothing short of a miracle. It would be hard to imagine a better testimony to the value Americans have found in nature—to the beauty they have chosen to celebrate in the wild New England woods.

The swampy lowland that forms the centerpiece of this forest ramble has over time been a great many things. When the massive sheets of ice that scoured this region finally began to retreat, some 12,000 to 20,000 years ago, they left in their wake a small lake, dammed on the south side by a thick wall of glacial till. Centuries later, from roughly 2,000 B.C. to 600 A.D., various Native American peoples came to this spot to hunt and to work stone into points. More than a thousand years after that, in the late 1700s, the place rang with the sound of axes, as European settlers busied themselves building great charcoal hearths to make the fuel that would fire the iron foundries of central and western Connecticut. And finally, from 1880 to 1915 this was an agricultural meadow owned by Johann Ullmann, who grew fine fields of hay on these rich glacial soils.

Today this lowland is in the hands—or perhaps we should say paws—of beavers, which for some years now have maintained a carefully regulated wetland filled with a remarkable braid of life. It is a place stitched with red maple, sedge, sensitive fern, cattails, elder, willow, alder, buttonbush, jewelweed, and blue flag; birds include red-winged blackbirds, swamp sparrows, tree swallows, yellow warblers, and yellowthroats. Indeed, here you'll have a chance to see many species of plants and birds you may have never seen before—all thanks to the hard work and tenacity of the beavers.

At just over 0.1 mile, in a quiet cluster of hemlock, yellow poplar, striped maple, and hobblebush, is an intersection with the Agnes Bowen Trail, marked with orange blazes. Continue to follow the yellow blazes of the Charles Pack route, reaching in 0.2 mile a bridge over Beaver Brook. In June much of this area will be dusted with the beautiful white to pinkish blossoms of mountain laurel. Because laurel seeds typically take root on moss beds, the plants are often found growing in old pasture sites like this, where the somewhat sterile, acidic soil promotes the growth of moss over grass. If the laurel is in bloom, note the way the stamens bend backward, their tips tucked into tiny pouches located around the outside edge of the flower. As an insect enters the bloom these stamens often spring free, spraying pollen onto the visitor's back.

After crossing Beaver Brook the trail veers left and makes a short climb up the face of a terrace, and about 0.1 mile later, passes the remains of two large charcoal hearths located on your left about 50 feet off the trail. These will appear as level areas, roughly 30 feet in diameter, encircled by a berm and ditch. Charcoal was produced on many such sites in this area. The procedure involved stacking 30 or so cords of wood, covering the pile with dirt, and then burning it; the finished product was then shipped to iron furnaces in western Connecticut. In the period from the American Revolution to the Civil War the hunger for charcoal was insatiable—a fact that left virtually no valley, hillside, or mountaintop untouched by logging, no matter how steep or inaccessible. Indeed, a hundred years ago the vast majority of the lands in western Connecticut were almost totally bereft of trees.

After passing nice patches of tree clubmoss and Canada mayflower, the latter in spring flying clusters of white, star-shaped flowers, in 0.7 mile the trail passes an old stone foundation. This remnant is from a home thought to have been built sometime before 1806 by a man named Jabez Bacon. Imagine the labor required to quarry these stones from nearby ledges, and then shape and lay them! The port located at the base of the chimney was used for smoking meat.

At just over 0.8 mile the trail crosses the Pack Grove Road (named for Charles Pack, a successful lumberman who donated lands to the Peoples Forest), winds through a forest thick with beech, and then 0.6 mile later crosses Pack Grove Road once again. Shortly afterward the path drifts through a picnic area and reaches the paved Beaver Brook Road. We'll take a left here, following the pavement for 0.75 mile past magnificent stands of white pine and patches of false Solomon's seal, hay-scented fern, and wild oats, and then turn left again onto the Agnes Bowen Trail, marked by orange blazes. Soon the Bowen trail joins the Greenwood Road, which you'll follow to the left for a short distance, and then drops back into the forest again. (This detour, by the way, is thanks to resident beaver, who have managed to raise the level of Beaver Swamp considerably over the past five years.)

Once back in the woods the trail winds through fine stands of yellow birch and hemlock before joining the Charles Pack Trail again at 2.9 miles, where you'll make a right turn to get back to your car. This latter stretch of pathway is a good place to look for Indian cucumber, a 1- to 2-foot-tall plant with an unbranched stem sporting two sets of whorled leaves; in May and early June several nodding, greenish-yellow flowers will be found hanging from the center of the upper whorl. True to its name, the root of this plant does indeed taste somewhat like a cucumber, and for centuries was a favorite food of native people and settlers alike. Naturalist Ernest Thompson Seton tells an intriguing tale about this plant. In the days of long ago, he explains, whenever Indians gathered for a council, the little people of the forest, known as the Pukwudjies, would do the same. These gatherings of the little people were always lighthearted—most taking on the atmosphere of a fair—and it was common for vendors to set up tiny umbrellas (the whorled leaves of this plant), and then sit beneath them throughout the day selling slices of cucumber. When it came time to go home the vendors would bury the cucumbers in the ground, using the leafy umbrella to mark the spot.

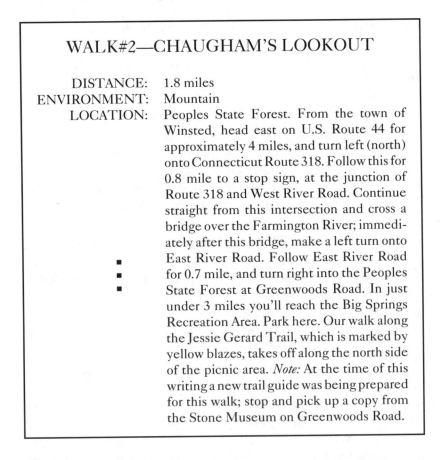

WALK#2—CHAUGHAM'S LOOKOUT

DISTANCE: 1.8 miles
ENVIRONMENT: Mountain
LOCATION: Peoples State Forest. From the town of Winsted, head east on U.S. Route 44 for approximately 4 miles, and turn left (north) onto Connecticut Route 318. Follow this for 0.8 mile to a stop sign, at the junction of Route 318 and West River Road. Continue straight from this intersection and cross a bridge over the Farmington River; immediately after this bridge, make a left turn onto East River Road. Follow East River Road for 0.7 mile, and turn right into the Peoples State Forest at Greenwoods Road. In just under 3 miles you'll reach the Big Springs Recreation Area. Park here. Our walk along the Jessie Gerard Trail, which is marked by yellow blazes, takes off along the north side of the picnic area. *Note:* At the time of this writing a new trail guide was being prepared for this walk; stop and pick up a copy from the Stone Museum on Greenwoods Road.

The initial 1,000 feet or so of this walk follows the historic Ore Road, so named because for nearly a hundred years, beginning with the Revolutionary War, iron was carried from the Salisbury furnaces over these hills and then either to the Newgate prison where inmates made it into nails, or to the armory at Springfield where it was turned into cannons. (During the Revolution northwest Connecticut was the principal site of cannon manufacturing, some 250 being turned out over the course of the war. Likewise, captured enemy cannon were brought back to Salisbury and Lakeville to be rebored, so that they could then be used with American munitions.)

Keeping fire in the region's 50 or so iron furnaces required tremendous amounts of charcoal, a significant amount of which was produced from trees harvested in what is now People's State Forest. Thus far 60 hearth sites have been identified in this area; one of these—the remains of which look like a large tent platform surrounded by a berm and ditch—can be seen about 500 feet into this walk.

Our ramble begins in what were the initial holdings of the Peoples Forest, passing beautiful stands of hemlock and white pine, as well as trailside gardens of sarsaparilla, Canada mayflower, and hay-scented fern. The two large boulders you'll pass early on in this walk are glacial erratics, carried to this location in the arms of mammoth ice flows that poured south out of Canada, finally retreating some 12,000 to 20,000 years ago. Just about the time these hushed woodlands have lulled you into a fine stupor, at 0.6 mile the path reaches an extraordinary rocky perch, hanging high above the dancing waters of the Farmington River. Visible upstream is the town of Riverton, home of the famous Hitchcock Chair Company, and beyond that a dizzy line of hills tumbling into southwest Massachusetts.

Besides the splendid views, our promontory is backed by lovely clusters of mountain laurel, their branches in June dripping with white to pinkish blooms, as well as wind-tossed huddles of red and chestnut oak.

From here our path heads southward, skirting the ledge through hemlock, laurel, and mayflower, reaching at just under 1 mile a second and equally magnificent rocky perch—this one more southerly in its orientation, offering sweeping views past the forested hills near Ski Sundown winter sports area, nearly to the city of Hartford. Right below you is a pair of stone abutments on either side of the Farmington River. These are the remains of a rather impressive footbridge constructed by the Civilian Conservation Corps in 1935; unfortunately, in the spring following its completion, it was destroyed by an ice flow.

This particular promontory is known as Chaugham's Lookout (some forest maps incorrectly assign this name to the perch just to the north). The Chaugham in question was a rather famous man—or infamous, depending on who you ask—of Spanish and Narragansett blood who arrived in this area around 1740. He eloped with young Molly Barber of Wethersfield, and eventually founded a settlement known as Barkhamsted Lighthouse, on the Farmington River just south of where you now stand. The couple had eight children, six of whom stayed in the area. In time, Barkhamsted Lighthouse would become one of the most ethnically diverse communities of its size in the nation; through his children's marriages Chaugham's extended family came to include Native Americans of various tribes, Creole settlers from the south, and even freed slaves. The "Lighthouse" part of the settlement's name, incidentally, referred to the fact that stage drivers on the Farmington River Turnpike would often use the lights of the Chaugham household as a marker, announcing to their passengers that they were at that point just 5 miles out of New Hartford.

This promontory came to be known as Chaugham's Lookout during the 1740s, when a group of ruffians living nearby got into the habit of making drunken forays into New Hartford to raise Cain with the settlers. Chaugham usually found out about these schemes ahead of time, and alerted the settlers of the town by building signal fires atop this rocky ledge.

From this point the path drops sharply down a series of stone slabs, and soon thereafter meets the Robert Ross Trail, which is marked by blue blazes. Turn left onto the Ross Trail and follow it to the end of Warner Road. Walk Warner Road out to the Greenwoods Road and turn left, back to the trailhead at Big Springs.

WALK #3—RAND'S VIEW

DISTANCE: 2.4 miles
ENVIRONMENT: Mountain
LOCATION: The Nature Conservancy. From U.S. Highway 7 in the northwest corner of Connecticut, turn east outside the town of Falls Village onto State Road 126 North; 0.6 mile from this turnoff you'll come to a stop sign. Turn left onto Point of Rocks Road, and continue 0.1 mile to Water Street, which takes off to the right, passing beneath a railroad bridge. In 0.4 mile Water Street makes a turn to the left across a bridge over the Housatonic River. Once across the bridge, stay right, and in 0.4 mile you'll turn left onto Sugar Hill Road. The trailhead and parking area are at the end of Sugar Hill Road, 0.9 mile from this last turn.

Despite a rather sharp climb toward the end of the walk, this 1.2 miles of former Appalachian Trail is a pure delight. Along the way you'll find a quiet mix of deciduous forest, fern gardens, and cool, tumbling water, ending in a yawning mountain view that, on a clear day, reaches all the way to the soft green shoulders of Mount Greylock in northwestern Massachusetts. Some of the climbing sections can be slippery; make sure your shoes are up to the task.

Our path begins on a small dirt road that starts as a private driveway, framed on both sides by that classic signature of early New England agriculture, the stone fence. While you may wonder why in the world someone would build stone fences through the woods, the truth is that when these stones were first piled here this was field, not forest.

Early farmers of the region cleared the land and then erected not stone, but wooden fences around each and every pasture. Of course this penchant for fences consumed enormous amounts of wood (an oak fence might have to be rebuilt every seven years), and caused the English, who used no fences, to question our sanity at erecting so many ugly enclosures around private property. By the early 1800s good wood was disappearing at an alarming rate, causing many farmers to simply pile field stones against their existing fences. In time the wooden portions of those fences— including a line of cap rails that likely topped the one you're walking along—rotted away, leaving only the stones. As the fields were abandoned various shrubs grew up around the lines, followed by the kind of forest you see here today.

In 0.3 mile we'll take off to the right along a small footpath. Look for hickory, birch, and an occasional white pine, growing from a forest floor carpeted with purple trillium, geranium, rue anemone, and miterwort. Miterwort, which in May is covered with a stalk of tiny, intricate white flowers, derives its name from the fact that its fruits resemble the peaked hat, or miter, commonly worn by bishops.

The major uphill portion of this trek begins at about 0.75 mile, alongside a series of stone and timber steps that trace the course of a small veil of falling water. Hemlock and yellow birch are both common here. Yellow birch, with its shiny yellow to silver bark and rough, double-toothed leaves, is commercially very valuable, used in great quantities for both lumber and furniture. Hemlock, on the other hand, an evergreen sporting needles colored dark green above with two white bands beneath, does well in cool, shaded places like this. Hemlock bark contains significant quantities of tannin, which has long been used to produce finished leather goods. To this end hemlocks were once cut down in New England by the thousands simply for their bark, the rest of the course, durable wood left to rot in the forest.

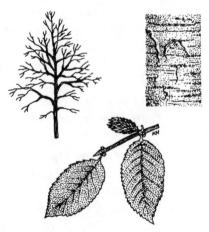

Yellow Birch

In 0.9 mile, very close to the crest of Barrack Matiff, are marker signs for a Nature Conservancy area, the 310-acre Patricia Winter Woodland–Hamlet Hill Preserve. This is one of more than 60 sanctuaries owned by the Connecticut Chapter of the Nature Conservancy, perhaps the finest, most capable preservation organization in the United States today. In Connecticut alone the Conservancy has protected more than 13,000 precious acres. The Patricia Winter Woodland is now slated for sale to the National Park Service.

Continue along a stream lined with hemlocks and an occasional Jack-in-the-pulpit. The fleshy, peppery taproots of Jack-in-the-pulpit were once enjoyed by native peoples, a fact that led to the common name of "Indian turnip." At 1.3 miles meet the Appalachian Trail. Going right leads in 0.7 mile to Prospect Mountain. We'll continue straight, though, following the blue-blazed trail for 500 feet to Rand's View.

Rand's View is a delightful place, a collage of rolling pasture and thick, wild forest melting into the high, hazy lines of the Berkshires. Though striking in the fall, to me this perch feels like a summer kind of place—somewhere to be when the sun is walking, not running, across the sky, pouring out enough warmth to send body and soul into a fine and certain stupor.

WALK #4—POND MOUNTAIN NATURAL AREA

DISTANCE:	2.2 miles
ENVIRONMENT:	Mountain
LOCATION:	Pond Mountain Trust, in cooperation with the Connecticut Chapter of the Nature Conservancy. From the intersection of U.S. Route 7 and Connecticut Route 341 in the village of Kent, head west on Route 341 for approximately 2 miles, and turn right onto Macedonia Brook Road. Follow this for 0.9 mile to Fuller Mountain Road, and turn right; proceed for another 0.9 mile to the parking area for Pond Mountain Natural Area, located on the right side of the road.

Traveling the back roads of western Connecticut, one soon loses count of the natural surprises that lie tucked among the feet and shoulders of these crumpled hills. Pond Mountain is among the best of those surprises—a hushed, restive place, at various times of the day dripping with the sounds of tree frogs and hermit thrush, with yellow warblers, scarlet tanagers, and red-eyed vireos also close at hand.

We'll begin our walk by following the Entry Trail for 0.2 mile and then taking a right onto the Mountain Trail, marked by yellow diamond blazes. At the intersection with the Escarpment Trail bear right, climbing over 0.4 mile to the summit of Pond Mountain. In places this ascent requires some rather hardy climbing. The good news is that the trail not only winds through a lovely forest of striped, red, and sugar maples, hemlock, yellow poplar, ironwood, paper and yellow birch, black cherry, chinkapin, scrub, and white oak, but ends at a rocky promontory offering views rarely seen by those who remain anchored to the pavement. On a clear day you can see all the way into the Catskill Mountains of New York. All things considered, the lands tumbling from this summit look better than they have for centuries. Once again forests lay on hills that were repeatedly stripped of timber—beech, oak, and hickory harvested for lumber and firewood; the bark of hemlock and oak used to tan leather; and for a hundred years, beginning with the Revolutionary War, nearly every kind of hardwood imaginable taken from lands lying to the north and east to make charcoal for the firing of iron smelters. There is not only beauty to be gleaned from this vista, but also a comforting sense of nature's remarkable patience and tenacity.

As you begin making your way back down the trail again, take time to notice the lovely trailside gardens—tufts of blueberry crouched near the top of the mountain, yielding to strawberry, wild geranium, sarsaparilla, hobblebush, trillium, Canada mayflower, and bedstraw as the path descends. Bedstraw is also known as "cleavers" and "catchweed"—names that allude to the bristly fruits that tend to attach themselves to the pant legs of passing humans and the fur of animals. As is true for many of the plants along this path, bedstraw has a long history of medicinal use. The shoots are loaded with vitamin C, and thus were once a common treatment for scurvy, while the powdered roots were routinely applied to wounds in order to stop bleeding and promote healing. Also in this forest is another plant with notable medicinal values—the Japanese barberry. Barberries in general have for centuries been used as a source of berberine, a substance not only effective in treating diarrhea, but also valuable as a wash to treat sore eyes. The next time you buy a bottle of eye drops to "get the red out," take a look at the label; more than likely you'll find berberine listed as a primary ingredient.

At the next trail junction turn right onto the Escarpment Trail—a broad pathway cradled by hemlock, sugar maple, and paper birch. Soon you'll reach an intersection with the Red Gate Trail; turn left, and in 40 yards or so turn left again onto the Pond Trail (Fuller Pond will now be on your right). The thick weave of ferns that comprise the bulk of the understory here lends a certain enchantment to this portion of our walk—a hint of mystical days of long ago, when fern spore was thought to render people invisible. Such dense fern growth is actually somewhat unnatural—the result of fire suppression—and not nearly as beneficial to wildlife as the more varied understory that tends to build in the years following a burn. At 1.9 miles is the junction with the Entry Trail; turn left and follow it back to the parking area, keeping your eyes and ears open for hairy woodpeckers, black-capped chickadees, robins, and brown creepers.

The existence of this beautiful preserve is thanks to the generosity of former Kent resident Myra Hopson, who wished it to be maintained in a natural state for scientific, educational, and cultural use. All of us must make a special effort to treat this area with respect—especially considering the limited staffing resources of the Pond Mountain Trust—so that it can remain open to delight and inspire visitors for generations to come. Please make a special point to stay on the trails. Refrain from picking plants. And carry out whatever litter you happen to find.

WALK #5—HOUSATONIC RIVER

DISTANCE:	2 miles
ENVIRONMENT:	Fresh Water
LOCATION:	Connecticut State and National Park Service lands. Head south out of the village of Kent, on U.S. Highway 7. At the stoplight at Bulls Bridge, turn west on Bulls Bridge Road. You'll pass through a covered wooden bridge, and a few yards farther, cross an open bridge over the Housatonic River. The trailhead and parking area will be on your left on the far side of this second bridge.

Nowhere in the state of Connecticut is the walking more pleasant than along the beautiful Housatonic. In this single mile of river, which is but a tiny slice of the Housatonic's 130-mile run to Long Island Sound, is a wonderful array of sights and sounds. One minute the river is roiling and splashing in great nosedives over sheer marble ledges and chutes, and the next, it becomes a sheet of clear, unbroken water, slipping past huddles of hemlock and red oak with barely a whisper.

The walk to Ten Mile River will also let you rub elbows with a wonderful mix of hardwoods, conifers, and ground covers. In the latter category, keep an eye out along the first several hundred yards for ferns, Solomon's seal, and round-lobed hepatica. This latter plant is easily recognized by its leaves, each of which contains three shamrock-shaped lobes that appear fused together at the base. The shape of this plant, said the botanist of long ago who named it, resembled the shape of the human liver. Thus, according to the *Doctrine of Signatures*—a theory that said all plants contain a sign of the treatment for which they were intended—he gave this plant the genus name of *Hepaticus*, derived from the Greek word for liver.

The Solomon's seal, with its smooth, lance-shaped leaves and delicate green to ivory flower bells, takes its name from an entirely different, though equally imaginative comparison. When the leaf of this plant is broken from the root stalk, the resulting scar is supposed to look like the official seal of King Solomon. Later in the year the plant forms blue-black berries, resembling small grapes.

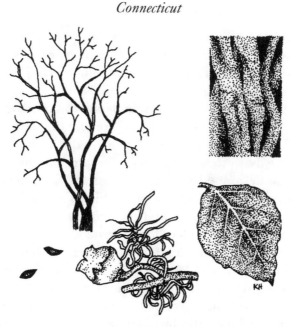

Witch Hazel

Interspersed with hemlock, sugar maple, and red oak in the first 0.4 mile are several clumps of witch hazel. Herbalists know this tree for the strong astringent that can be made from its leaves and smooth brown bark. But medicine is hardly the only story the witch hazel has to tell. The young shoots of this tree have long been a favorite of dowsers for making *devining rods*. (Devining rods are the forked branches that dowsers claim can be used to locate underground water; more optimistic practitioners suggest that they can also be used to locate precious metals.) Over the centuries dowsing has had no shortage of skeptics. Sixteenth-century religious leaders like Martin Luther were emphatically opposed to the idea, some going so far as to suggest that it wasn't water that pulled the rod toward the earth, but the hands of Satan! Nevertheless, even today there are thousands of otherwise conservative farmers who wouldn't think of digging a well without the advice of a dowser.

If you're taking this walk in the fall, don't be surprised if a witch hazel seed or two comes flying your way. When the hazel's fruit capsules open, they propel their cargo like bursts of gunfire, some seeds landing 25 feet or more from the parent tree.

In just under 0.5 mile the trail forks. Our walk follows the path on the left, along the blazes of the Appalachian Trail. Watch the ground here for red columbine, ginger, violet, and that delicate orchid known as pink lady's slipper. Besides being lovely to look at, the pink lady's slipper was long used to treat nervous conditions ranging from insomnia to epilepsy. Please note that this plant does not propagate well, and should not be picked.

At 0.6 mile is a fine view of the Housatonic River. The fact that the Housatonic has cut a beautiful gorge in this particular place is no accident. Underlying this corridor are thick layers of marble that yield easily to the erosive lick of water. The high hills and plateaus that lie immediately to the east and west, on the other hand, are made up of rock like granite, which is much more difficult to erode. The Housatonic poked and probed, and, like all rivers, ended up working the path of least resistance.

At 0.9 mile you'll descend through a cleared area with lovely spatters of dogwood and Japanese honeysuckle. Our turnaround point is a short distance past this, on the far side of a footbridge crossing the Ten Mile River. To stand on this footbridge is to immerse yourself in an absolute symphony of rushing water—the Ten Mile fast-stepping out of the high, wild hills of eastern New York, and the Housatonic rolling strong and fast across the smooth gray bedrock of the Marble Valley.

Pink Lady's Slipper

WALK #6—HEZEKIAH'S KNOB

DISTANCE: 1.7 miles
ENVIRONMENT: Mountain
LOCATION: Sleeping Giant State Park. Heading north on State Highway 10 (Whitney Avenue) from Hamden, turn right onto Mount Carmel Avenue. Go past the Mount Carmel entrance to Sleeping Giant State Park to Chestnut Lane, which is located approximately 2.1 miles from Whitney Avenue, and turn left. Our trailhead is 0.8 mile up this road on the left side, in the bend of a sharp right turn. Begin walking on the trail blazed with white squares.

With all due respect to Hobbomock, that evil deity of local Indian lore who collapsed into a deep sleep here under the weight of a spell placed on him by good spirit Kietan, I must say that geologists have an equally engaging, if only slightly less fanciful tale to tell of the origin of the sleeping giant. According to them, hot igneous rock streamed up through fissures cut deep within a bed of 300-million-year-old sandstone, pushing the sedimentary rock upward until it formed a series of rounded ridge lines, rising and falling like waves frozen against the ancient sky. Quick to yield to the forces of wind, water, and ice, this relatively soft sandstone was eroded away, leaving the hard igneous outcroppings that today make up the giant's legs, arms, body, and head.

Whatever creation story you prefer, there can be no argument that Sleeping Giant is one of south-central Connecticut's greatest treasures, a tumble of high, windswept knobs and ridges—places to put into fresh perspective the hodgepodge of traffic and sirens and barking dogs lying far below. Our walk begins on a trail marked by white square blazes, taking off through mats of white wood and large-leafed asters, wild oats, Canada mayflower, blue violets, round-lobed hepatica, and Solomon's seal.

Solomon's seal gets its name from the fact that the scar left on the rhizome when the old leaf stalk breaks away resembles the seal of that wise old King Solomon. What's more, some early herbalists claimed that the good king (and respected magician) somehow managed to

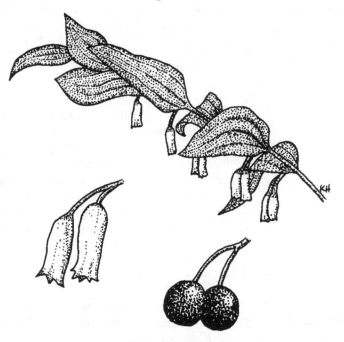

Solomon's Seal

put that little seal on the roots by his own hand, in an effort to guide us to the plant's medicinal values. Well, who knows? Although centuries-old claims that Solomon's seal can stop severe bleeding may be somewhat overoptimistic, the roots of the plant do contain allantoin, which is a substance used even today for treating cuts and abrasions. Solomon's seal has bell-shaped blooms that hang down from the leaf axils; the somewhat similar false Solomon's seal, which also grows here, bears its flowers in white clusters at the tip of the stem.

We'll get down to the business of climbing fairly quickly. Take your time moving up these steep rock stair treads, noting not only the beautiful redcedars beside you, but the increasingly fine views opening up behind you to the west. At just over 0.4 mile you'll cross a blue-blazed trail, and just beyond, the open, rocky perch of Hezekiah's Knob. From here you can look west and see the stone observation tower located on the left hip of the giant—at 739 feet, the highest point in the park. The tower was a WPA project completed in 1939, and it immediately became a major tourist attraction. From this perch there are also sweeping views to the south and southeast, into a quilt of streets and factories and neighborhoods, much of it well wrapped in deciduous forest.

Less than 10 miles to the south and barely out of sight is the city of New Haven, home of the hallowed halls of Yale. The act of incorporation for Yale College, by the way, was an unusually strong commitment to education—one that grew to exempt all students not only from the military, but also from taxes.

A particularly interesting way to date Yale is to look at a sampling of its early rules and customs. There was a time, for example, when scholars in their chambers were required to speak only Latin. Instructors were to call an undergraduate by his surname "unless he be the son of a noble man or knight's eldest son." Newtonian science began filtering into the classrooms in the 1730s, yet it seems there was a bit of a lag before acquiring scientific equipment became much of a priority. Former student Lyman Beecher writes that in 1793 there was "a four-foot telescope, all rusty: nobody ever looked through it, and if they did, not to edification."

From Hezekiah's Knob we'll take a right (heading north) on the blue-blazed trail through a mix of chestnut, red and white oak, witch hazel, maple, and mountain laurel, the latter growing especially thick at 0.6 mile. Cross a green trail at 0.7 mile, and 0.1 mile later, take a right on the red trail. (If you'd like to sample another view first, this time of the more rugged country to the northeast, go a short distance past the red trail intersection and up a small hill to a ridge-top overlook.) The red trail will hit a violet trail at 1.1 miles, where you'll take another right. Follow this 0.6 mile, staying left at the fork that occurs not far from the parking area.

WALK #7—CASCADE GORGE

DISTANCE:	1.7 miles
ENVIRONMENT:	Forest
LOCATION:	Sleeping Giant State Park. Heading north on State Highway 10 (Whitney Avenue) from Hamden, proceed past Mount Carmel Avenue (this is the southern entrance to Sleeping Giant), and turn right 0.55 mile later, onto Tuttle Avenue. Our parking area and trailhead is 1.1 miles down Tuttle Avenue, on the right.

To the Indians of this area, the giant known as Hobbomock was no pleasant fellow. His name was tantamount to death and disease, and his presence was considered akin to the color black and the cold, angry fury of the north wind. Some young warriors went through great rituals of physical hardship for this god, including drinking false white hellebore juice (also used to poison arrow tips). The general idea was to use such an ordeal for making a covenant with Hobbomock, whereby he would protect you from death by the arrows and knives of your enemies.

It was after Hobbomock had gone on a particularly nasty rampage against his human subjects, during which he thundered his foot down upon the earth 14 miles northeast of here and changed the entire course of the Connecticut River, that the good spirit of Kietan came to the rescue. She placed a special spell on Hobbomock that caused him to grow very tired, and finally collapse into a deep sleep. And thus this park is distinguished by the profile of a sleeping giant. On this walk we'll climb to the old boy's left thigh, where a beautiful tumble of hemlock, beech, and maple has taken root. The high point of the park occurs at the giant's left hip, which rises to an elevation of 739 feet, and is located approximately 0.75 mile southwest of our turnaround point.

Throughout this walk we'll be following a north-south trail blazed with red circles, winding along a forest floor sprinkled with tufts of mountain laurel, white wood asters, Canada

False Solomon's Seal

mayflower, violets, false Solomon's seal, sarsaparilla, trillium, and jewelweed. If you've visited the other side of the park, near the main entrance, you may recall that it contained fewer ground plants; this is because those south-facing slopes receive more sunlight, which tends to leave less moisture in the soil to support the growth of such vegetation. (Species like hickories actually prefer their feet to be a bit drier; thus you'll find more of them on the other side of the park.)

By 0.2 mile you'll have gained a high ledge from which you can look down into a wonderful gorge. In many places this shady, twisted ravine is lined with beautiful huddles of hemlock, the dark lace of their branches lending an almost mystical quality to the scene. You'll find in this park several variations of the Canadian hemlocks that cradle this gorge. (Botanists have identified nearly 100 varieties of this tree throughout North America, many of which show up as dwarf, shrublike plants or as braids of thin branches running across the forest floor.) Unfortunately, many of the hemlocks at Sleeping Giant are now infested by the hemlock woolly adelgid, an insect thought to have been introduced from Asia in 1924. These insects suck sap from young twigs, resulting in the loss of new shoots and needles; defoliation and death of the tree can occur within a few years. Evidence of hemlock woolly adelgid infestation shows up as white cottony sacs at the base of the needles, looking rather like the tips of cotton swabs.

At 0.5 mile we'll cross a flat section of pathway through an open, sunlit hollow with chestnut oaks, red maple, Christmas fern, round-lobed hepatica, wood sorrel, beech, and ground cedar. From here the trail climbs again, though much more gently, to a great talus pile. This massive jumble of gray rocks contains pieces of igneous basalt, a material that was forced up as molten material through cracks in the sandstone some 200 million years ago. Unlike sandstone, however, this basalt is quite hard, having easily survived thorough scouring by ice, wind, and rain. Among these rocks look for clumps of the delightful little plant known as herb Robert, which produces attractive pink flowers from May through October. Just who the "Robert" is in herb Robert is a matter of debate. Popular candidates, however, include a 12th-century Duke of Normandy, a French monk, and Robert Goodfellow, also known as Robin

Hood. The plant was long used to treat a severe skin disease known as erysipelas, and, thanks in large part to its tannin content, made an effective compress with which to stop bleeding.

Just past this talus pile, in a garden of jewelweed, violet, wood aster, and Christmas fern, our path crosses first a lavender trail and, a few yards later, a blue trail. If you continue straight for another 100 yards the route will make a left turn into a sheltered nook cradling a slice of swamp habitat. There's little water visible here, though the variety and density of plant life is remarkable; look for clumps of sweet pepperbush, chestnut, sassafras, and sweet birch. It's the oil of sweet birch, incidentally, obtained from a distillation of the twigs and bark of young trees, that once gave wintergreen flavor to hundreds of candies and medicines. Unfortunately, the fact that it took nearly a hundred trees to produce 1 quart of wintergreen oil did not bode well for the survival of the species. (Wintergreen oil is now synthesized from wood alcohol and salicylic acid.) In addition, it was the sap of the sweet birch, gathered with taps in early spring, that was fermented and turned into birch beer.

Nearby are pockets of cinnamon, sensitive, and royal ferns. This latter plant, often growing 4 to 6 feet tall and looking somewhat like a locust tree, is considered by many to be the most beautiful of all the ferns.

WALK #8—COCKAPONSET STATE FOREST

DISTANCE: 2.4 miles
ENVIRONMENT: Forest
LOCATION: From State Highway 9, head west on State Highway 148 for 1.6 miles, and turn right. Follow this road for another 1.6 miles and turn left, into the Pataconk Lake State Recreation Area. Proceed for 0.4 mile, past the southern end of the reservoir, to a set of parking areas, one on either side of the road. You'll find our blue-blazed Cockaponset Trail just past these parking lots, heading off to the right (northwest).

Walking New England's woodlands often lulls me into aimless, ambling thoughts about all manner of things. On the backside of this particular loop, amid quiet groves of beech, red maple, hickory, and yellow poplar, I ended up wondering how a small state like Connecticut could possibly have been responsible for such a long line of significant world "firsts." These range from the somewhat trivial, such as the first Graham cracker, Frisbee, can opener, corkscrew, and lollipop (named for a winning racehorse), to others that were rather profound. Not only was the planet Mars officially discovered by Connecticut professor Asaph Hall in 1877, but the first documented meteor in the United States hit the dirt in Weston. The man behind the cotton gin, Eli Whitney, was from New Haven. Likewise the first model of the steamboat, the first American bicycle, the first helicopter, nuclear submarine, commercial gramophone, FM radio station, etc., all came from the people of Connecticut.

Of course mixed in with all that were a few questionable achievements. The first American witch to be executed met her maker at the end of a rope in Hartford. The first blue law was enacted here, consisting of a 1647 prohibition against "social smoking." Such things point to the fact that, at least in Puritan times, breaches of behavior here weren't taken lightly. Consider these items from the Code of 1650: First-time burglars had a letter "B" branded on their foreheads. (Unless, of course, you robbed on the Sabbath, in which case you got your ear cut off to boot.) If caught cursing you were required to hand over 10 shillings, or, if short the cash, off you went for a couple of hours in the stocks. As of 1650 you could also no longer play that wild and crazy game known as shuffleboard, during which "much precious time is spent unfruitfully and much waste of wind and beer occasioned." Getting caught would cost you 5 shillings, or if you owned the public house where the game was being played, 20 shillings. Shuffleboard, then, was obviously quite an evil, seeing that it cost some men twice as much as a good curse.

But on with our walk. While you're hardly going to be the first to traverse this popular trail along Pataconk Reservoir, hitting it on a cool morning in late autumn will offer you a few stretches where it just might seem that way. At just over 0.1 mile the Cockaponset Trail meets our path, the Pataconk Trail, which takes off to the right along the lake shore, marked by a series of blue blazes with

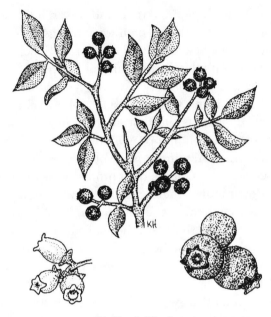

Highbush Blueberry

red dots in the middle. Once past a string of picnic tables things quiet down considerably, the waterside path winding past jumbles of rocks and clumps of beech, maple, highbush blueberry, and clubmoss. At 0.4 mile is a small inlet, which you may see peppered with a blanket of yellow pond lilies. The seeds of this beautiful plant were once toasted like popcorn, while the tubers can be either roasted or boiled for a food that tastes rather like a potato. (An odd, and in no way appetizing, addendum to this bit of folklore claims that the roots of yellow pond lily can be steeped in milk and set out to kill cockroaches, while the smoke from burning them will send crickets off to new chirping grounds.)

In 0.5 mile you'll cross a very quiet, brackish-looking brook sprinkled with water striders. These amazing water walkers stay afloat on six legs, each of which is covered with water-repellent hairs. Only four of these legs are out to the side of the insect; the other two are underneath the front of the body, and serve both for grabbing onto things and as oars with which to paddle. Some researchers maintain that water striders can communicate with each other by tapping out messages with their legs. If you're tempted to submerge a strider to see what happens, don't. The poor fellow will likely be unable to break through the surface again, and will quickly drown.

In 1.2 miles you'll reach Pataconk Brook, an absolutely delightful forest stream tumbling head over heels across a braid of rocks. It's here you'll find our blue-blazed path, the Cockaponset Trail, coming in from the left. This is the path we'll take back to the parking area, a quiet but rather sublime route crossing the wooded crown of a 500-foot hummock. The latter portion of this stretch, a lowland where beech and maple have attained significant size, is especially appealing—a kind of forest cathedral that on spring and summer mornings is filled with an impressive array of birdsong.

WALK #9—BRIDE BROOK

DISTANCE: 1.6 miles
ENVIRONMENT: Coast
LOCATION: Rocky Neck State Park. From Interstate 95, take exit 72 to State Highway 156 and head east, following the signs into Rocky Neck State Park. Once inside the park, follow the day use road for just over 1.5 miles. Just past a bridge crossing Bride Brook is a large parking area on the right. Our trail takes off from the far northwest corner of this parking lot, near a group of picnic tables, and is marked by a wooden post with a red blaze on it.

Belted Kingfisher

The deep woods of Rocky Neck, or the thick carpets of marsh grass cradling the weary windings of Bride Brook, are worlds away from the jumble of volleyballs and bikinis and baking bodies typically strewn across this beautiful pocket beach. *(Pocket beach,* by the way, is the geological term used to describe sandy, crescent-shaped beaches framed on either side by a prominent headland. Rocky Neck is one of the finest examples of a pocket beach in the state.) When you've heard too many rock-and-roll countdowns or gotten one too many whiffs of suntan oil, slip up this gentle trail and hang out for a while with the bitterns, snowy egrets, cormorants, and kingfishers.

Just a few steps down the path you'll cross a rich tidal flowage; immediately to your right, on the top of a large elevated platform, is a beautiful osprey nest. Osprey are renowned for building substantial nests, the male collecting most of the twigs and small branches that form the exterior of the structure, while the female gathers the mosses, grass, and bark used for the lining. Not long ago, high concentrations of DDT in the fish that osprey feed on nearly brought the demise of these magnificent birds. The poison altered the shell structure of the egg, causing it to break when the female tried to incubate it. This was particularly trouble-some given that, unlike some other species, osprey do not lay a new clutch of eggs if their first one is destroyed.

If the tide happens to be out during your visit, take a look in these pockets of mud for tracks of raccoon, whose forefoot prints are easily recognizable by their resemblance to the human hand.

On the far side of this marsh the path plunges back into a tangle of red maple, highbush blueberry, and black oak, as well as an abundance of what for over three-quarters of a century has been Connecticut's state flower, the mountain laurel. Mountain laurel sometimes grows in extremely dense clusters (some locals call these "laurel hells"), and may reach heights of 12 to 15 feet. In winter these thickets are frequented by deer, which browse on the leaves. They also provide excellent protection for a variety of small mammals.

At 0.25 mile is a cross trail, where you should take the fainter, white-blazed right branch toward the edge of Bride Brook. From here the path winds along the water's edge, past thick clusters of sweet pepperbush, bittersweet, and sassafras. Pause at breaks in the vegetation to make careful scans of Bride

Snowy Egret

Brook. Here you may see a marsh hawk, or even a belted kingfisher cruising the stream banks looking for fish. Also common is the snowy egret, spindly legs flashing as it sprints through the shallows in a mad dash for minnows.

One of the best view spots is found at just under 0.5 mile, at a place where the trail seems to dwindle under an onslaught of shrubs. You can either turn around here, or pick your way along the path another 0.3 mile to a beautiful garden of cinnamon, hay-scented, and Christmas ferns, framed on the east by dense thickets of witch hazel, winterberry, dogwood, hickory, bittersweet, and rose. If you do follow this path to, or even beyond the fern garden mentioned above, you'll be rewarded with a rich feeling of wildness—a sense that you've penetrated some kind of inner sanctum of peace and quiet.

Unfortunately, settlement along this coast has not always come with a strong ethic for the careful conservation of natural resources. The wolf disappeared early on, especially once the legislature in 1647 approved a bounty of 10 shillings; bobcat and eastern mountain lion weren't far behind. Likewise, the abundance of shellfish began to thin in places by the middle of the 17th century. (At one point the town fathers of Fair Haven issued a complete ban on the harvest of oysters, exceptions to be made for pregnant women who had sudden cravings for them.) Snowy egrets, hunted for their feathers, disappeared for a time in the late 1800s. Writing about the effects of war on the countryside in *The Red Badge of Courage,* author Stephen Crane said it was a surprise "that Nature had gone tranquilly on with her golden process in the midst of so much devilment." Perhaps much the same could be said for times of peace.

Fortunately, today there is strong movement toward a better conservation ethic. Once-absent or endangered species such as great blue herons, peregrine falcons, barn owls, and long-eared owls, for example, are slowly increasing their numbers.

It's good to know the calm of places like this, to feel your imagination opening up again at the sight of soaring red-tailed hawks or at the soft flash of a startled white-tailed deer. Perhaps that's a secret for keeping the human heart from growing harder: to preserve these kinds of connections, to make ample room for them in our daily lives.

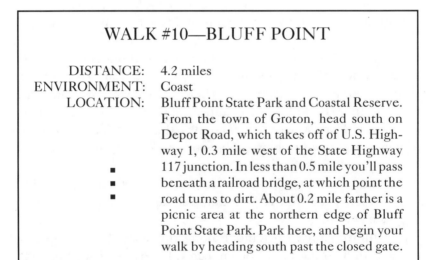

WALK #10—BLUFF POINT

DISTANCE: 4.2 miles
ENVIRONMENT: Coast
LOCATION: Bluff Point State Park and Coastal Reserve. From the town of Groton, head south on Depot Road, which takes off of U.S. Highway 1, 0.3 mile west of the State Highway 117 junction. In less than 0.5 mile you'll pass beneath a railroad bridge, at which point the road turns to dirt. About 0.2 mile farther is a picnic area at the northern edge of Bluff Point State Park. Park here, and begin your walk by heading south past the closed gate.

Connecticut

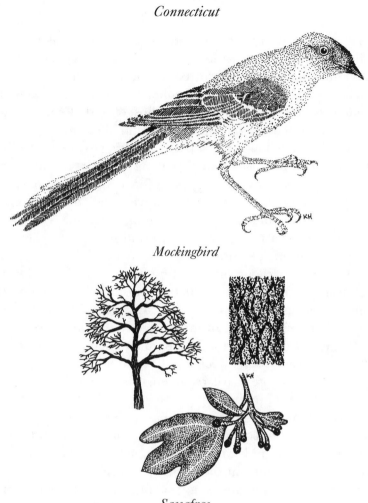

Mockingbird

Sassafras

Bluff Point is an especially beautiful slice of southern New England. Other than a little noise pollution from the airport across the Poquonock River, these 800 acres form one of the few pristine slices of real estate on the entire Connecticut coast. Stitched across the length and breadth of the preserve is a delightful mix of vines, hardwoods, and conifers, framed to the south by a shoreline peppered with great and little blue herons, mute swans, snowy egrets, buffleheads, and mallards. During winter you'll also find scaups here by the thousands; it's great fun to watch these birds making dive after dive in search of crabs and barnacles, a feast often accompanied by a fresh sea lettuce salad.

One-tenth mile into the walk is a fork in the road. We'll be returning on the left branch, but for now stay to the right, past fine mats of strawberry and Canada mayflower. A short walk away is a small meadow dappled with oaks, cradled on three sides by an almost impenetrable weave of pepperbush, bittersweet, green-brier, honeysuckle, grape, black raspberry, and rose. These tangles provide excellent food and cover for a host of birds; keep eyes and ears peeled for mockingbirds, catbirds, and bluebirds.

At 0.5 mile follow a grassy path branching to the right off the main road. This less-used trail runs along the quiet reaches of the Poquonock River, through a young forest of cherry, oak, and redcedar; if you're quiet you may spot white-tailed deer nibbling on the bark, buds, or leaves of these young trees.

This area is also a good place to find sassafras, a plant that produces some of its leathery leaves in the shape of mittens. Sassafras root has a long history of medicinal use for everything from purifying the blood to curing syphilis; for a time during the colonial era it was second only to tobacco as an export. As late as the 1950s sassafras was used as an antiseptic in dentistry, as well as for flavoring everything from toothpaste to root beer. Unfortunately, 25 years ago the USDA decided that the safrole contained in sassafras oil was a potential carcinogen, thus bringing to an end its use in commercial products.

A break in the vegetation occurs at 0.75 mile, offering lovely views of the Poquonock River estuary. In just another 0.1 mile a small path to the right leads to a grassy glade on the river shore— a perfect place for watching the swans, herons, and other waterbirds that reside here during various times of the year. The nesting boxes you see on short posts are for wood ducks, while the taller platforms are for osprey.

In another 0.1 mile veer to the left, following a well-worn path back to the main road, where you'll turn right. At this point views of the coastline begin to open up, and in 1.6 miles, just past a boardwalk leading out to Bluff Point Beach, the trail splits. Stay right, and climb up onto the headland of Bluff Point itself. From here you can see Fishers Island ahead and slightly to the left, and, still farther to the left, Rhode Island's Watch Hill, which was used as an observation point by soldiers during the Civil War.

Continue to make your way eastward around this small peninsula of gneiss rock, past beach plum, salt spray rose, bayberry, and beach pea. At 1.7 miles take the right fork in the road, which leads along the rocky beach. In 2.1 miles you'll join a well-used, grassy roadway. Make a gentle climb past a small trail taking off to the right, to an intersection at 2.8 miles. Turn right here, and then stay to the left. This path winds gently through a pleasant blend of forest and birdsong, finally arriving back at the main road, where you'll make one last right turn toward the parking lot.

I found it easy to imagine the first Puritan settlers standing here in 1636, marveling at this rich tapestry—a far cry not only from places they knew on the other side of the Atlantic, but also from the Massachusetts colonies they abandoned to take up new lives in the Connecticut River Valley. Besides trees of tremendous stature there were birds and mammals beyond counting: wild turkeys, quail, partridge, otter, mink, deer, fox, and mountain lion. Even wolves were fairly abundant.

With fearless Puritan Thomas Hooker in the lead, the "Newtown Contingent" had loaded guns, cooking pots, and 160 head of cattle and moved out of Cambridge on a 100-mile trek into this new wilderness. Like thousands of restless Americans in later years, Hooker and his followers found the Massachusetts Colony too crowded for their liking. "My people must leave," Hooker explained in his petition to the Massachusetts court; "it is the strong bent of their spirits to move thither."

WALK #11—RHODODENDRON SANCTUARY

DISTANCE:	2 miles
ENVIRONMENT:	Fresh Water
LOCATION:	The Mount Misery unit of the Pachaug State Forest. From State Highway 138 east of Voluntown, head north on State Highway 49. In 0.6 mile, on the left, is our entrance to the state forest. Immediately after you make this turn is a fork; stay right. Follow signs for the public use area until, at 0.9 mile, you arrive on the east side of a large playing field. Park here. The trail takes off from the north side of the field, beside a small sign marking the Rhododendron Sanctuary.

Rhododendron

Of all the members of the heath family—a clan that includes blueberry, cranberry, and huckleberry—there is none more striking than the great *Rhododendron maximum.* In this rich bog of the Pachaug State Forest the rhododendron reaches its greatest potential, a tangle of sprawling, free-form trunks corkscrewing 20 feet into the air, flying rosettes of thick, leathery leaves and, in early July, delicate puffs of pink and white flowers.

Though beautiful, the tendency of rhododendrons to grow in vast, almost impenetrable thickets has sometimes led to the plant being reduced to "nuisance" status. Furthermore, the leaves and flowers of all rhododendrons and azaleas are poisonous. (Even honey made from the flowers is toxic.) Despite its drawbacks, though, early settlers had at least a modest appreciation for rhododendron, since they could use the amount of curl in the plant's evergreen leaves as a guide to air temperature. Below about 60 degrees Fahrenheit, leaves will droop in distinct increments that roughly correspond to 10-degree drops in the temperature; by the time the thermometer hits a point just above freezing, each displays a distinct backward curl.

Our walk begins in a pleasant, open forest of hemlock, white pine, and an occasional red or white oak. In 0.1 mile you'll begin a short descent, marked at first by a loose weave of highbush blueberry, starflower, and Canada mayflower, giving way as the ground becomes wetter to cinnamon ferns, sweet pepperbush, rhododendron, Atlantic white cedar, and skunk cabbage. Atlantic white cedar was especially valued by early New England settlers, who used it for everything from floors to roof shingles to pipe organs. In fact, so prized is this durable wood that as standing timber became scarce, bogs were often dredged to extract dead cedars, many of which had been submerged for decades.

Continue to follow the trail deeper and deeper into a wonderful rhododendron-cedar jungle. The bird life is especially interesting, and you should have no problem seeing (or at least hearing) Canada and Audubon's warblers, red-breasted nuthatches, brown creepers, and, in the very tops of trees, olive-sided flycatchers.

In less than 0.2 mile is a trail heading off to the left—this is a return path for the loop trail you're on now. Continue straight. From here on there's no real path, just blazes to guide you through

Olive-sided Flycatcher

Brown Creeper

a very wet, spongy bog. With appropriate footwear you'll surely enjoy this delightful amble through a dark, delicate world of cedar and rhododendron thickets, with occasional flushes of moss, arrowleaf, sweet gale, and pepperbush.

Another resident you'll spot here is the pitcher plant. The leaves of the pitcher are joined in such a way that rainwater collects at the base, forming a small reservoir. An insect comes along and is drawn in for a closer look by a series of brightly colored veins and nectar glands located along the upper edges of the leaves. Once inside, though, a fine mat of downward curving hairs makes it nearly impossible for the bug to crawl out again. Furthermore, beneath these hairs is yet another trap, this one consisting of layers of sticky, loose cells that break away and adhere to the insect's feet as it tries to make a break for freedom. Eventually the tired, hapless victim falls into the pool of water and drowns. Using digestive enzymes produced during certain months of the year, the pitcher plant then slowly breaks the insect's body down to release the bounty of nutrients stored there. Indigestible pieces of the insect are collected in a narrow stalk at the base of the plant.

Curiously, there's a small moth (*Exyria rolandiana*) that actually lays her eggs on the inside of pitcher plant leaves; once caterpillars hatch in the spring they distribute themselves, feeding on plant material that grows along the inside of the fluted leaves. This is low-maintenance living at its best. The only spinning the caterpillar has to do is to throw up a couple lines across the opening of the plant to keep from being eaten by other visitors.

One-tenth mile after leaving the nature trail is a "T" intersection at a small road. Turn left, continuing to follow the trail (which soon leaves this road) until you reach a dirt road near the campground entrance. Turn left at this second road, following it back to the parking area.

▪ RHODE ISLAND ▪

RHODE ISLAND
. . .

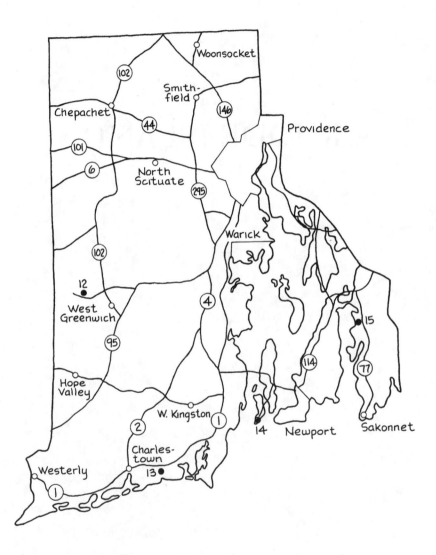

Woonsocket
(102)
Smith-
field
(146)
Chepachet
Providence
(44)
(101)
(6)
North
Scituate
(295)
(102)
Warick
12
4
West
Greenwich
15
(95)
114
77
Hope
Valley
W. Kingston
2
1
14
Newport
Sakonnet
Charles-
town
Westerly
13
1

Rhode Island

WALK #12—RATTLESNAKE LEDGE

DISTANCE: 1.9 miles

ENVIRONMENT: Mountain

LOCATION: Wickaboxet State Forest. From Interstate 95 in Rhode Island, head northwest on State Highway 102. In 3.4 miles you'll come to Plain Meeting House Road; turn left. In 3 miles, on the right side of the road, is the small parking area and trailhead.

Wickaboxet (a Narragansett Indian word) was Rhode Island's first state forest; today it remains a quiet, untrammeled mix of rocky ledges and rolling hills cloaked in varying measures of pine and deciduous woods. While you may see some weekend activity at Rattlesnake Ledge itself (the face is popular with beginning climbers), the tree-lined roadways that meander beyond are washed with little more than the sounds of wind and birdsong, along with the occasional scolding of nervous red squirrels.

Depending on what time of year you visit, the fringe of roadside vegetation just beyond the parking lot can in itself be a small feast for the eyes. Here are the ivory blooms of Canada mayflower, starflower, and strawberry, lightly seasoned with a sprinkling of Rhode Island's state flower, the blue violet. The leaves of the common blue violet, incidentally, are extremely high in vitamins A and C and were, in some parts of the east, common fare as salads or cooked greens. (A couple of old folk remedies actually recommend them for measles.) The root of a close relative, the garden violet, has a long history of use by herbalists in treating respiratory ailments.

Forty yards from the parking area, turn left onto a small, grassy roadway climbing gently up a hill forested with white pine and red

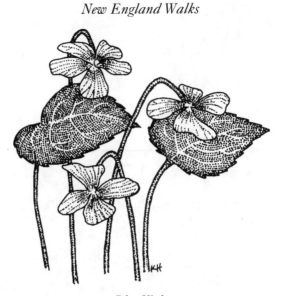

Blue Violet

oak. Watch the roadside for clusters of ground cedar, a plant that looks like an elf's version of a Christmas tree plantation. Also here are birdfoot violets, so named for the plant's leaves, which are clustered in the shape of a bird's foot. Unlike the blue violets you saw in the moist ground near the beginning of this walk, birdfoots like drier, sandier soils. Interestingly, the five petals of these blooms often come in two colors—an upper pair of deep purple, and then three lower petals in a light lavender. This striking combination has led some nature writers to refer to the birdfoot as the most beautiful violet in the world.

Continue past clusters of blueberry, and, at 0.5 mile, a huddle of bigtooth aspen on the right. The leaves of aspen will shimmer in the slightest puff of air. This phenomenon was once credited to the belief that aspen was used for Christ's cross; so tragic was this event that it caused all other aspens to tremble forever after. A more pragmatic explanation is that the leaves are flat and extremely supple at the point where they join the stems; this causes them to quake in breezes that humans can't even feel.

At about 0.6 mile turn back on a road coming in from the right, and then, immediately afterward, turn left at a "Y" intersection. This stretch of the walk is much drier than where you began. Here you'll find a loosely woven forest of pitch pine, which is an irregularly shaped tree with three needles and furrowed, dark gray bark. Pitch pine derives its name from high concentrations of resin

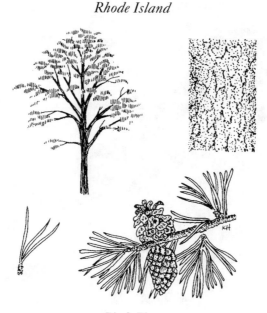

Pitch Pine

in the bark—so high, in fact, that colonists used to fasten the knots to poles for use as torches. Great quantities of pitch pine were used during the 1600s and 1700s as a source of turpentine and tar. Because both these products were needed to maintain sailing fleets, pitch pines were protected under a set of "no cut" laws handed down from the king. Though such regulations were rarely adhered to or enforced, they stayed on the books right up until the American Revolution.

Pass a smattering of sassafras at 0.9 mile, just before turning right and descending a small hill. Long before the arrival of the Pilgrims, the discovery of sassafras in New England was touted by politicians as a commodity that could help sustain colonial expansion in the Americas. At the time the tree was valued not only for flavoring and perfume, but as a treatment for syphilis.

Soon the road makes another right, and, at approximately 1.25 miles, crosses a faint "T" intersection. Just past this intersection you'll see Rattlesnake Ledge on the right. Make your way past a mixed deciduous forest to the base of the ledge. This is a good place to see several types of birds, including northern orioles, black-capped chicadees, mourning doves, and white-breasted nuthatches. On the far right side of the rock mass is a fairly easy trail up Rattlesnake Ledge, the top of which affords wonderful views to the south.

Northern Oriole

It was the timber rattlesnake that lent its name to this rocky perch. Connoisseurs of small birds, squirrels, and mice, timber rattlers were once extremely common here. In fact, throughout most of the 1700s groups of men would head out to these ledges every spring and fall for "snake hunts," during which the poor creatures were killed by the hundreds. Today timber rattlers are quite rare (in fact, it's illegal to kill them), and should pose no danger to you.

The rolling landscape before you was forested until the first half of the 1700s, when farms began spreading across the countryside. Besides cattle and sheep, turkeys were also a popular stock. Turned into pasture with the cattle, turkeys got nicely plump simply by feasting on the chestnuts that at the time were found in nearly every nook and cranny of southern New England. When the chestnut blight wiped out this source of food in the early 20th century, wild turkeys had to be satisfied with acorns and beechnuts. The combination of tired farm soil and growing job opportunities in nearby cities led to many farms being abandoned in the 1800s; the forest, ever on the march, wasted no time in reclaiming them.

WALK #13—TRUSTOM POND

DISTANCE: 1.9 miles

ENVIRONMENT: Coast

LOCATION: Trustom Pond National Wildlife Refuge. From the intersection of State Highway 2 and U.S. Highway 1 near Charleston, head east on Highway 1 for 3.7 miles, and turn right (south) onto the Moonstone Beach Road. Proceed down this road for 1.1 miles, and then make a right onto Matunuck School Road. The parking area and trailhead for the refuge is 0.7 mile down this road, on the left.

Despite development that has nearly overwhelmed the southern New England coast, the state of Rhode Island still retains a couple of natural jewels perfect for slow, sweet saunters during virtually any month of the year. It seems somehow appropriate that the state founded by Roger Williams—one of very few New England leaders who genuinely respected other cultures ("Nature knows no difference between European and American [Indian]," he once said)—today has a place like Trustom Pond, the management of which reflects some measure of respect and admiration for the vast underpinnings of nature.

Our trail takes off from the far side of the parking area, leading quickly to an interpretive display that will tell you about both the natural and cultural history of this area. We'll be following the trail marked by a sign displaying the profile of a hiker. At a "T" intersection not far from these interpretive panels you'll take a right, and immediately afterward, a left, into an open field of alfalfa, flushed with the whistles of meadowlarks. The females of this species weave beautiful dome-shaped grass nests in the hollow of small depressions on the ground. This preference for ground floor living, often in farmers' fields, leaves meadowlarks more vulnerable than most birds to trampling and predators.

At the south end of these fields is a good example of how nature would manage things if left to its own devices. Shadbush, honeysuckle, viburnum, blueberry, and raspberry are all doing their best to lay rights to this sandy, acidic soil. The greenery grows

Sweet Pepperbush

steadily more intense, and by 0.3 mile you'll be totally immersed in beautiful thickets of cherry, scrub oak, red maple, grape, apple, and arrowwood. Like most of Trustom Pond, this habitat has no shortage of bird life, including orioles, robins, towhees, catbirds, brown thrashers, and sparrows.

At 0.7 mile is a "T" intersection. Take a left here, following a narrow peninsula of land out to Osprey Point. At the tip of this peninsula, wrapped in a blanket of pepperbush and framed by spartina grass, is a small observation tower surrounded on three sides by the brackish waters of Trustom Pond. A long, narrow barrier beach completely separates this pond from Block Island Sound, although each spring during high water refuge managers cut a small channel through the sand to help replenish nutrients in the pond.

Of course the birds available for your viewing depends on what time of year you visit. Safe bets are mute swans, Canada geese, teals, pintails, mallards, wood ducks, terns, cormorants, egrets, and great blue herons. True to the name of Osprey Point, you'll also have a good chance of seeing one of these graceful raptors scanning the pond for a fresh fish dinner; a short distance away, red-tailed hawks will be perusing the meadows for mice.

On your return, stay to the left at the first intersection you come to, following the western half of the loop trail back to the parking area. Here again is a marvelous variety of plant communities, brimming with everything from catbrier and scrub oak to fox grape and Austrian pine.

WALK #14—BEAVERTAIL STATE PARK

DISTANCE: 1.5 miles
ENVIRONMENT: Coast
LOCATION: Bay Island Park System. From State Highway 138 South (Wolcott Street) beside the Jamestown docks, go approximately 0.5 mile and turn right. This leads to Beavertail Road, which will take you directly into Beavertail State Park. Once inside the park, continue around the tip of the peninsula past the lighthouse, and park at parking lot number 3. Begin walking back south along the rocky shoreline toward the lighthouse.

If you're the kind of person who relishes a surging sea, the somber song of the foghorn, and the sight of terns spinning cartwheels in the salt air, then Beavertail is sure to satisfy. Although there are easier footpaths farther inland, this particular walk is best suited to those willing to work their way along the braid of sod cliffs and somewhat precarious bedrock ledges that rise and fall along the outer perimeter of the park; if possible, plan to take a little extra time for exploring the shallow tidal pools and inlets you'll find along the way.

A short distance south of the parking area is the Beavertail Light, constructed in 1749 as the third lighthouse in New England, and the fourth to be erected anywhere in America. There's no question that this celebrated sentinel has seen its share of excitement. It was burned by the British in 1775, and then rebuilt 11 years later on funds approved by President George Washington. The light keeper's dwelling collapsed under strong winds in 1815, was swept out to sea by spring ice flows on the Providence River in 1875, and damaged once again during a hurricane in the fall of 1938. It was this 1938 hurricane, by the way, that exposed the foundation of the original 1749 tower, which you can see just south of the current lighthouse.

The Egyptians were among the first to make wide use of signaling ships with lights, relying on fires set atop special towers. Curiously, the Egyptians were also responsible for building what is thought to be the tallest lighthouse ever; constructed around 250 B.C. the "Pharos of Alexandria" stood more than 400 feet high, and was used off and on to guide ships for nearly 1,500 years.

Well before there were any guiding lights in this particular region, the seaman William Kidd, or, as you may know him, Captain Kidd, made a call to see his friend Thomas Paine. Aware that the captain had been declared a pirate by the English government (somewhat unjustly, some still maintain), Paine tried to dissuade Kidd from making his planned landing in Boston the following day. Unfortunately, Kidd dismissed the warning, and upon his landing was immediately nabbed, shipped back to England, and hanged. Hardly was the poor old pirate cold in his grave before people started writing tales and songs about him. One of these ditties, titled "The Ballad of Captain Kidd," was sung by schoolchildren on both sides of the Atlantic for years.

Make your way around the tip of the island past tufts of English plantain and pasture rose, toward the more protected eastern flank of the peninsula. In winter a remarkable variety of seabirds can be found on this more protected side of the island, including scoters, eiders, brants, and scaups. Walking northward, immediately below you will be an abundance of two common intertidal plants. The first is bladder rockweed (sometimes called bladder wrack), easily identified by the pairs of air bladders attached to its fronds. With these floats the plant can stay nearer the surface of the water where the sunlight is stronger, thereby producing more food. The one drawback to this adaptation is that the air pods tend to act as handles for the

Lesser Scaup

surf, which sometimes grabs with enough force to rip the plant from its moorings. To compensate, bladder rockweed grows fewer air chambers in exposed, rough-water sites than it does in more protected locations.

The other common resident here is Irish moss, a beautiful, multibranched red to purple algae that often forms thick, dense mats along the low tide line. This is as tough a species as can be found on the Atlantic coast, able to withstand the assaults of the strongest waves. With the possible exception of the blue mussel, Irish moss, once established, will ward off invasion by virtually all competitors. Irish moss is the source of carragheen, a substance used for everything from a stabilizer for salad dressings and chocolate milk, to a thickening for paints, pies, and toothpaste.

Three-tenths mile into the walk are lovely spatters of yellow buttercups, as well as tufts of horsetail and redcedar. Up ahead is a small inlet, which at low tide is lined with long piles of blue mussel shells. To say that blue mussels are prolific is an understatement; a single female may spawn more than 10 million eggs! Such reproductive strategies are essential, considering that mussels in all stages of development are prey to a host of creatures, including starfish and crabs.

The larvae of mussels settle onto the sea floor at the will of the waves. Then during the summer months they migrate up the tidal zone with the aid of a special "foot," eventually fastening themselves to the surface of a shoreline rock, using protein threads as tough and resilient as any synthetic fiber. If the rock the mussel chooses proves to be in a bad location (not enough food, for instance), it can easily detach itself from its lifelines and move to a better one nearby.

At about 0.6 mile, near a small fresh-water rivulet, is a tall wooden post on your right. Proceed up the shoreline as far as you wish, but on your return trip head east at this post on a grassy pathway back to the entrance road. You'll find a wonderful array of bird life on this part of the walk, including flickers, sparrows, meadowlarks, and robins. What a delight to hear their morning and evening songfests, floating out against the slow, soothing drum of ocean waves.

WALK #15—EMILIE RUECKER WILDLIFE REFUGE

DISTANCE:	1.4 miles
ENVIRONMENT:	Coast
LOCATION:	From the intersection of state highways 77 and 177 in Tiverton, head south on Connecticut Route 77 for 1.7 miles to Seapowet Avenue, which takes off from the right (west) side of the road. The parking area and trailhead are 0.25 mile down Seapowet Avenue, on the right.

Given the right location, it's amazing how much natural beauty can be folded into just 50 acres. And Emilie Ruecker's farm, which she donated to the Massachusetts Audubon Society in 1965, is definitely the right location. Besides being a haven for well over 100 species of birds, there are beautiful wildflowers here, wrapping the land in splashes of color from spring to fall.

Begin your walk by heading north along the Yellow Trail, past lovely mats of cultivated lily of the valley. Though this hearty plant was brought over from Europe to grace American gardens, it wasted no time breaking free from such confines to colonize the surrounding countryside. For centuries the white, heavily perfumed flowers have symbolized purity, a notion that eventually led to their use in bridal bouquets. This link to purity is also reflected in another common nickname, "our-lady's-tears," which is a reference to the Virgin Mary. Although normally considered poisonous, extracts of the plant were long used by folk healers to strengthen the heartbeat, as well as to ease the discomfort of gout.

The Yellow Trail continues past clusters of pine, honeysuckle, and spruce; keep an ear cocked for northern orioles, cardinals, hermit thrushes, Carolina wrens, and cedar waxwings. Cedar waxwings, with their wiry-sounding song of *seeee*, are an extremely social lot, and in late summer come together in great berry brigades that scour the countryside for edible fruits. Adults have a special pouch in their throat that allows them to store up to a couple dozen small berries, carry them back to the nest, and then

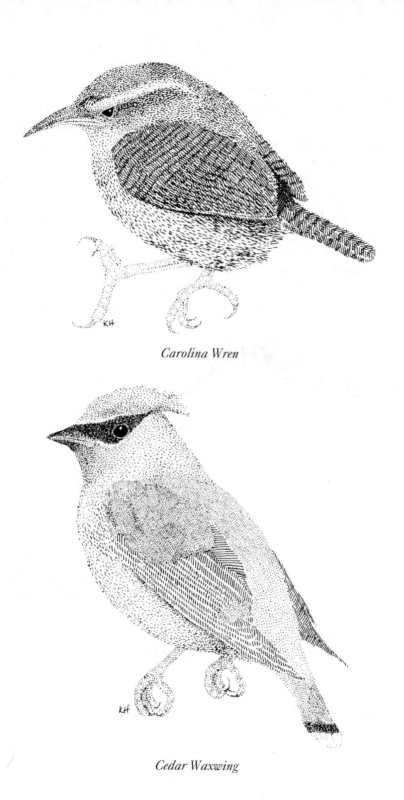

Carolina Wren

Cedar Waxwing

regurgitate them one at a time into the mouths of hungry young-sters. One of the more curious behaviors of cedar waxwings is seen when several of the birds line up on a tree branch or fence rail, and begin passing berries down the row; the game ends when one of the birds decides to eat the hand-off.

Turn left at the Blue Trail and then almost immediately take another left, past black cherry trees, Canada mayflower, and starflower. This path will cross a bridge at 0.17 mile. If you stay to the right you'll move counterclockwise around a small peninsula jutting into the Sakonnet River—much of it covered with thickets of ground juniper, bayberry, and shadbush. (The name shadbush, incidentally, refers to the fact that clusters of delicate white flowers bloom in the spring about the time that shad are swimming upstream to spawn.) As you make your way

Black-crowned Night Heron

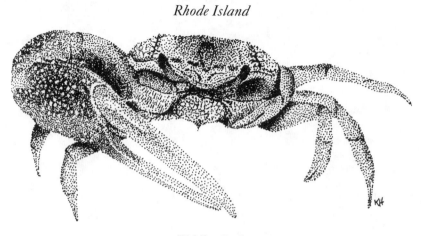

Fiddler Crab

westward along this peninsula keep your eyes open for the glossy ibis, black-crowned night heron, great and little blue heron, and snowy egret. Like many of the more striking waterbirds, snowy egrets almost went extinct during the last half of the 19th century, killed off by the thousands to obtain their feathers for use as decorations in women's hats.

When you get back to the Yellow Trail, take a left, and loop clockwise around another small peninsula, this one rimmed by cordgrass, rushes, spike grass, seaside goldenrod, and saltwort. Besides clams and mussels, there's an abundance of fiddler crabs rushing back and forth across these flats, each with a single large claw held aloft, the scene looking rather like a convention of lunatic bass players.

Leave the shore and head back south along the Yellow Trail. In open, grassy areas keep your eyes out for the beautiful swamp buttercup. Soon after you complete the loop and begin heading south on the main stem of the Yellow Trail again, you'll see a red-blazed path taking off to the left. Passing by a beautiful cluster of mature sugar maples, the Red Trail sinks deeper and deeper into a hushed woodland of alder, arrowwood viburnum, oak, and hickory—a great place to see or hear woodcocks, olive-sided flycatchers, redstarts, and yellow-rumped warblers.

At 1.4 miles is an intersection; continue straight along a faint trail back to the parking area. (The left branch will take you back to Seapowet Avenue, at a point just east of the trailhead.)

▪ MASSACHUSETTS ▪

MASSACHUSETTS

· · ·

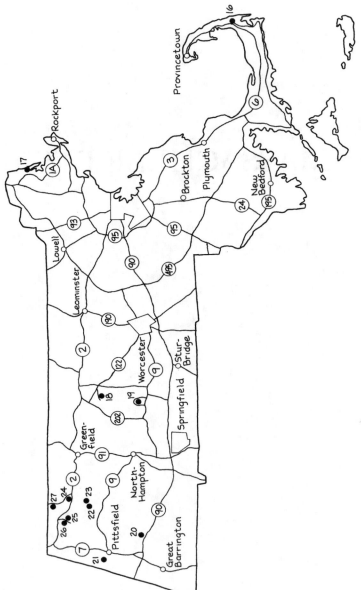

Massachusetts

WALK #16—FORT HILL–RED MAPLE SWAMP

DISTANCE:	2 miles
ENVIRONMENT:	Coast
LOCATION:	Cape Cod National Seashore, Massachusetts. From the Orleans Rotary on U.S. Highway 6, continue north on Highway 6 for approximately 2 miles to Governor Prince Road, and turn right. Park at the first parking lot on the left, just across the road from the Penniman House historic site. You'll find our trail behind the Penniman house, taking off on the right side of the barn.

> With the landless gull, that at sunset folds her wings and is rocked to sleep between billows; so at nightfall, the Nantucketer, out of sight of land, furls his sails, and lays him to his rest, while under his very pillow rush herds of walruses and whales.
>
> —*Herman Melville*
> Moby Dick

Long before Edward Penniman, whose stately 1868 house stands at the beginning of our walk, left Eastham at the tender age of 11 to seek a life on whaling ships, southeast New England had established itself as one of the premier deepwater whaling centers of the world. Crews from this region would literally roam the globe in search of whales, often making a spring to autumn run behind mass migrations stretching all the way from Brazil to Greenland. Of special value to New England whalers were the sperm whales, much coveted for the rich pools of *spermaceti* in their heads. Spermaceti was a kind of waxy oil that, besides being used in lamps, was added to tallow to make longer burning, nearly smokeless candles. What's more, the ivory teeth found in the lower jaw of the sperm whale were highly valued for use in scrimshaw.

Once a whaling crew sighted a whale, one of several small boats were quickly lowered off the mother ship. Into this craft climbed six hearty men, none of whom wasted any time laying his muscled arms to the oars, every mighty sweep pushing them closer and closer to a sounding whale. Once in position, one of the men would plunge a harpoon into the whale's side. Attached to the other end of the harpoon was a 1,300-foot coil of rope that the crew members tried to measure out carefully, or as carefully as one could measure out a rope anchored to a panicking 60-foot-long creature making a life and death dash for freedom. It was this boisterous, hell-bent pull across the sea in a whaling boat that would one day come to be known around the world as a "Nantucket sleigh ride."

Just past the barn behind the Penniman house the trail enters an old orchard, now a cool, almost impenetrable thicket of black locust, poison ivy, black cherry, multiflora rose, redcedar, and black oak. But in just under 0.3 mile you'll reach a sunny, open area at the base of Fort Hill (actually one of three grassy hummocks so named on the Cape). Along the short climb to the top are fine mats of milkweed, Queen Anne's lace, and chicory, whose beautiful blue flowers open at about the same time each day. While you may be aware that the young leaves and roots of chicory have long been used for seasonings and

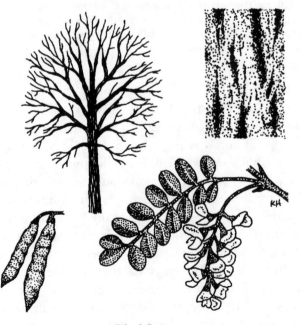

Black Locust

coffee substitutes, the plant has also had a long history of use by herbal healers. The Romans used chicory to treat disorders of the liver, while people of the Middle Ages made poultices from the leaves to bring down the swelling of bruised muscles.

At the top of Fort Hill is one of the finest views in all the Cape. To the east is the edge of Nauset Marsh, a mix of golden salt meadow grass laced with long, twisted braids of tidal streams and mudflats, all bound by the arms of the Atlantic.

As lush as this land may look now, it wasn't always this way. The Plymouth colonists who founded Eastham in 1646 had a fiery determination to subdue the land, just as the book of Genesis had commanded them. In remarkably little time their axes cleared the forest to make room for crops, and hundreds of cattle were turned out on the lush salt grass meadows. Unfortunately, the layer of topsoil that overlay these sand plains—what had given rise to the illusion that this was an inexhaustible land of plenty—was a frightfully thin one. Despite laws handed down by the Massachusetts General Court prohibiting grazing and requiring the planting of beach grass in devastated areas, by the late 1700s the plains of Eastham were worn out. "What was once a fertile spot," wrote one traveler to this area in 1794, "has become prey to the winds, and lies buried under a barren heap of sand."

Make your way down Fort Hill, past pokeweed, black cherry, black locust, redcedar, Japanese honeysuckle, and salt spray rose.

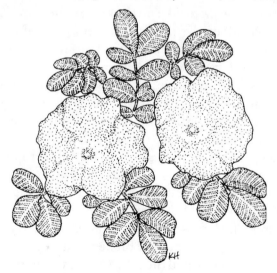

Salt Spray Rose

At 0.5 mile is a fork in the trail, with a short spur taking off to the right to the edge of a tidal stream. Stay to the left here and continue 0.4 mile to a shelter at Indian Rock. Pause here at least long enough to read the interpretive signs, which offer excellent natural and cultural history of the coast.

Straight ahead, about 0.2 mile past Indian Rock, follow a pathway taking off to the left into Red Maple Swamp. I found this lush forest of second-growth maple especially intriguing. Those looking through different eyes, though, might find it unsettling—an appropriate backdrop for chilling ghost stories. Many of the trees sport gnarled trunks with arthritic-looking branches, held up to the sky like a huddle of old men begging to be delivered from this onslaught of fox grape and moonseed vines.

Also along this portion of our walk are wonderful clusters of sweet pepperbush, elder, catbriar, netted chain fern, bayberry, baked-apple bush, arrowwood, and swamp azalea. Everywhere you look, in fact, are mats of leaves of one sort or another. At 1.3 miles is a junction with a path going off to the right. Stay to the left, continuing to wind through the hush of the red maple forest; you'll meet this same trail again 0.45 mile later, this time on the right, so be sure to stay left. Finally, at 1.9 miles is yet another junction where you'll stay to the right, almost immediately after which you'll take one more right back to the parking lot.

This latter section of trail through the Red Maple Swamp is an especially good walk to take on days when the Cape is wrapped in fog. (Fog, incidentally, provides a significant amount of the moisture that many of these plants need to survive.) According to Indian legend, the fogs of Cape Cod are no simple matter of condensation. One day while returning from a successful raid against the Nausets, the great warrior Maushop heard the death wail of his wife wafting through the forest. Running to her side, to his horror he discovered that the Great Devil Bird from across the South Sea had swooped down and made a meal out of his 16-year-old son.

Enraged, Maushop set off across the waters toward what is now Martha's Vineyard, calling on the heavens to lend him the strength to slay the evil bird giant. Finding the monster asleep in a great oak tree, the bones of Indian children scattered around its trunk, Maushop crept up into the branches, raised his tomahawk, and in one great swoop killed the bird. On the way home, Maushop paused on the island for a smoke, but found that his tobacco was so wet from his earlier ocean crossing that it would not burn. Covering the wet tobacco with pokeweed, Maushop was finally able to light his pipe, which burned with great, thick clouds of smoke. So dense did the smoke become, in fact, that the morning breezes eventually carried it across the sound to Maushop's village, which his people immediately recognized as a sign that he had triumphed over the monster bird.

And always after that, whenever a bank of summer fog drifted onto the Cape from across the sound, Indian children would hear of the great bravery of Maushop, and how once again, the smoke from his pipe was coming to them in the arms of the wind.

WALK #17—KETTLE HOLE

DISTANCE: 0.6 mile
ENVIRONMENT: Coast
LOCATION: Parker River National Wildlife Refuge. Traveling north on Interstate 95 north of Boston, take the exit for State Highway 113, and then proceed eastward, following the signs for State Highway 1A. In the town of Newburyport you'll see signs directing you to Plum Island and the Parker River Refuge. Once you pass the main entrance gate, proceed south and park at lot 3, located on the east (left) side of the road. Begin walking on the boardwalk that heads east toward the beach. *Note:* Visitor hours at Parker River are a half hour before sunrise to a half hour after sunset. Because on summer days the refuge often fills to capacity by 9:00 A.M., you would do well to rouse yourself for a dawn visit. Boardwalks at parking lots 1 and 7 are handicapped accessible, with observation decks overlooking the beach.

This 5,000-acre stretch of barrier beach, stitched with forest and marsh and capped by a long tumble of sand dunes, is one of the loveliest slices of coast in southern New England. An astonishing 300 species of birds frequent this refuge during various times of the year. In the cool of November you may find more than 20,000 ducks alone, as well as great clatters of snow and Canada geese, longspurs settling in from the Arctic, and mixed groups of pipits and snow buntings cartwheeling on the autumn winds. The only sensible way to traverse the trails and beaches of Parker River is slowly and deliberately. Do keep in mind that in order to protect fragile vegetation (as well as to help you avoid deer ticks), park regulations require visitors to stay on boardwalks and beaches.

Heading east from parking lot number 3, about 10 yards down the boardwalk is a tangle of barberry, rose, and bayberry. It's the waxy coatings on the fruits of this latter plant that have long been boiled off and then used as scent, most commonly in bayberry candles. Beyond this fringe, and for the most part out of sight, lies the oldest forest on Plum Island—a mix of aspen, maple, alder, black cherry, and oak, much of it bedecked in a lush cloak of grape and poison ivy. The reason this forest is so lush is that it lies in a protected depression—sometimes referred to as a *blowout*—carved by the wind in the back side of a large dune field. Out of reach of sea and sand it's been able to enjoy the kind of steady growth not possible elsewhere on the island.

As you move ever closer to the sea, you'll be entering places where it's increasingly difficult for plants to survive. On the back side of the foredunes are clusters of beach plum, poison ivy, golden heather, and the leathery leaves of bearberry. Colonists often stretched their supplies of tobacco by mixing it with bearberry leaves, while some coastal Indians used the plant as a treatment for bladder infections.

By the time you're standing in full face of the ocean, there's little left of the plant kingdom. Still hanging on are clumps of beach pea and seaside goldenrod, but soon even these dwindle away. Here the world belongs to American beachgrass, a plant that not only doesn't mind sand, but in fact requires a 3- or 4-inch layer of it to even survive. This blanket of sand stimulates beachgrass to send out horizontal root runners. Every 10 inches or so these rhizomes sink another set of roots and then pop out a cluster of leaves—a kind of root race to grow just fast enough to stay one step ahead of the blowing sands. The interesting thing about beachgrass is that once a sizeable colony gets established, it has a remarkable stabilizing effect on shifting dunes. When the colonists' cattle overgrazed the native beach grass at Truro on Cape Cod, the dunes immediately began to overtake the town's meadows. In 1739 the general court passed a law giving full protection to these areas. Yet even with such protection, combined with vigorous planting efforts, the settlers never did fully recover the acres they lost.

The beach itself is the final fringe of a peninsula fashioned by wind, waves, and great layers of rocky debris carried to the sea from the mainland first by tongues of glacial ice, and later by melt water. Perhaps nowhere more than at a barrier beach–dune complex like this one do the dynamics of nature seem more striking, while the exact borders of an ecosystem remain more uncertain.

If you have the time, by all means plan on hiking the 2-mile-long Hellcat Swamp Nature Trail, which is accessed south of here, at parking lot number 4. With its fresh and saltwater marshes, this is an especially good place to enjoy birds. An excellent interpretive brochure is available at the trailhead.

WALK #18—SOAPSTONE HILL

DISTANCE: 2.4 miles
ENVIRONMENT: Mountain
LOCATION: Quabbin Watershed. From the intersection of state highways 32A and 122 near the village of Petersham, head west on Highway 122 for 0.4 mile, and turn left onto West Street. Proceed for 2.6 miles to a crossroads, and turn left. Follow this road for 0.9 mile to a gate, marked by number 37. Park here and begin walking west along this gated road.

The Soapstone Hill walk is ideal for anyone willing to drive a few miles of twisted, potholed country roads in exchange for a yawning view of the Quabbin Watershed. Encompassed in that view are an 18-mile reach of blue water, thick blankets of hardwoods tossed across the crumpled hills, and eagles, osprey, and red-tailed hawks hanging from the summer skies.

Our walk takes off from access gate 37, winding gently downward through a young forest of hemlock, birch, red and black oaks, witch hazel, white pine, and red maple, seasoned here and there with mats of whorled and white wood asters, cinnamon,

Red Pine

bracken, and interrupted ferns, twisted stalk, and sarsaparilla. The route levels out as it continues to the west, and in 0.6 mile meets a road taking off to the left (south) through a grove of red pines. As beautiful as red pine can be, Quabbin managers are systematically eliminating many of the old groves that were planted shortly after the reservoir was built. In their place will be young hardwoods, whose growth patterns and lack of acidic needles promote more under-story plants, ultimately offering more food and protection for wildlife.

Just past this road you'll cross a bridge over the west branch of Fever Brook, a rather brackish flow in its final, sluggish drift before joining Quabbin Reservoir just to the south. At the first road on the right past this bridge, turn to the north and follow this watercourse to a beautiful marsh. Beaver sign is plentiful here, as are the beating wings of great blue herons, black ducks, red-winged blackbirds, blue-gray gnatcatchers, and that herald of spring, the tree swallow. Tree swallows are fascinating to watch as they make dramatic swoops and dives above the water in tight, fast pinwheels. Although there has never been a shortage of research on this bird, a few of its habits remain downright puzzling. For one thing, during some years on the breeding grounds, every member of a tree swallow colony may suddenly disappear for several days. Sometimes this mysterious, hasty departure even occurs during the female's incubation of the eggs, though with no apparent damage to the next generation. No one has been able to say for sure where, or why, the swallows go.

Other unusual behaviors include flying in small groups high above the breeding grounds and then diving down en masse back to the nests, as well as the old game of feather catch. This is where one or more birds drop a feather from high in the air, swoop down to catch it, and then release it again for yet another dramatic on-the-wing snag. (Think what baseball would be like with these guys in the outfield!)

At 0.8 mile (about halfway down the marsh), you'll see a faint footpath taking off into the woods to the left. This is our route to the top of Soapstone Hill, rising 300 feet above where you now stand. There are some steep sections of trail here, so be sure to take your time with it. Less than 0.2 mile from the marsh you'll reach the rocky top of Soapstone Hill, with a beautiful, sweeping view to the south of Quabbin Reservoir (once the Swift River Valley) and its glittering braid of mountain-top islands. If you continue north along this faint pathway for another 0.1 mile you'll find another promontory. This one is perched at the edge of a rugged escarpment, tumbling to the northeast toward the rolling woodlands of the Federated Women's Clubs State Forest.

WALK #19—QUABBIN PARK

DISTANCE: 2.7 miles
ENVIRONMENT: Forest
LOCATION: Metropolitan District Commission Watershed Management. From Belchertown, head east on Massachusetts Route 9 for 2 miles to the west entrance to Quabbin Park. (This is the first of three park entrances.) Proceed past the Metropolitan District Commission headquarters, across the dam, and turn left. Continue on this road past the Enfield Lookout and a picnic area on the north side of the road, to a trail along the south side of the highway marked by number 32. You can park directly across the highway from this trail. (This walk ends at marker 34, on the same road you parked on. If you can't arrange for someone to pick you up, turn left at the highway and walk 2 miles to return to your car, which would increase the total distance to 4.7 miles.)

While "Quabbin" is a Nipmuc Indian word meaning "many waters," today it's come to mean just one water—the more than 400 billion gallons of Swift River and Beaver Brook held by Quabbin Reservoir, built a half-century ago to supply the faucets of Boston. Beneath these shimmering waters lie the remains of four small communities: Dana, Prescott, Greenwich, and Enfield. And yet the real heyday of these towns was over long before Quabbin started to fill, overcome when local cotton and woolen milling jobs were lost to the urban industrial revolution. During the building of the reservoir 7,500 graves had to be relocated from 34 cemeteries—three times the number of living residents who packed up their memories and headed for higher ground.

Ironically, the drowning of the Swift River Valley ended up providing critical protection for this 55,000-acre watershed. These lands are well managed, and have long served as an expansive field laboratory for studies of wildlife, acid rain, and general watershed productivity. It's at Quabbin that you'll have the best chance of seeing bald eagles, wild turkeys, bobcat, red fox, fisher, and coyote. This walk is set up as a one-way trek, though of course you can simply turn around at any point and retrace your steps. Major Quabbin Park trails are blazed by circles of yellow paint on the trees, while most starting points and junctions are marked by numbered posts. (Before starting, pick up a park trail map from the Visitor's Center.) Our trek begins at marker post 32, located on the south side of the peninsula circle drive, just east of a developed picnic area. It ends on the east side of the park, about 0.5 mile north of State Highway 9.

The walk begins in a fairly young mixed forest of spruce, hemlock, red and black oak, beech, birch, red maple, and white pine. Especially common here are ferns, which in places form a tight weave of fronds sprawling across the forest floor as far as the eye can see. You'll see bracken, hay-scented, and New York ferns, as well as beautiful mats of large cinnamon ferns; this latter plant is named for the lovely cinnamon-colored fertile leaves visible in late spring. Cinnamon fern, along with the interrupted fern, which grows on somewhat drier soils, are among the most common ferns in the Northeast.

At 0.5 mile, through the forest off to your left, is a marsh in the last stages of succession. As plant debris accumulated at the edges of this water pocket, they formed fertile layers on which even more plants took hold—sedges, rushes, cattails, and arrowhead. Over

Red Fox

Northern Red Oak

time such vegetation squeezed the open water into a smaller and smaller pool, until one day there was no longer any visible water left at all. Such is the fate of all ponds; the rate of fill depends on the initial size of the pond, water supply, and climate.

Just after passing a stone wall and making a right turn, look to your left for beaver-gnawed trees. The descendants of these dedicated engineers, which were likely responsible for the existence of the pond in the first place, have long since moved on to wetter pastures. Over the years beavers have created more than 1,500 acres of marshes and ponds in the Quabbin.

Wind your way through nice stands of red pine at 0.7 mile, followed shortly thereafter by a more deciduous mix. Along this stretch of trail are more ferns, as well as clumps of twisted stalk, huckleberry, round-leafed dogwood, and Japanese barberry. Common barberry, incidentally, a relative of the Japanese version you see here, was widely used by the Egyptians as an ingredient for fighting plagues. (Barberry does in fact have antibacterial qualities which may have helped protect people against such disease.) In more modern times it was used for treating irritated eyes. (The next time you're trying to "get the red out," look and see if the solution you're using contains berberine. If so, it may well have been extracted from common barberry.)

At 1.2 miles is a "V" junction with a trail coming in over your right shoulder. Make the sharp turn onto this fainter path, following the yellow circles carefully as they drift through a forest of red, black, and white oak, spruce, red maple, and white pine, as well as occasional gardens of maidenhair, interrupted, and sweet fern. Soon after this junction visible signs of a trail begin to fade. From here on, for a distance of roughly 1.3 miles, you'll be ambling through an open forest guided only by a line of marks on the distant trees. Hiking this way through a deep forest is a wonderful experience. What was before just another slice of woods is now a heartland of unspoiled, untrammeled nature. You'll likely find yourself going slower here, not just because you have to look for the next blaze, but because you begin choosing routes according to the blooms and sprouts that most pique your curiosity. Bear left at marker 35, and in just over 0.1 mile you'll reach trail's end at marker 34. For me the conclusion of this walk came all too quickly. The initial rush of cars flying over the blacktop was startling, much too abrupt an end to the deep, restive hush of a Quabbin woodland.

WALK #20—FINERTY POND

DISTANCE: 4 miles

ENVIRONMENT: Forest

LOCATION: October Mountain State Forest. From the town of Lee, head east on U.S. Route 20 for 4.5 miles to Becket Road, and turn left. Just under 0.5 mile from this intersection turn left onto a small wood road; park off this road on the right, being sure to not block access. *Note:* This walk has been identified as appropriate for blind visitors with sighted guides. However, there are several rough sections along the last mile, any of which could prove to be difficult for the visually challenged.

The next time you have a few spare hours burning a hole in your day, you'd be hard pressed to find anything more enjoyable to spend them on than a slow ramble through the rich weave of forest, pond, and wildflower gardens that make up the October Mountain State Forest. Most of our trek is along old wood roads that cut through third-growth stands of red and white oak, sugar and striped maple, yellow poplar, beech, paper and yellow birch, hemlock, white ash, and cherry. White-tailed deer, as well as an occasional coyote and black bear, amble through the somber shadows of the woods, and after a good summer rain shower, coral-colored Eastern newts can be seen scurrying across the thick, damp beds of oak leaves. (Curiously, in warmer climates Eastern newts not only never leave their homes in local ponds, but for their entire lives wear an olive green skin bedecked with small red dots. In cool places like this, however, young adults emerge from the water to spend a couple years roaming on land—a kind of terrestrial grand tour, if you will—taking on a beautiful reddish-orange color in the process.)

Walking along broad trails and old roadways like these can be especially enjoyable, since the extra sunlight available from the cut gives rise to a remarkable variety of plants. Get out your identification books and see if you can spot sarsaparilla, pointed blue-eyed grass, purple trillium, wild oats, false Solomon's seal, the fronds of cinnamon, Christmas, maidenhair, and inter-rupted ferns, pink lady's slipper, and an occasional Jack-in-the-pulpit. There are a number of stories about how this latter plant got its name. One of the more amusing centers around a preacher named Reverend Jack T. Arum, who was bound and determined to save the souls of the local Indians. Unfortu-nately, Reverend Jack had a biting, spiteful tongue, and his sermons were filled with belittling remarks about the Indians and their way of life. In time the natives had all they could stand of such disrespect, and so dispatched a small band of warriors to kill the preacher and bury him in the woods. Imagine their horror when from his grave came a new plant, shaped like a pulpit, with Reverend Jack right in the middle of it, serving up another nasty round of preaching.

At just under 1 mile from Becket Road is a "Y" intersection; we'll take a right here, soon passing over a stretch of cobblestone roadbed laid down by Civilian Conservation Corps workers in the 1930s. From here continue making a gentle climb, reaching an intersection with a white-blazed trail in another 0.7 mile. This is the famous Appalachian Trail, making its twisted run from Geor-gia to Maine. You can turn left here and follow it down to a path running along Finerty Pond, or else continue straight on the old wood road, which also makes for the pond. Either way, you'll probably want to follow the pondside path until you find a clear spot from which to enjoy the view.

WALK #21—BERKSHIRE HILLS RAMBLE

DISTANCE: 1.1 miles

ENVIRONMENT: Mountain

LOCATION: Pittsfield State Forest. From Park Square Traffic Circle in the center of Pittsfield, head west on West Street for about 2.5 miles, and turn right onto Churchill Street. Continue for almost 2 miles to Cascade Street and turn left; at the next "T" intersection turn right again into the State Forest. Once past the park Contact Station, continue driving straight onto the Berry Pond Circuit Road, a one-way loop climbing 1,000 feet to the crest of the range. As you reach this crest, watch for a sign on the left marking the Berkshire Hills Ramble; park in the small turnout on the right side of the road. (An interpretive guide for this walk is available from the forest administrative office. To reach this office, turn left just after passing the Contact Station at the entrance to the forest.) *Note:* This walk has been identified as appropriate for blind visitors with sighted guides.

Though beautiful from spring to fall, this trail is especially appealing in late May and throughout much of June, when great sweeps of pink azaleas are flying their showy blossoms in the summer breeze, and the path is dusted with starflowers, buttercups, and lady's slippers. This is Taconic Range rambling at its very best. Indeed, a long, quiet walk through this forest can make it seem as if New England had changed little since the days when Herman Melville sat staring into these same hills from his farm near Pittsfield, resting his mind in these forests as he struggled to turn his recent adventures on a Nantucket whaler into a novel called *Moby Dick.* (Melville also liked to picnic at Balanced Rock, a 165-ton limestone boulder located on the northeast edge of the state forest; this rock became an important setting in another of Melville's novels, this one titled *Pierre or the Ambiguities.*)

If you happen to be here outside the blooming season, the azaleas are easily recognizable as a tall shrub with oblong leaves clustered at the ends of the branches. The species name of this plant, *nudiflorum*, means "naked flower"—a reference to the tendency of flowers to appear when the leaves are not yet fully formed. Another showy flower you're likely to see along the grassy pathways of this walk is hawkweed—a small, foot-high plant sporting orange, dandelionlike flowers. Hawkweed takes its name from a very old and rather mysterious European belief that hawks bathed their eyes in the juices of the flower in order to sharpen their vision. New England farmers, who considered this rapidly spreading introduced species nothing but a nuisance, had a somewhat more disparaging name for the plant, calling it devil's paintbrush.

At about 0.2 mile you'll see a faint path heading off to the left into a red pine plantation; go left, passing lovely patches of hayscented fern. The trail ducks into the red pines, which later are mingled with balsam and spruce; this is a hushed, richly scented woodland with an understory of Canada mayflower, starflower, tree and bristly clubmoss, as well as smatterings of hobblebush.

At 0.75 mile the path reaches the edge of Berry Pond—a beautiful spot, and at 2,150 feet the highest natural body of water in the state of Massachusetts. Summer visitors will see the edges of the pond dappled with the waxy, lemon-colored blooms of yellow pond lilies. This plant, along with the white water lily, has long been employed by herbalists to treat diarrhea, as well as to soothe sore throats. Further, the roots are not only edible, but various New England Indian tribes dried them for use in treating cuts and abrasions of the skin. The seeds can be eaten as well, and when roasted make a delicious snack, not unlike popcorn.

As the forest interpretive brochure points out, the edge of this pond is home for a number of frogs. Most of these are green frogs, a species that never strays more than a long jump from the safety and comfort of fresh water, as you'll note from the chorus of plops and splashes that will surely attend your approach. (To get a sense for just how wary and alert these guys are, see how difficult it is to sneak up on them without their noticing.) If a hungry snake happens along looking for lunch, the green frog will sometimes fill its lungs and then use its front and rear legs to lift its body off the ground; such a position makes it far more difficult for the snake to swallow it.

Both Berry Pond and Berry Mountain take their name from 18th-century Massachusetts resident William Berry. Appreciative of Berry's performance in the Revolutionary War at the Battle of Bennington, George Washington granted Berry a slice of the land that now makes up this beautiful state forest.

WALK #22—HALLOCKVILLE POND

DISTANCE: 1.5 miles
ENVIRONMENT: Fresh Water
LOCATION: Kenneth Dubuque Memorial State Forest. From the Intersection of state highways 2 and 8 in the town of North Adams, head east on Highway 2 for 18.1 miles, and turn right onto State Highway 8A. Follow this southward for 8.7 miles to the north end of Hallockville Road, and park here. Our walk begins around the north end of the pond, circling it in a counterclockwise direction.

This round-the-lake loop trail is a nearly perfect mix of water and woods. There are rocky coves blanketed with rubbery mats of pond lilies, and hushed, towering forests of hemlock and white pine. Here you'll find beautiful clumps of birch leaning out over the water, straining their necks for a better view of the sun. In autumn the sky drops deep shades of blue onto the surface of the lake; framed in splashes of gold, red, and evergreen, the place almost seems to vibrate with color.

Park in the small turnout adjacent to the northeast corner of the lake and begin walking counterclockwise around the north shore, past a cluster of state forest buildings. Pay close attention to the plant communities on this western side of the lake, since they'll change fairly dramatically as you round the southwestern tip and begin walking back to the parking area again—testimony to the fact that orientation to the sun has a profound effect on what plants will grow in any given area.

At 0.2 mile pass through several beautiful gardens of New York fern, and shortly afterward, fine clusters of red and white pine, easily two of the more striking members of the pine family. (Red pine has two needles, incidentally, while white pine has five.) Notice how few understory plants grow at the feet of these stately trees—in part because of the amount of shade they cast, but also due to the high levels of acidity present in these thick carpets of needles. This is a good spot to look and listen for red-breasted nuthatches, golden-crowned kinglets and, high up in the canopy, Blackburnian warblers.

"Water," wrote Leonardo da Vinci, "is the driver of nature." With that in mind, by all means pick out one of the many stony perches along the south side of the lake and let this lovely liquid world show you a few of its mysteries. If you happen to be near a collection of lily pads, watch for sudden pops coming from underneath the leaves. The undersides of lily pads—well anchored and close to sunlight, food, and oxygen—make perfect homes for a variety of snails, worms, beetles, and caddis flies; the popping you may hear is the sound of fish nipping a meal from the undersides of the leaves. Some floating pads are relished by beaver, who at a young age learn to roll them up with their forefeet like a fine cigar, and then munch them as if they were so many hot dogs.

As you round the tip of the lake look for mats of American yew, as well as increasingly dense stands of mountain laurel, which in June fly beautiful clusters of pinkish-white flowers. Also along the trail are blue violet, Canada mayflower, sarsaparilla and, near the very end of the walk, the tightly wrapped blooms of closed gentian.

Notice that several of the trees along this back side have been gnawed by beavers. Access tunnels to a beaver lodge in the middle of a lake are underwater. Once ice forms, the nonhibernating beaver will have to depend on a submerged cache of branches, along with an occasional tuber from the bottom of the pond, to sustain it until spring thaw. Venturing out beneath the ice cover for a leisurely snack is no problem, since adult beaver can easily hold their breath for 15 to 20 minutes.

Like many of the rest of us, beaver aren't particularly eager to have winter settle in on them. They'll maintain a hole in the ice sheet as long as possible by bumping it open from below, and then enlarging it by breaking off pieces from the perimeter with their nimble front feet.

Scarlet Tanager

WALK #23—MOODY SPRINGS

DISTANCE: 0.8 mile

ENVIRONMENT: Forest

LOCATION: Kenneth Dubuque Memorial State Forest. From the intersection of state highways 2 and 8 in the town of North Adams, head east on Highway 2 for 18.1 miles, and turn right onto State Highway 8A. Follow this southward for 8.7 miles, and make a sharp left onto Hallockville Road, a dirt road that climbs through the forest toward the northeast. (This intersection is near the north shore of Hallockville Pond.) Go 1.3 miles down this road and turn left, just past a small pond on the right. There will be a "Y" intersection 0.4 mile from this turn where you'll stay to the left, following Moody Spring Road. Our parking area and trailhead will be on your right next to a camping shelter, 0.7 mile from this last "Y" intersection.

For anyone heading into the western hills of Massachusetts looking for peace and quiet, Kenneth Dubuque Memorial State Forest is the place to go. Here you'll find a twisted maze of dirt roads and trails, some of the latter all but lost beneath thick mats of vegetation. On those paths that are still navigable there's little to distract you from the pleasures at hand: watching the flash of a scarlet tanager, or the bold stripes of a black and white warbler as he circles tree trunks looking for insects; listening to the *teacher! teacher!* cry of the ovenbird, or the staccato rap of a northern flicker as he announces his territory.

Before we get started, take a short walk down to the outflow of Moody Spring and help yourself to a swig of cold, fresh water; residents have been drinking from this spring for decades—not just to quench their thirst, but to treat a long list of physical disorders. Standing with your back to the spring (facing downhill), you'll see a small trail taking off to the left, marked by a series of blazed trees. This is our walking path. Be forewarned that there are a few places where the trail itself is a little hard to see, but never is the next blaze far away. The route basically takes you on a short but sweet romp through a variety of hardwood nooks and crannies—moist ravines, lined with patches of violet, orchid, Canada mayflower, and sarsaparilla. In the distance are hauntingly beautiful clumps of white birch, their trunks drawing you ever farther into the cool, deep shadows of the forest.

Though white-tailed deer are plentiful here, they can be difficult to see. Deer not only have excellent hearing (you can watch their ears constantly scanning the surroundings), but are thought to be able to detect movement down to the blinking of a person's eye. What's more, few large animals know their surroundings better than deer. An eastern white-tail will typically have a range of about a square mile, which she knows like the back of her hoof. Deer that have been tagged and moved to other areas, perhaps a dozen or more miles away, have quickly found their way back to their home turf.

The female white-tail bears fawns in the spring. If it's her first birth she may have only one youngster, but in succeeding years twins will be the rule. A fawn can stand just 10 minutes after birth, is gulping milk by the cupful in less than a minute, and can walk in less than an hour. Mom takes advantage of this fact by quickly prodding the youngster away from his birth spot, just in case the

White-tailed Deer

scent of birthing should attract a predator. (The fawn itself has so little smell during the first days of life that even hunting dogs walking nearby may fail to detect it.) Defenseless young fawns tend to lie quietly for the first few days after birth, well-camouflaged by the spots on their coats. During this time the mother will keep away from the fawn except to nurse it, since her own scent might otherwise reveal the youngster's location. Should the fawn wander off the mother will be able to track it by following a slight scent trail left by a special gland on the hoof.

Would-be deer watchers should keep in mind that a feeding white-tail will sometimes shake its tail immediately before it looks up to survey its surroundings. If you're trying to get close for a better look, advance quietly, and stop as soon as you see the tail move. Also, since deer relish many different types of nuts, plan to take a few evening walks in the fall through forests of oak, beech, and hickory.

At just over 0.4 mile the blazed trail comes out on Moody Springs Road; turn left and walk through the hardwood forest back to the Moody Springs shelter. If it's late in the evening, wait to walk this final stretch until a flush of darkness has covered the land. Slow your pace way down, and listen for the first faint stirrings of the night crew. Authors who write about their experiences in the dark woods seem to do so at a deeper, more profound level of imagery, as if in losing clear sight, they gain a sixth, more mystical sense of perception. Thoreau walked along a moonlit lake in Maine and later wrote about seeing "the shores of a new world" which "left such an impression of stern, yet gentle wildness on my memory as will not soon be effaced." Henry Beston, author of *The Outermost House,* cautioned that "with the banishment of night from the experience of man, there vanishes as well a religious emotion, a poetic mood, which gives depth to the adventure of humanity." Even the rather matter-of-fact Americana grassroots poet Stephen Vincent Benét got a bit mysterious when writing about happenings under the cloak of darkness:

> When Daniel Boone goes by at night
> The phantom deer arise
> And all lost, wild America
> is burning in their eyes.

WALK #24—THE MEADOWS

DISTANCE: 3.5 miles
ENVIRONMENT: Forest
LOCATION: Mohawk Trail State Forest. Located on the north side of State Highway 2, 14.2 miles east of the intersection of State Highways 8 and 2, in the town of North Adams. Cross the bridge and turn left, parking just outside of the entrance station to the campgrounds. The walk begins along the main campground entrance road.

This forested ravine, pared down to bedrock by the tumbling waters of the Cold River, is among the more beautiful stretches of an old Indian pathway known as the Mohawk Trail. The Mohawk Trail was blazed sometime in the middle of the 17th century—not by the Mohawks, but by the Pocumtucks of the Connecticut River Valley. The Pocumtucks are thought to have punched this path westward to gain better raiding access to their archenemies the Mohawks, who at the time were located in what is now extreme eastern New York state. For years early Dutch settlers found themselves in the middle of this ping-pong game of pillage, flying back and forth across the Hoosac and Teconic mountains.

The diplomatic Dutch cajoled the two tribes into stopping their mutual slaughter, and were ultimately able to formulate a peace treaty that allowed everyone concerned to save face. Alas, a couple of Pocumtuck warriors murdered Mohawk Prince Saheda, even as he was traveling along this trail to put his mark on the Dutch treaty. The Mohawks were outraged, and wasted no time setting out on the warpath once again. Fueled by a burning drive for revenge, it took them less than two days to, for all practical purposes, wipe the Pocumtucks from the face of the earth.

Of course this Mohawk victory was, in the grand scheme of things, hardly a winning of the war. The real struggle would be against an even more zealous tribe from across the Atlantic Ocean, whose battle cries were fueled with the fire of a Christian God. "The blasphemy, and insolence, and prodigious barbarity of the savages," wrote Cotton Mather in 1702, "was come to a sufficient height for the 'Lord God of Zaboath' to interpose his own revenges."

The taking of Indian lands throughout New England was at least in part justified by the notion that the natives were not subduing their lands as instructed by the biblical book of Genesis, and therefore forfeited any claim to them. Under this notion, then, lands that the Indians had cultivated were, for a time, at least, protected by law. "What landes any of the Indians ... have by possession or improvement, by subduing of the same," the Massachusetts court ruled, "they have just right thereunto, according to that Gen: 1:28, chap: 9:1, Psa 115,16." Unfortunately, the Indians in northern New England were for the most part not farmers, and therefore had no rights whatsoever.

Though the first portion of our walk is along the campground road system, it would be hard to find a more enjoyable slice of coniferous forest. Just to the north of where you parked is a beautiful stand of planted Norway spruce. This beautiful import is found throughout much of northern Europe, and holds the distinction of producing the largest cones of any spruce in the world. As you make your way up the entrance road you'll also see the first of many large hemlocks, which in places hover over patches of mountain laurel, as well as an occasional clump of closed gentian. The genus name for this latter plant, whose lavender flowers are held in tight, bottle-shaped clusters, comes from a 2nd-century B.C. King of Illyria named Gentius, who is often credited with discovering the healing powers of the gentians. Historical records, however, indicate that the Egyptians were using gentian in their medicine 1,000 years before the good king came to power.

By 0.3 mile the road plunges into a corridor of towering white pine, their nearly branchless trunks rising into the sun like a battalion of soldiers snapped to attention. Looking at these beautiful giants, which are not yet close to reaching their full potential, it's easy to see why England's Royal Navy coveted them for use as ship's masts. It was for just such purpose that when Massachusetts received its charter in 1691, settlers were forbidden to cut any public tree "of the diameter of twenty-four inches and upwards at twelve inches from the ground."

Take a right at 0.4 mile, following the signs to the group camping area. The broken trees you see just past this junction are from a tornado that roared through the campground in the summer

Whorled Wood Aster

of 1988, snapping off massive hemlocks and white pines as if they were so many matchsticks. Soon you'll come to a dirt road taking off to the right, which we'll follow past the group campground and into the more untrodden forest beyond. Past the campground are still more white pine and hemlock, as well as an occasional maple, beech, and yellow birch. Watch the ground here for starflower, bracken fern, and both white and whorled wood aster. The blooming of these asters is a sure sign that summer is coming to a close.

At 1 mile, a short distance past a faint road taking off to the left, turn left onto a blue-blazed nature trail. Along this quiet stretch of path are some extensive mats of clubmoss. Like ferns, clubmosses also reproduce by releasing millions of spores into the air in early autumn; if you're here in September, a pass of your hand through these carpets will launch a veritable cloud of yellow spores. Each of these tiny spores is extremely uniform in both shape and size, a trait that led to their use in everything from coating pills to make them easier to swallow, to providing a standard for measuring the size of microscopic objects. Furthermore, clubmoss spore also tends to burn rapidly. This made it popular not only in fireworks, but as a prime source of that famous "poof!" flash system employed by early photographers. Also along this stretch are remnants of stone walls, built in the 1700s to contain sheep that were being raised in the area.

At 1.4 miles you'll intersect a small road at the edge of a meadow, the first of two such clearings on this walk. Our path follows this small road to the end of the first meadow, enters the woods again, and finally enters another, lower meadow at the west end, passing a natural pond and several bluebird houses along the way. About halfway through this upper meadow, on the south side, is one of the oldest maple trees in the Northeast. (Not long ago it was revealed that this state preserve contains one of Massachusetts' few remaining old growth forests; in general this means trees 200 or more years old, which show few signs of human interference, fire, or blowdown. Also, along the ridge of Todd Mountain is an unaltered section of "Indian Trail"—a path thought to have been in nearly constant use since prehistoric times.)

Plan to spend some time in the arms of these lovely clearings, fringed on the near edge by huddles of conifers, and beyond that, by a swell of uplands thick with hardwoods. In spring these openings are covered in magnificent carpets of wildflowers, the various species bursting with the warm roll of the season like the carefully orchestrated movements of a symphony. The show will continue on a more subdued note throughout the summer, as the land quietly fades into blends of milkweed, bindweed, yarrow, rough-fruited cinquefoil, orange hawkweed, and pokeweed.

At the edge of the lower meadow our road turns to the right along a fast run of the Deerfield River. Just past the grave site of Revolutionary War soldier John Wheeler and his wife Susannah, you'll come to a "Y" intersection where you'll turn right. Wrapped once again in the hush of the conifer forest, this road will lead you back to the parking area in 1.2 miles.

WALK #25—BOG POND

DISTANCE:	1.4 miles
ENVIRONMENT:	Fresh Water
LOCATION:	Savoy Mountain State Forest. From the intersection of state highways 8 and 2 in the town of North Adams, head east on state highway 2 for 4.5 miles. Turn right on Central Shaft Road, and follow the signs for just over 3 miles to Savoy Mountain State Forest. Continue to follow this road toward the park campground. Our walk takes off on a small dirt track known as Haskins Road, located 0.2 mile past the campground on the left.

Some residents of eastern New England consider Boston and Massachusetts to be one and the same. Yet within the nearly 8,000 square miles of the Bay State are slices of nature rich almost beyond belief, not the least of which lie in the shadows of the ancient Berkshires. This is the home of bear and deer and even an occasional moose—a place steeped in blue sky, a land of drooping mountain shoulders cloaked in thick blankets of northern hardwood forest.

From the entrance to the park campground walk south for just under 0.2 mile, and turn left (east) onto a small dirt two-track called Haskins Road. Immediately the world shifts from sun to shadow, as thick stands of birch, hemlock, maple, and beech crowd together in a race to snatch the light before it can fall to the forest floor. Along the first few yards of this road is jewelweed, its spotted orange blossoms hanging like hand-made lanterns from tufts of soft, gray-green foliage. When fully ripe, the elongated seedpods of jewelweed fire off their batteries of seeds at even the slightest touch, hence another one of its common names—spotted touch-me-not. The juice of this plant is well known for relieving the itching of poison ivy, and has also served well as a fungicide for treating athlete's foot.

At 0.4 mile a small trail takes off to the right, marked with a blue blaze. Follow this path through clusters of conifers, birch, and beeches, with smatterings of hobblebush and ferns growing underneath. You'll spot Bog Pond shimmering through the trees at 0.6 mile.

Bogs are highly acidic places; some, in fact, will have acidic levels a hundred times that of clean rainwater. And yet that hasn't stopped certain plants from thriving here, including Labrador tea, leatherleaf, pitcher plant, and round-leaved sundew. Pitcher plant and round-leaved sundew are *insectivorous*, which means that at least some of their diet is made up of bugs. Since members of the vegetable kingdom can't flick a tongue or snap a beak to grab visiting insects, they rely on more subtle means. The pitcher plant has a pool of water at the base of its leaves that hapless visitors fall into and drown. The sundew, on the other hand, has sticky glandular hairs that catch insects' feet when they land for a meal. (There's some evidence to suggest that a type of anesthetic is also released by short hairs on the inner leaves.) The movements of the insect to set itself free stimulate the plant to begin wrapping hairs around its body. This response begins less than 2 minutes after the bug lands, and is complete 15 to 20 minutes later. Once the insect is digested, the tentacles open again, ready for the next unsuspecting victim.

WALK #26—BUSBY TRAIL

DISTANCE:	3 miles
ENVIRONMENT:	Mountain
LOCATION:	Savoy Mountain State Forest. From the intersection of state highways 8 and 2 in the town of North Adams, head east on Highway 2 for 4.5 miles. Turn right on Central Shaft Road, and follow the signs for just over 3 miles to Savoy Mountain State Forest. Our walk takes off on the right side of the road, 0.3 mile past the entrance to the forest, and approximately 75 yards beyond the forest headquarters on Old Florida Road. At the fork 50 feet into the walk, take a right on Busby Trail.

There is no better way to get a sense for the ruggedness of this slice of New England than to survey it from a towering, rocky perch like Spruce Hill, rising 2,566 feet along the extreme western fall line of the Hoosac Range. This long tumble of high country, created by the marriage of the Green and Berkshire mountains, is unbroken by a single valley for more than 150 miles. For centuries this was considered to be the western wall of the American wilderness, a howling, treacherous land of wild men and beasts, a region dissected only by the Mohawk Trail a few miles to the north of where you now stand. It was along that path that Massachusetts native peoples made raids on neighboring tribes in the forested uplands of eastern New York. The route also felt the feet of a young man from Boston named Paul Revere, who hurried westward along the Mohawk Trail on his way to defend British fortifications during the French and Indian War.

Our walk begins in a beautiful patchwork of fern and forest—red maple, birch, beech, hemlock, and oak, with hay-scented and lady fern growing at their feet. Also common are mats of whorled wood aster, Japanese knotweed, and an occasional hobblebush. At 0.2 mile, a short distance after passing a power line thick with meadowsweet and hardhack, is a particularly fine fern garden. Tight clusters of lacy green leaflets are spread across the ground nearly as far as the eye can see, as if the gods had tried to ease their footsteps through the forest by wrapping the land in a carpet of fronds.

Ferns, along with the clubmosses and scouring rush that can also be found along this trail, were in their prime 200 million years ago, growing to tremendous size in the warm forests of the Mesozoic era. Ferns release spores—perhaps as many as 50 million from a single plant—a few of which land on bare soil or on carpets of moss and germinate, growing into small, heart-shaped plants called *prothallia*. Prothallia contain both male and female reproductive organs. If a thin film of water is present, a swimming sperm outside the prothallium will join with an egg produced in a tiny vase-shaped female organ. This fertilized egg divides and begins growing into a plant. For a time this plant obtains nourishment from the parent prothallium; eventually, though, it will send a root into the earth and unfurl a small leaf to begin the manufacture of food. Upon maturity the fern releases its own spores, and the whole cycle begins again.

Our path continues past a mix of bluebead lilies, violets, jewelweed, false Solomon's seal, white wood aster, and an occasional Indian cucumber. If you're here in the fall, watch at about 0.5 mile for spiny balls of beechnuts littering the ground. While today beech is primarily known for its wood, which is used to produce furniture and tool handles, there was a time when you could find beechnuts on the shelves of nearly any New England grocery. Besides being delicious to eat raw, these nuts were roasted and used as a substitute for, or at least an additive to, coffee beans. The oil of the beechnut was frequently used for cooking, and herbalists long prescribed it as a remedy for worms. Indians and colonists alike made decoctions of beechnut leaves to help relieve the pain of burns and rashes. Today beechnuts remain a staple food for many forest animals.

Continue climbing past a diverse mix of conifers and hardwoods, through sunlit openings and cool, deep shade. Christmas ferns, which remain green throughout the winter, are found at 0.8 mile, and a short distance later, look for baneberry, Canada mayflower, sensitive fern, bunchberries, and wild oats. In 1.5 miles is the rocky top of Spruce Hill. From here the world is a grand sweep of hill and valley, capped by a sky that on most days will be flushed with birds of prey. In the fall watch for migrating broad-winged, red-tailed, and sharp-shinned hawks, as well as American kestrels.

Directly below you to the west is the Hoosic River Valley, framed on the far side by Mount Greylock—at 3,491 feet, the highest point in Massachusetts. Mount Greylock is actually part of an entirely different set of mountains than is Spruce Hill. Members of the Taconic Range, Greylock and its compadres are actually thought to have once been located on the east side of Vermont's Green Mountains. Five hundred million years ago there were grand collisions and uplifts occurring along geologic plates lying deep within the earth. The slow, dramatic rise of the Green Mountains actually lifted portions of what would become the Taconic Range and slid them westward, where they finally came to rest roughly in the region you see them today. Add millions of years of wind and water erosion, the patient downward slicing of rivers, and the mighty grind of glacial ice, and you end up with the mountain masterpiece spread before you.

Mount Greylock, by the way, takes its name from the crest of snow that tends to cloak it during winter months. In 1946 scientists seeded clouds around this peak with dry ice, producing the first artificial snowstorm.

WALK #27—DUNBAR BROOK

DISTANCE:	1.8 miles
ENVIRONMENT:	Forest
LOCATION:	Monroe State Forest. From the intersection of state highways 8 and 2 in the town of North Adams, head east on Route 2 for approximately 5.6 miles to Tilda Hill Road, and turn left (north). (This turn will be just east of the Florida Fire Station.) Proceed northward on Tilda Hill Road for 6.3 miles to Kingsley Hill Road, and turn right. In approximately 1.4 miles you'll reach a "T" intersection in the village of Monroe Bridge. Turn right. The trailhead parking area will be on your right in 1.75 miles, across from a New England Power Company picnic area. *Note:* To find the trail from the parking area, you must walk roughly 20 yards south up a two-track road that parallels a power line; at the top of a small hill, you'll see our pathway taking off into the forest toward the west.

While the steely web of power lines woven across the Deerfield River Valley doesn't exactly inspire one to plunge feet first into nature, beautiful Dunbar Brook, protected from development by a thick veil of state forest, is most certainly worth a closer look. The blend of cool stream waters dancing through shady slices of mature maple, hemlock, and yellow birch forest creates a very serene, almost cathedrallike atmosphere, delightful in nearly any kind of weather.

Straddling the lovely Hoosac Range, meeting place of the Berkshire and Green mountains, this walk passes a medley of round-shouldered plateaus and steep, dizzy plunges through the forest, all dissected by a braid of dark, forested valleys lined with running water. Three centuries ago this line of mountains marked the end of New England and the beginning the frontier, a boundary held in check largely through the tenacious efforts of a few small towns to the east. (In Deerfield's Memorial Hall Museum you can inspect the front door of settler John Sheldon, laced with gashes from flying tomahawks, courtesy of angry Indians in 1704.)

Yet long after the threat of attack ended, the mountains themselves remained a formidable barrier to westward movement. Unable to find a practical overland railroad route, in the 1870s, with the aid of a marvelous new explosive known as nitroglycerine, the 5-mile-long Hoosac Tunnel was blasted through these mountains just south of where you now stand. This was an incredible feat of engineering; by the time the tunnel was completed in the fall of 1873, it had claimed more than 200 lives.

Our path begins in a beautiful hemlock forest, the branches woven into a dark curtain that all but blocks out the fingers of the sun. Many of those who settled on the Bershire Plateau did so with

Eastern Hemlock

American Beech

an eye to harvesting the forest. To this end hemlock was cut in great quantities and the bark sold for tannin, which was used in preparing leather; for many years the nearby town of North Adams was a leading producer of manufactured leather.

Where there is hemlock, there is usually beech. A beautiful example of this latter tree is found at 0.1 mile on the right side of the trail, its smooth "elephant trunk" bark lending color and texture to the forest. Both hemlock and beech grow and reproduce best in shaded areas, their feet planted in acidic soil. Interestingly, you'll find that most of the beech-hemlock forests you come across in New England are located in moist areas, even though both trees are capable of growing on drier sites. This may have to do with fires that for centuries rolled across much of the New England landscape. Since neither hemlock nor beech is capable of sprouting new growth from burned trunks, these lowland areas may have at one time been the only safe refuges for either tree. As we continue to suppress fires, these fellows may well get their chance to venture out onto drier horizons.

By 0.25 mile yellow birch has come on the scene, along with maple, witch hazel, bluebead lily, and whorled wood aster—all crowded into a narrow corridor framed on the south by a steep, forested hillside, and on the north by the delightful rills and pools of Dunbar Brook. Notice the carpets of apron and white-tipped moss growing on this hillside. In this particular instance the old adage about moss growing on the north side of trees and hills, out of reach of the drying rays of the sun, is true. (If you're lost in the woods, however, you'd better have more lore up your sleeve than just this. Moss will in fact grow wherever it's damp and shady—east, west, south, or north.) Growing on these massive boulders, moss serves as the leading force in the manufacture of soil. Tiny pieces of rock are loosened by the moss, which, when combined with its own dead leaves, forms a base for other plants—even young trees—to take root and grow.

Continue past mats of sarsaparilla, violets, partridgeberry, and Indian cucumber, along with fine gardens of wood-, hay-scented, and Christmas fern. (The hollylike evergreen leaflets of this latter fern have made it a popular holiday decoration for centuries, hence its common name.) At 0.5 mile, on a small hill just this side of a small streamside campsite, is a wonderful view into the depths of the forest. The dark green of hemlocks is broken here and there by shimmering, ghostly trunks of white and yellow birch. Young striped maples lean their supple trunks into the light of the trail, while overhead are magnificent eastern cottonwoods, their high-flying canopies all but lost to sight in a tangle of lesser trees. Pause here for a moment and listen. You may hear the flutey music of the wood thrush, the sleepy song of the warbling vireo, or, if you're lucky, the rich, haunting song of the veery.

From this perch the trail again descends to the creek, passing clumps of wild oats, false Solomon's seal, tall meadow rue, blue violets, shinleaf, baneberry, and foamflower. Our turnaround point is at a wooden footbridge across Dunbar Brook, reached in 0.9 mile, just after taking a right turn at a fork in the trail. Those not yet ready to turn around can continue up the path for several more miles to Main Road, much of the route running cheek to cheek with this delightful stream.

▪ VERMONT ▪

VERMONT

∎ ∎ ∎

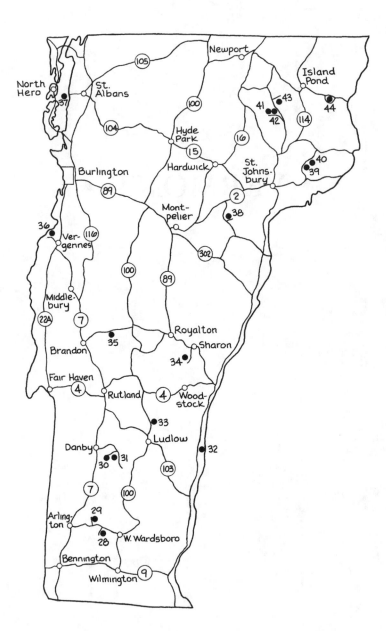

North
Hero

St.
Albans

Newport

Island
Pond

(105)

(100)

41 43
42
44

(37)

(104)

Hyde
Park

(16)

(114)

Burlington

(15)

Hardwick

St.
Johns-
bury

40
39

(89)

(2)

36

Ver-
gennes

(116)

Mont-
pelier

38

(302)

(100)

(89)

Middle-
bury

(22A)

(7)

Royalton

Brandon

35

Sharon

34

Fair Haven

(4)

Rutland

(4)

Wood-
stock

33

Danby

Ludlow

32

30 31

(103)

(7)

(100)

Arling-
ton

29

28 W. Wardsboro

Bennington

Wilmington

(9)

Vermont

WALK #28—GROUT POND

DISTANCE:	2.9 miles
ENVIRONMENT:	Fresh Water
LOCATION:	Green Mountain National Forest. Coming from the north, follow State Highway 100 to the single bridge in the town of West Wardsboro. From this point head south for 0.2 mile and turn right (west) onto Forest Road 6. Proceed for 6.4 miles to the Grout Pond entrance road, and turn left. Follow this road for 1.2 miles to a parking lot and picnic area at the bottom of a hill on the northwest corner of Grout Pond. (A boat ramp is nearby.) Our walk continues east along this road, running along the north shore of the pond.

This easy 2.9-mile stroll winds in and out of forest and clearing, the rippling waters of Grout Pond never more than a stone's throw away. But for a few scratchy patches of wood nettle growing on the back side of the pond, the route traverses what is essentially a very friendly environment—in warm months a gentle mix of shade and sunlight that can slow the most harried walker. Henry James once said that "summer afternoon" were the most beautiful words in the English language. Head down, feet up along the shore of Grout Pond, it's hard to disagree.

From the parking area at the end of the road we'll be heading clockwise around the lake, beginning on a roadway that eventually narrows to a footpath. Besides commonly celebrated trees like sugar and striped maples, beech, and balsam fir, you'll also be passing a couple of species that you may have overlooked, such as mountain maple and hop hornbeam. The bark of the mountain maple is an important food to deer, while ruffed grouse—which in summer nest along the grassy fringes of the woods—relish the young buds. (Then again, ruffed grouse relish a lot of things. Studies in various parts of the country have identified a diet consisting of more than 600 types of plants!)

True to form, ruffed grouse also feed on the buds of the hop hornbeam you'll see along the first 0.5 mile of this walk. The "hop" in this name refers to the resemblance that the fruits have to beer hops. Hop hornbeam is also sometimes called ironwood, a reference to the extremely hard wood which for centuries has been used to fashion tool handles.

The walkway inches closer and closer to the shore, with several nice side trails going off to small picnic areas. At 0.5 mile you'll be able to look across the pond to the southeast and see the forested flank of 3,556-foot Mount Snow. Just about the time the road yields to a footpath, keep your eyes out for fine stands of both mountain holly and witherod. This latter plant is a *viburnum*, and like most members of that genus, has very slender, supple branches. In fact the first part of the plant's common name—"withe"—is a term referring to any flexible branch used in basketmaking. The fruit of the witherod, which appears in August and September, tastes a great deal like a raisin.

In 1 mile turn right to keep following the loop path around the pond. This next part of the walk is through a cool, moist forest, the trailsides lined with ferns, bunchberry, wood sorrel, and bluebead lily. Listen here for both the lilt of warblers, and the soft rattle of downy woodpeckers. As you round the southeast corner of Grout Pond, off to your right will be a wonderful wetland. The birdhouses in this corner pocket of the lake are for wood ducks; the homes are maintained year-round by adding fresh wood shavings to the floors of the nests. Wood ducks aren't the only ones who like this housing. Mice, bees, and wasps have been found inside the boxes, as have flying squirrels. (These marvelous little creatures don't actually fly, but rather use a special membrane located between their front and rear feet to glide out of trees—sometimes for distances of up to 150 feet. Because they're nocturnal, they are rarely seen by humans.)

At 1.8 miles is a "T" intersection, where you'll take another right. This is the stretch of trail to watch out for wood nettle, whose stinging hairs can irritate the skin. (Appropriately, along the wetland

Downy Woodpecker

Flying Squirrel

area you just passed are clusters of jewelweed, the leaves and stems of which can be ground up to produce a juice which substantially reduces the irritating effects of both nettles and poison ivy.) Also here are selfheal, tall meadow rue, whorled wood aster, and red-berried elder.

Across the lake to the north lies Stratton Mountain, where, in 1840, Daniel Webster delivered a stirring oratory in support of William Henry Harrison's bid for the presidency—part of the famous "Log Cabin and Hard Cider Campaign." (Webster would later lend his masterful editing to President Harrison's inaugural speech.) It's interesting to note that New Hampshire–born Webster was once so petrified at the thought of public speaking that he couldn't even get out of his seat when called to do so at Exeter Academy. Yet he went on to become one of the greatest orators in American history. Enormous gatherings—sometimes upward of 100,000 people—would show up to hear just about anything that Daniel Webster had to say. Across the water at sleepy little Stratton Mountain, he drew a crowd of more than 15,000.

Champion of New Englanders, praised at one time or another by everyone from Lincoln to Emerson, Webster was an extremely influential statesman. It was under the direction of this staunch Federalist that American currency eventually gained a solid position within the U.S. Bank. The Monroe Doctrine, which announced to the world that the American continents "are henceforth not to be considered as subjects for future colonization by any European power," had a great deal of Daniel Webster in it. Famous patriotic statements such as "One country, one constitution, one destiny" and "The people's government, made for the people, made by the people, and answerable to the people," were Webster's. It is reported that lying on the cusp of death in 1852, the last words this statesman ever uttered were "I still live." For a long time, in the hearts of many, many Americans, indeed he still did.

At 2.5 miles you'll reach a dirt road. Other routes lead off from this one, but if you continue circling to the right you'll reach the entrance road at 2.7 miles. Turn right once again, and in 0.2 mile you'll arrive back at the trailhead parking area.

WALK #29—BRANCH POND

DISTANCE: 1.6 miles
ENVIRONMENT: Fresh Water
LOCATION: Green Mountain National Forest. Coming from the north, follow State Highway 100 to the single bridge in West Wardsboro. From this point head south for 0.2 mile and turn right (west) onto the Arlington-Wordsboro Road. Proceed for 11.3 miles to Forest Road 70, and turn right. Follow this for just under 2.5 miles to the end of the road. Our trail takes off on the right.

> And the pond's stillness rippled as if
> by rain instead is pocked with life.
> —*Maxine Kumin*

Though you can reach the hidden southern finger of Branch Pond via a short walk from the parking area, this pathway through a cool mixed forest to the pond's east side is an even nicer way to get acquainted. The woods are lush with ferns and patches of wood sorrel. Bluebead lily and purple trillium line the trail, with mats of hobblebush hugging the great, shining trunks of the yellow birch. This is also a good place to catch the beautiful song of the hermit thrush. Each performance of this camouflaged ground nester is delivered at a slightly different pitch, and in a somewhat rearranged crescendo of clear, fluid notes; dripping off the leaves of the forest like drops of fresh rain, they form as sweet a birdsong as any in America.

At just under 0.3 mile is the Branch Pond Trail; take a left, winding through the woods to the fringe of a quiet marsh. Watch here for green heron gliding silently past twisted tree skeletons, looking like the last survivors of some ancient spirit world. Soon the path ducks into the forest again and, in a beautiful stand of yellow birch at 0.7 mile, intersects the trail to Branch Pond. Take a left and walk 0.1 mile to the edge of the pond. The last few yards of this path will take you past a beautiful collection of sheep laurel, their pink, spotted saucer-shaped flowers looking like miniaturized versions of that showiest of eastern upland plants, the mountain laurel. In June, you may also be treated to the striking blossoms of blue flag iris.

Perhaps more than any other inland environment, ponds are thoroughly flushed with life, though much of it goes unnoticed by human visitors. It's a very complex, interwoven web of life, thousands of events unfolding in any given hour, on any given summer day. As sure as you stand here, somewhere a fish is eyeing a group of whirligig beetles floating on the surface of the pond. Those beetles, on the other hand, are scanning the depths for danger with one set of "underwater eyes," while watching for their own dinner of insects to fall onto the surface of the pond with another set. Water striders strike at young mosquitos emerging from their larval stage. A dragonfly nymph zips quietly through the water, propelling itself by first drawing water into its digestive tract, and then using special muscles to squeeze it out again. A diving beetle grabs a bubble of air with his wing covers—an instant scuba tank, of sorts—and dives beneath the water, perhaps not to surface again for many hours. And of course there are frogs and newts and turtles and crayfish, toads and birds and worms and spiders and snakes.

Underlying all this semivisible activity are the one-celled *phytoplanktons*. While these *algaes* and *desmids* and *diatoms* maintain methods of locomotion fully two billion years old, under the microscope some are as uncannily futuristic looking as anything dreamed up in the studios of Hollywood. These "invisible" organisms are what form the very foundation for all the life in the pond—the rich underpinning upon which rests virtually every ascending level of the food chain.

Red-spotted Newt

WALK #30—OLD JOB

DISTANCE:	6.1 miles
ENVIRONMENT:	Forest
LOCATION:	Green Mountain National Forest. From Rutland, head south on U.S. Highway 7 to the small village of Danby. From here, head east on Forest Road 10 for 6.75 miles, and turn right onto Forest Road 30. Our parking area and trailhead are at the end of Road 30, 2.3 miles from this last turn. Begin by following the closed roadway west across the bridge.

Although longer than most of our treks, this pleasant loop through lovely Green Mountain scenery is easily managed by most walkers. Here you'll find grasses and wildflowers typical of lands laying bare to the sun, as well as rich slices of mature hardwood forest. The back side of the walk follows beautiful watercourses, the tempo of their rocky dances winding down as the days drift further into summer.

Our route begins on a roadway now closed to motorized vehicles, climbing in various grades toward an intersection with the Appalachian and Long trails. Beyond the dirt mound across the road at 0.5 mile you can get a fine sense of how rapidly nature reclaims landscapes altered by the hand of man. Closed in 1984, this road is already populated with sizeable striped maples and pin cherries—a kind of advance guard for the more shade-tolerant yellow birch, sugar maple, and beech.

This is an especially good place to study the kinds of plants that thrive in open areas. While gardeners may lump many of these species into the catchall category of "weeds," here in the wild, free from our notions of what is either useful or sublime, they certainly manage to cast their own brand of beauty. Besides, many of our opinions about what is and isn't worthless in the plant world is to some extent a matter of fashion. Fifty years ago, for example, lamb's quarter and curly dock—both of which are now considered weeds—showed up regularly on many people's dinner tables.

Look here for horsetail, yarrow, wild indigo, and selfheal, as well as tall meadow rue, bladder campion, cow vetch, milkweed, and sweet and hop clovers. Purple-flowered raspberries lend splashes of lavender, while buttercups and golden Alexander add touches of gold. Cutleaf and red-banded sedges tickle your thighs, while ferns peek out from a cover of striped maples.

Be prepared along the grassy edges of the woods to be surprised by sudden explosions of ruffed grouse—a bird prone to scaring the daylights out of humans by fleeing the nest when we're almost on top of it. When young chicks are present, if threatened the mother puts on an impressive bit of acting, in the form of a "near-death" scene that plays quite nicely to predators, which tend to go for sick or injured animals. Feigning a broken wing is part of the show, and if that doesn't work, she may emit a series of mournful, high-pitched squeals. In the case of humans too stupid to be lured by even that, she may lie on her back and beat the ground with her wings! Once the threat has passed the mother circles back to gather up her chicks. By autumn young grouse are able to fly, at which time the birds will roost in the safety of trees.

At 2.6 miles, after a stretch of moderate climbing, you'll reach the intersection with the Long and Appalachian trails, where you'll turn right toward the Lost Pond Shelter. It's striking to move from an open, sunlit road cut into a quiet forest of hemlock, beech, and yellow birch. No longer is the path lined with composites, vetches, and milkweeds, but with the more shade-tolerant, moisture-loving bluebead lily, clearstem, wood sorrel, Indian cucumber, and false nettle, as well as the increasingly rare Jack-in-the-pulpit.

Continue to descend on this pathway for approximately 1.5 miles to the intersection of a trail to Old Job Shelter; turn right here, beginning the final leg of our loop. This is in many ways the finest stretch of the walk, marked by a gentle, smooth climb through the forest, much of it beside boulder-choked streams. At 4.9 miles you'll reach Old Job Clearing, which in summer sports huddles of tall fireweed spikes, each one practically screaming its purple color to you as you pass.

At Old Job Shelter the trail turns right into a forest of yellow birch, beech, and maple. Beside you is Lake Brook, which will, over 0.75 mile, guide you gently home. To celebrate your return is a beautiful plunge pool at the trailhead, delicious to the touch on any warm summer afternoon.

WALK #31—FOREST ROAD 301

DISTANCE: 2.2 miles
ENVIRONMENT: Mountain
LOCATION: Green Mountain National Forest. From Rutland, head south on U.S. Highway 7 to the small village of Danby, and turn left onto Forest Road 10. Follow this route eastward for 6.75 miles, and turn right onto Forest Road 30. Follow this for 1.4 miles, and turn left onto Forest Road 301. Park at the gate, and begin walking along this road.

Despite a few logging scars near the end of the path, this is a more engaging trek than the rather ho-hum name of "Forest Road 301" might imply. The old roadway, located in an area closed to all motor vehicles, carves a gentle line through a beautiful mature hardwood forest, ending at a high perch from which you can survey a great, green swell of mountains rising to the north.

Because the forest has yet to reclaim the land cleared to make this road, you'll find it covered by many of the tenacious plants that are so good at growing in disturbed, compacted soils. Some of these plants are so adept at claiming poor ground that they're often used as a means of measuring the general health of a place. Though most of these species are seldom thought of as anything but weeds (and foreign weeds at that!) some have rather interesting tales to tell.

Throughout much of this walk, for example, you'll find bladder campion, oxeye daisy, curly dock, scented bedstraw, and mullein. Use of mullein, with its tall, woolly stem and thick basal leaves, goes back 2,000 years, to a time when Roman soldiers dipped the tips of the plant in grease and then lit them for torches. Tea from the leaves was not only taken by both Native Americans and Europeans for a variety of ailments, but colonists routinely put them in their socks to help stay the biting cold of a New England winter.

Curly dock (or yellow dock), on the other hand, has been a food source in America for a long, long time; during the Depression, steaming bowls of young curly dock leaves routinely made their way to the dinner table. The plant tastes rather like spinach with a hint of lemon, and has half again as much vitamin A and twice the vitamin C as does that more common garden vegetable. Indians routinely made flour from curly dock seeds, and some people continue to use the stems of the plant for what can best be described as a mock rhubarb pie.

Likewise, the young leaves of that ever-present biennial, oxeye daisy, have long been cooked as well as used with other raw vegetables in salads. The bitter oil from older oxeye daisy leaves was at one time a medicine for gout, while European doctors used it to clear the sinus tract.

You'll come to a grassy clearing 0.2 mile down the road on the right. These areas are sometimes known as deer parks, since white-tailed deer browse at their edges, bed down in them, or just plain loiter, chewing their cud before heading back into the woods. Come to this clearing late in the evening and you may well see several of these graceful creatures.

When I took this walk I happened to see several piles of coyote scat lying in the road. While some may view this clever creature as an indication of untouched wilderness, the coyote is actually very good at adapting to the reckless, blustering ways of humans. He can run extremely fast—40 miles per hour in short bursts—swim remarkably well, and has amazing recuperative powers. Healthy coyotes have been caught with severe bullet wounds completely healed over; one male was still going strong after having his lower jaw shot off! In many parts of the country coyotes have thrived not only in the face of development, but against extraordinary efforts by ranchers to wipe them from the face of the earth.

Though coyotes will occasionally eat a young sheep or deer, the take is negligible. Indeed, one of the things that makes coyotes so tenacious is their broad diet, consisting of everything from birds to berries. Coyotes make up one of the best mechanisms for cleaning the forest of carrion, and go a long way in keeping a lid on rodent populations. Nevertheless, a mere 20 years ago the Maine legislature was considering a $50 bounty on them, despite the fact that there were fewer than 500 of the animals in the entire state.

In 0.8 mile is a comely little stream, followed by an area that was once intensively logged. This land is being reclaimed through a natural process known as forest succession, whereby shrubs like raspberry are replaced by fast-growing but short-lived trees such as aspen, paper birch, gray birch, and pin cherry. These in turn yield to more shade-tolerant varieties of trees, including yellow birch

Eastern Coyote

and red maple, to which later may be added trees of the climax forest, such as beech, sugar maple, and hemlock. Some species, such as the birches, start growing fairly quickly after logging because they can sprout new saplings from stumps or roots.

Toward the back of the large, flat cleared area at the end of the main road, hidden at first by a modest wall of brush, is a small dirt road. Follow this upward at a fairly steep angle for roughly 0.5 mile to our turnaround point, just a few miles from the Peru Peak Wilderness. (There will be one faint intersection along the way; stay left.) From these heights you can look northward into the graceful rise and fall of the Green Mountain country, the forest lying thick and beautiful on the distant, crumpled hills.

WALK #32—WILGUS STATE PARK

DISTANCE:	0.6 mile
ENVIRONMENT:	Fresh Water
LOCATION:	Take the Ascutney, Vermont, exit off of Interstate 91, and follow U.S. Highway 5 south for approximately 1.5 miles. The park entrance will be on your left. Immediately after entering the park, make a right turn into the picnic area parking lot. We'll be walking along a riverside nature trail, located on the far side of the picnic area.

Just a stone's throw from U.S. Highway 5, this short, shady amble along the Connecticut River is a refreshing pause for road-weary travelers. The Connecticut, whose name is derived from an Indian phrase meaning "long tidal river," is New England's longest watercourse, winding its way 410 miles from the crumpled, forested uplands of the Canadian border to the waters of Long Island Sound. Thanks to a massive clean-up effort, the Connecticut is once again a resource that charms and inspires. "This stream," wrote former Yale president Timothy Dwight in the early 1800s, "may with more propriety than any other in the world, be named *THE BEAUTIFUL RIVER*. The purity, salubrity and sweetness of its waters; ... the uncommon and universal beauty of its banks ... the rude bluff and the shaggy mountain, are objects which no traveler can thoroughly describe and no reader can adequately imagine."

Beyond beauty, however, this river valley has long been a stage for the comings and goings of various cultures. Great villages of Penacooks and Abnaki Indians once lived here, raising crops, tapping sugar maples, and spearing shad along the riverbanks. Although the river was "discovered" in 1614 by a Dutch sea captain named Adriaen Block, the first European settlement along these upper reaches was a square fort of pine, built south of here by the British in 1724. After this there seemed to be no end to the skirmishes—battles with the Indians, fights with the French, onslaughts from the British, and a tirade of verbal warfare between Ethan Allen and Eleazer Wheelock (co-founder of Dartmouth) over who would ultimately control this verdant land.

Besides the pleasure of the Connecticut River for company, one of the more enjoyable aspects of this walk is the fact that several trees along the trail have been identified, making the trek perfect for those anxious to get a close-up look at a handful of New England's more common trees. Since names are only a beginning, though, let's spend some time talking about a few of these long-time Connecticut Valley residents:

White Pine: (at the beginning of the walk, on the left) White pine has an illustrious history in New England. Capable of growing straight and tall to enormous size, white pines were perfect for making strong, one-piece masts for sailing ships. In colonial times it was strictly against the law for colonists to cut down any white

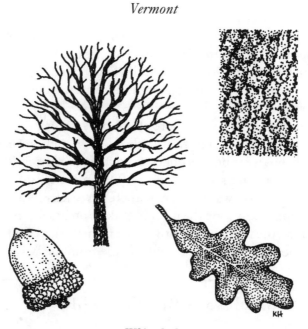

White Oak

pine measuring over 3 feet thick at the stump (just one of many laws that the colonists chose to ignore). So big were these trees that loggers sometimes needed 70 pair of oxen to skid one out of the forest!

White Oak: (0.1 mile in, on the left) While no group of trees was more important to natives of the Northeast than the oaks, most people had a special place in their hearts for certain white oaks. Some white oaks produce acorns with fairly low levels of tannic acid—that bitter, disagreeable taste that puckers your mouth (and, if you ate enough, would eventually harm your digestive tract). Removing tannic acid from acorns required long periods of leaching in water, which the Indians accomplished either by burying them in the ground or hanging them in streams—sometimes for several months. Only then would they be fit to grind into flour, or mix into mush or pemmican. Obviously, locating a white oak with fairly sweet nuts on it, whose tannins could be leached quickly and easily, was something to celebrate.

Yellow Birch: (1.8 miles in, on the left) Of all the birches, yellow birch has the longest, most varied history of commercial use. Carriage makers chose yellow birch to craft their hubs, since the wood is very resistant to cracking, and could be counted on to hold wheel spokes tightly in place for many years. Likewise, many New England shipbuilders preferred yellow birch for making any part of a vessel that was to remain underwater. Tool handles are also constructed of this birch.

Curiously, much of the lore about birch trees in general has nothing to do at all with practical applications. For instance, slender birch branches were not only once used for spanking children, but for flogging prisoners as far back as Roman times. (One legend claims that Christ was beaten with birch sticks.) In addition, witches supposedly rode the midnight skies on brooms made from birch. Light, pleasant teas are still made from the leaves of birches, and Europeans once favored a wine made from the twigs and sap.

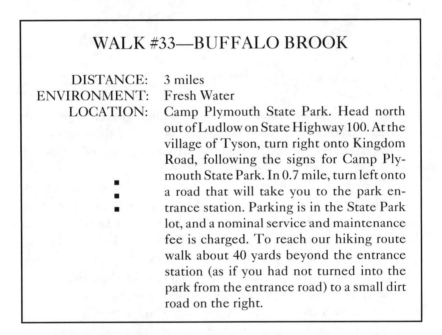

WALK #33—BUFFALO BROOK

DISTANCE: 3 miles
ENVIRONMENT: *Fresh Water*
LOCATION: Camp Plymouth State Park. Head north out of Ludlow on State Highway 100. At the village of Tyson, turn right onto Kingdom Road, following the signs for Camp Plymouth State Park. In 0.7 mile, turn left onto a road that will take you to the park entrance station. Parking is in the State Park lot, and a nominal service and maintenance fee is charged. To reach our hiking route walk about 40 yards beyond the entrance station (as if you had not turned into the park from the entrance road) to a small dirt road on the right.

This walk is particularly pleasant during early morning or late evening, when the buzz of the chickadee and the shout of the ovenbird can be heard ringing through the woods, punctuating the sound of stream water falling over smooth folds of rock.

A half-dozen miles to the east, between Cavendish and South Woodstock, was the location of the eastern main line of Vermont's underground railroad. For three-quarters of a century countless slaves moved north toward the promise of freedom on Canadian

Vermont

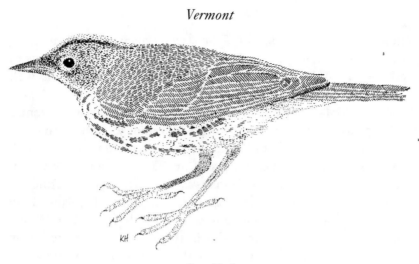

Ovenbird

soil; they were carried much of the way in wooden crates or in wagons with false bottoms. Indeed, Vermont had a long history of anti-slavery sentiment. In 1777, while still a republic, it drafted the first constitution in which slavery was prohibited. Furthermore, open defiance of the Fugitive Slave Law of 1793 was fairly common in Vermont courts. (This defiance gained considerable ground in 1815, when a Middlebury judge stated that the only proof of ownership he would honor in extraditing a man back into slavery was "a bill of sale from God Almighty.") Per capita, more Vermonters fought for the Union in the Civil War—one out of every four men— than in any other state; only one in ten of those were drafted.

Seven years after Lee surrendered to Grant at Appomattox, a boy named Calvin Coolidge was born just north of here, near the town of Plymouth. After wading through a sea of scandals inherited from Warren Harding (Harding died in office), in 1924 Coolidge was elected the 30th president of the United States. Coolidge was an extremely serious man, often referred to as "Silent Cal." One story has it that during a formal dinner, an attractive woman seated next to Coolidge informed him that she had just made a bet that she could get more than two words out of him. "You lose," was all Coolidge said.

As you make your way along the roadway, keep your eyes out at 0.1 mile for nice clusters of shinleaf, a ground cover with elliptical leaves and stalks of fragrant, waxy white flowers. The leaves of this rather common member of the wintergreen family contain a chemical similar to aspirin. They were once used to make a plaster—known as a shin plaster—placed on cuts and wounds to reduce pain. Also in this area is the beautiful bluebead lily, as well as Canada mayflower and wood sorrel.

The walk continues to follow the stream at a very gentle grade, passing through a lovely forest of hemlock, birch, beech, and maple, with fringes of tall meadow rue, clearstem, and selfheal. Common to dry, gravelly sites is an early bloomer, coltsfoot. Coltsfoot was known to the Romans as "cough dispeller," while the English called it coughwort, both names hinting at the plant's long use as a remedy for persistent coughs, asthma, and bronchial congestion. For years asthmatics in this country found relief by smoking coltsfoot leaves, a practice that began to wane only when more effective antihistamines arrived on the scene.

You'll cross Buffalo Brook several times during this walk, giving you a perfect chance to explore some of the easily over-looked wonders of a stream environment. Here are net-winged midge larva, hanging onto rocks in the middle of the current by means of special suction cups. Suction can be increased or de-creased at will by retracting or extending a pistonlike device located in each cup; by letting some of the suction cups loose, and then re-anchoring them in a new spot, the midge larva moves over rocks without being swept away by the current.

In general, stream dwellers have adapted to the forces of flowing water in truly fantastic ways. The sleek, supple body of a fish, for instance, allows it to swim upstream with a minimum of energy. One species of caddis fly actually weaves a net in the fork of a tiny twig, which it uses to snare food drifting by in the current. Blackfly larva, which grow into one of the most detested insects of northern New England, anchor themselves to webs of silk spun against a rock, snatching food from the current with a pair of hairy appendages. If a blackfly larva is accidentally dislodged, it can return by reeling itself back upstream with a safety line anchored to the home web.

At 1.3 miles is a fork in the stream; stay right. You'll come to our turnaround in another 0.2 mile, at a point where Buffalo Brook comes in from the left, along a faint roadway, and Reading Pond Brook continues straight up the main forested ravine. You may want to sit on the point of land that lies between these two watercourses, savoring for a while what John Milton once called the "liquid lapse of murmuring streams."

WALK #34—AMITY POND NATURAL AREA

DISTANCE: 0.9 mile

ENVIRONMENT: Mountain

LOCATION: Vermont State Lands. From the intersection of State Highway 12 and U.S. 4 in downtown Woodstock, head north on Highway 12 for approximately 1.1 miles, turning right at a sign for Suicide Six Ski Area. In 2 miles you'll reach a fork in the road at the village of South Pomfret, where you'll stay right. (Suicide Six Ski Area is to the left.) In just under 5 miles you'll see a road taking off to the left, marked by a sign reading "To Interstate 89." Take this left, and veer left once again in approximately 1.7 miles. Amity Pond Natural Area is down this road 2.2 miles, on your left. (The entrance is marked by an identification sign located just off the side of the road.) A small parking area is across from the entrance.

"It is our hope that this park may be a true refuge," wrote Dick and Elizabeth Brett, who donated this land 20 years ago to the state of Vermont. "It is our hope that the sportsmanship of those who travel by machine will permit this small area to be a sanctuary for wildlife, native plants, and the people who cherish these things in an atmosphere of quiet relaxation."

And indeed Amity Pond provides just that. The high spine of this preserve offers striking views of Ascutney, Killington, and the Pico Mountains to the south. And yet here nature doesn't so much shout down rocky escarpments and soaring vistas, as it whispers across grassy knolls and highlands. Having been heavily grazed and doggedly timbered for centuries, Amity, it seems, has at last come to rest. You can almost feel a sigh of relief—in a summer breeze through the sedges, in the sleepy look of a green frog waiting for flies at the edge of a pond, in the rose-breasted grosbeaks flitting from forest to field looking for spiders and seeds.

We'll be walking along a gentle, blazed route that can be followed virtually any time of the year. Those who want more of Amity are encouraged to pursue trails to the many other

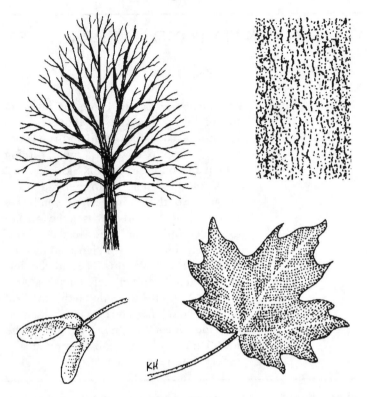

Sugar Maple

nooks and crannies of the preserve, each as delightful as those presented here. Do be aware, however, that some paths are hard to follow, especially at the height of summer when covered in thick cloaks of grass.

The first few feet of our path is through a small grassy meadow, framed by a plantation of red pine—a tree that's long been planted along highways throughout New England. The trail forks immediately, at which point we'll take the right branch, sinking quickly into a cool canopy of birch and sugar maple. The sugar maple, incidentally, the famous signature tree of Vermont, has only had a firm hold on the New England landscape for a relatively short amount of time. When a mile-thick sheet of ice finally began to retreat from the northeastern United States some 12,000 to 20,000 years ago, it of course left a landscape entirely bereft of trees. Nearly two millennia passed before spruce began to invade the region, followed by fir, and then, ever so slowly, aspen and alder. It was much later that trees like the sugar maple migrated up from the south. Barely 2,000 years have passed since this tree, along with yellow birch and American beech, became the dominant members of the northern New England hardwood forest.

The path climbs gently through the forest, coming out on a high, sunny meadow peppered with milkweed and raspberry. Immediately to the right, on the other side of a fence post with a blue diamond cross-country ski marker, is tiny Amity Pond. According to local legend, many years ago two girls attending the East Barnard School made a solemn vow to each other that they would always remain the best of friends. Unfortunately, one wed a man from the village of Pomfret, and the other a beau from Barnard. Remaining true to their promise, though, each year without fail the girls arranged by letter to meet for a summer picnic at this small pond; thus it became known as Amity's Pond.

Today Amity Pond, with its fringe of red pine, maple, and aspen, is every bit as delightful a place for a picnic as it was in the days of old. And yet as water and shore plants continue to die and accumulate on the bottom of the pond, it grows ever smaller. There will come a day in the not too distant future that best friends may share lunch not at the edge of a pond, but in the arms of a grassy meadow.

Just past Amity Pond you'll reach a crest of land offering beautiful views to the south and west. From here continue straight down the hillside, which in mid-to late summer will be splashed with asters. Though the path may be faint here, use the blue diamond cross-country ski markers to guide you. At the bottom of the hill the Woodstock Trail comes in from the left, but you continue straight into a fine woodland. Our path continues to meander down to a tiny stream at 0.5 mile—a mere trickle of water flowing through a hushed cathedral of maple, beech, birch, and an occasional mammoth white pine. This is our turnaround point.

On the way back, when you again reach the crest of the grassy hill you descended on the outbound walk (the "view spot," beside a large slab of rock), turn to the right (east) and head toward a blue diamond cross-country ski marker. You'll reach the starting point by first passing a camping shelter and then another small pond—this one fringed with clusters of aspen and willow, as well as by lovely mats of strawberry, red clover, milkweed, and sensitive fern.

WALK #35—CHITTENDEN BROOK

DISTANCE: 2.5 miles
ENVIRONMENT: Forest
LOCATION: Green Mountain National Forest. From the intersection of state highways 53 and 73, head east on Highway 73 for just over 9 miles, then turn right (south) onto the entrance road to Chittenden Brook Campground (Forest Road 45). Follow this road to the campground entrance, where you'll see a small two-track road taking off to the left, marked by a sign that reads "Campground Loop Trail." Park here, out of the way of campground traffic, and begin your walk along this path.

There's a lot packed into this 2.5 miles of pathway—meadows splashed with wildflowers, cool, tumbling streams, beaver ponds, and thick blankets of forest. A few walkers will be fortunate enough to see moose along the latter stretches of the trail, and nearly everyone will have a good chance at hearing the splendid singing of red-eyed vireos, chestnut-sided warblers, and one of Thoreau's personal favorites, the wood thrush.

Wood Thrush

Chestnut-sided Warbler

Both the campground and the brook accompanying you for much of this walk take their names from a colorful farmer and barkeep who was to become Vermont's first governor, Thomas Chittenden. Chittenden, whose one eye gave him a formidable appearance, served almost continuously as governor of the Vermont republic and state from 1778 to 1797. It was this man who held the fledgling republic together during Ethan Allen's imprisonment during the late 1770s—no small feat, considering the packs of land-hungry New Yorkers and various others who stood by waiting to lay into the lands of the Green Mountain Boys. Royall Tyler, a lawyer who eventually gained appointment to the Vermont Supreme Court, is credited with writing this rousing little ditty about Governor Chittenden:

> Talk not of your Washingtons,
> Hancocks and Sullivans,
> And all the wild crew;
> Our Tom set on high
> With his single eye
> Can more espy
> Than they can with two.

The first part of this walk climbs along a wide, grassy path fringed with sugar maple, yellow birch, and striped maple. Black-eyed Susans nod their sunny yellow heads in the breeze, while patches of red clover (Vermont's state flower) and fireweed lend striking touches of pink and lavender to the broad strokes of green grass. Fireweed, a tall plant sporting spikes of bright purple blossoms, is not only beautiful to look at, but is considered by many to be quite tasty. The stem has a sweet inner pith, and the leaves are often used both for making teas and as a cooked green. For that matter, the red clover you see here is hardly without virtues of its own. Herbalists in Europe have long prescribed a tea made from clover blossoms to aid in constipation, while clover poultices are used even today in treating athlete's foot.

As you continue a gentle climb, watch the edges of the path for ruffed grouse, which may flush suddenly. At your approach a female with chicks will likely run off through the brush feigning a broken wing, all the while making the most amazing whimpering noises—a well-orchestrated ruse to distract you from her young. In 0.75 mile the path makes a sharp turn to the right, nuzzling up to a fine thicket of hobblebush. This *viburnum*, easily recognized by its large, round, opposite leaves displaying prominent veins, is so named because its low-slung branches often take root, forming trip lines that catch, or "hobble" those wandering through the forest. Hobblebush is one of the first shrubs to flower in May, displaying flat clusters of tiny white blossoms encircled by much larger white blooms. (These outer blossoms are actually sterile.) Later in the summer the smaller flowers produce berries that turn from red to blue-black; these are quite sweet, and so much like a raisin that many people refer to hobblebush as "wild raisin."

Soon the grassy path meets and crosses Chittenden Brook. When you reach the other side turn right, following the Campground Loop Trail as it makes its way along the brook downstream through the forest. Notice the difference in the plants growing in this slice of cool forest compared to what thrived in open, drier grassy patches. Suddenly there's a riot of trillium, bluebead lily, and wood sorrel, as well as Indian cucumber, partridgeberry, and hair cap moss. As you gain a high bench overlooking the brook, the walk becomes a gentle amble through a myriad of soft shadows, muted summer light dripping like honey into the deep ravines of the forest.

At 1.5 miles is an intersection with the Chittenden Brook Trail. Follow the signed pathway to the beaver ponds, located at the end of an easy 0.2-mile walk to the west. The beaver activity in this area varies from year to year, but in late evening those willing to brave the bugs and thickets may well spot these furry engineers. If you're ever close enough to a beaver to get a really good look, you'll notice that the animal's rear feet, which lie at the end of short, powerful legs, are webbed between the toes to aid in swimming. (For truly "high-speed" swimming—perhaps 2.5 miles per hour—beaver alternate use of these feet with strokes of their large, flat tails.) A beaver's front feet are without webs and shaped like small hands. With these he can drag sticks, dig holes, comb fur, and a host of other tasks.

Beaver families vary in number, but typically consist of an adult female, male, yearlings, and kits—generally five to seven animals in all. Adult females call the shots in beaverland, but on the whole the family is extremely sociable. In late evening they can be seen grooming one another and generally frolicking together before they all settle back into their large, cone-shaped lodges. In the spring of their second year—the age of sexual maturity—teenagers either volunteer or are persuaded by their parents to set up house somewhere else, often several miles away.

While you're tromping around these wet areas, watch the muddy ground for tracks of another common visitor here—the moose. When you're ready, return to the Campground Loop Trail the same way you came. Turn left, and in just over 0.25 mile, after a delightful walk along the stream, you'll find yourself on the far side of Chittenden Brook Campground.

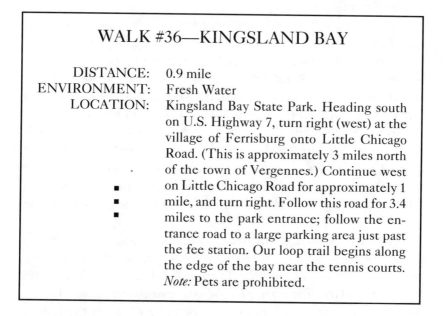

WALK #36—KINGSLAND BAY

DISTANCE: 0.9 mile
ENVIRONMENT: Fresh Water
LOCATION: Kingsland Bay State Park. Heading south on U.S. Highway 7, turn right (west) at the village of Ferrisburg onto Little Chicago Road. (This is approximately 3 miles north of the town of Vergennes.) Continue west on Little Chicago Road for approximately 1 mile, and turn right. Follow this road for 3.4 miles to the park entrance; follow the entrance road to a large parking area just past the fee station. Our loop trail begins along the edge of the bay near the tennis courts. *Note:* Pets are prohibited.

Kingsland Bay State Park is not only small, but is reached only by leaving the beaten path and heading down a twisted braid of narrow country roads. The benefit of such remoteness is that the park remains a relatively quiet place, where local chums get together on hot summer days for burgers and Frisbee and sailboarding. The one trail here is along a small peninsula that juts out into the bay, offering an easy amble through a typical Vermont lowland forest, complete with fine, cool views of Lake Champlain.

Unfortunately, we know little about the various Indian peoples who lived here in the centuries before the arrival of the Europeans. For the most part our tales begin with the French explorer, military man, and mapmaker who would ultimately lend his name to this long, blue reach of water—Samuel de Champlain.

In the fall of 1608, four years after Champlain had first mapped the coasts of Maine and New Hampshire, an Algonquin chief persuaded Champlain to lead an expedition into this lake to strike down the Algonquin's archenemies, the Iroquois. After a couple of rather uneventful days, on the night of July 29, across the water from where you now stand, Champlain and the Algonquins did indeed meet their enemy. Messengers were sent from the Iroquois, and, since the darkness of night made it nearly impossible to know who was friend and who was foe, both sides agreed to begin the battle at first light.

As darkness lifted, Champlain saw that he was easily outnumbered three to one. Undaunted, he led the Algonquin on a slow, confident march toward the advancing front line of the Iroquois. When the fearless Frenchman got to within about 30 yards, he reports seeing the Iroquois leaders make a move to draw their bows. "I took aim with my arquebus and shot straight at one of the three chiefs," he writes in his journal, "and with this shot two fell to the ground and one of their companions was wounded who died thereof a little later." Champlain's Algonquin friends could hardly have been more encouraged. They erupted into a boisterous attack, sending the alarmed Iroquois running into the shadows of the forest.

Some have suggested that with this single shot from his arquebus, Champlain set in motion a new level of hostility between the Algonquin and the Iroquois—a feud that France and Britain would use in their battle against each other for control of the New World. In truth, this interpretation probably gives the July 30 melee more consequence than it deserves. And yet it most certainly fueled the anger of the Iroquois, who, 32 years later, em-

Shagbark Hickory

barked on a series of some of the bloodiest raids in history against the French and their Algonquin friends.

Our walk begins in the cool shade of a forest thick with sugar maple, white cedar, hemlock, black cherry, and shadbush, the ground peppered with white trillium and an occasional false Solomon's seal. At about 0.1 mile are nice huddles of white oak, shagbark hickory, hemlock, and hop hornbeam, or, as it is also known, ironwood. At 0.2 mile a short spur trail heads left to a fine view spot. From here you can see the long sweep of the Adirondacks, rising into the New York sky from the far shores of Lake Champlain.

Leaving this rather pleasant perch you'll pass through a stately stand of red pine, the name derived from the tree's beautiful thick, reddish-brown bark. Although for over 200 years people have been calling this tree Norway Pine, this is a complete misnomer, since the mighty red is most certainly a native of the New World. Red pine grows well even on poor soils, sometimes able to push out a remarkable 18 to 24 inches of growth in a single year! As such, it's a favorite tree for replanting forests that have been cut or burned.

Our path rounds a small headland at 0.4 mile, and then, after a short climb, doubles back toward the main park. Just after this climb another spur trail takes off to the left, leading to another view spot, this one surrounded by some lovely clusters of honeysuckle.

Continue to make your way back through the forest, accompanied by white oak, hobblebush, and basswood. In 0.9 mile the path emerges near the tennis courts, just a few yards from where you started your trek.

WALK #37—BURTON ISLAND

DISTANCE: 2 miles
ENVIRONMENT: Fresh Water
LOCATION: Burton Island State Park. From the town of St. Alban's, Vermont, head west on State Highway 36 for approximately 5 miles, and turn left (south), following signs for Kill Kare State Park. A ferry will then take you from Kill Kare to Burton Island State Park. Once you arrive on Burton Island, you may want to stop in at the park office just north of the dock slip for a map of the park. To reach our trailhead, walk through the camping area until you reach the westernmost camping shelter. (All of these shelters have been named after trees; the one beside our trailhead is called "Juniper.") We'll be walking along the North Shore Trail, which heads west from beside this last lean-to.

Though it lies only a couple of good stone skips from the mainland, Burton Island, where automobiles are not allowed, seems like another world. How refreshing it is to find beautiful campgrounds bereft of a single sedan, to be able to peruse 250 acres of beaches and meadows and woodlands accompanied not by honking horns or racing engines, but by birdsong, the scamper of raccoons in the middle of the night, and the whisper of waves lapping against shoreline rocks. So appealing is the absence of cars here, so easily do campers transport their beer, bicycles, and bags of groceries from the ferry by simple wheeled carts, that it begs the question why we haven't created many more such recreation areas throughout the country.

Before you begin this walk, stop at the park office for a map, as well as a copy of a fine new guide to the North Shore Trail. The path we'll be walking begins 0.6 mile from the dock slip, beside the camping shelter tagged "Juniper." Things get interesting almost immediately, your first steps framed by fringes of cow vetch, and behind that, stately lines of staghorn sumac. Both staghorn and smooth sumac were used by Indians for a refreshing drink (the hairy fruits were soaked in water), as well as for making a bark tea that was reportedly effective in treating sore throats; a decoction of smooth sumac root and branches, on the other hand, was used as a treatment for gonorrhea.

Roughly 40 yards into the walk the trail passes between two large northern white cedars, and then meanders into a small huddle of aspen, their leaves dancing in the slightest puff of air. Nearby is common milkweed. Though sometimes viewed as a pest, milkweed has a rather impressive history of use. (It's also one of the few flowers along this stretch of trail native to America.) There are reports of native peoples in what is now Virginia using milkweed to treat skin disorders more than 400 years ago. Some 200 years later European-based medicine got behind the plant, proclaiming it to be an effective treatment for respiratory ailments. Finally, in the 20th century, long after most American doctors had stopped using the plant as a medicinal, the milkweed harvest started up again.

Northern White Cedar

This time the goal was to collect the mature pods, full of silky seed hairs, which became the primary stuffing material in Navy life jackets during the last years of World War II.

Thus far beautiful Lake Champlain has been a constant companion, and a particularly nice view of it opens up at about 0.1 mile. Twenty thousand years ago, during the height of the Wisconsin Ice Age, this beautiful valley was covered in a mass of ice stretching all the way to Long Island. After the end of glacial advance, when the icy fingers that had scoured and gouged the land finally started to recoil, meltwater began accumulating here in tremendous quantities. By the time the plug of ice to the north in the St. Lawrence Valley melted, creating a passage to the Atlantic, the level of the lake was actually hundreds of feet higher than you see it today.

The North Shore Trail continues to hug the waterline, past clusters of two European introductions—white campion and purple loosestrife. Like milkweed, loosestrife was once considered far more than just a garden pest. Greeks burned the plant to keep bugs at bay and, in a more mysterious vein, hung large garlands of it around the necks of their oxen, believing that it encouraged the animals to work together as a team. Today some herbalists still prescribe the plant as a treatment for diarrhea.

The scene changes abruptly as the path enters a forest of white pine, spruce, and speckled alder. Notice the thick carpet of pine needles here. Conifer needles are very slow to decompose, in part because they're covered by a waxy coating that helps the tree conserve moisture by allowing less water to escape through the pores.

At 0.2 mile are the quiet waters of Eagle Bay. This is a fine place to picnic, nap, or simply invest in a long, lazy Vermont daydream. What grand times there must have been here in the 1850s for the children of Burton Island's sharecropping caretakers. Done for the season with daily boat rides back and forth to St. Albans' school, it's easy to imagine them hurrying through their farm chores in order to make fast tracks to sun-drenched Eagle Bay. Great men of the day may have been wrapped up in their own countryside adventures—Thoreau at Walden Pond, Whitman on the back roads of New York—yet none of that would have seemed of any more consequence than being a kid right here, smack in the middle of a slow, sweet Burton Island summer.

Leaving the bay and its flocks of ring-billed gulls behind, we'll begin our return trip along the Eagle Bay Trail, which heads into the woods beside a large birch snag. Unlike the bare floor of the coniferous forest we passed earlier, the ground in this mixed deciduous forest is washed with shade-tolerant plants, including ferns, violet, twisted stalk, bunchberry, and Solomon's seal. At 0.5 mile the path enters a more open area. Just past a stretch of wooden treadways are fine samples of red osier, pin cherry, and white ash, the latter tree being the preferred wood for making everything from snowshoes to baseball bats.

At just over 0.6 mile, just this side of a dirt roadway, is a trail coming in from the left; turn back onto this pathway. Our starting point is reached in about 0.1 mile, after passing a lovely cattail marsh on the left—complete with the buzz of red-winged blackbirds—as well as a magnificent swamp white oak on the right.

Ring-billed Gull

WALK #38—PEACHAM BOG

DISTANCE: 4.8 miles
ENVIRONMENT: Fresh Water
LOCATION: Groton State Forest. From Interstate 91, head west on U.S. Highway 2 for 18.2 miles to State Highway 232, and turn left (south). Follow this road south for 8.4 miles to the main entrance into Groton State Forest. The nature center and parking area are 1.7 miles down this road on the left, just past the Big Deer Campground. Our walk takes off from the far side of this lot.

> I have frequently found that I was attracted solely by a few square rods of impermeable and unfathomable bog—a natural sink in one corner of it. That was the jewel that dazzled me. I derive more of my subsistence from the swamps which surround my native town than from the cultivated gardens in the village.
>
> —*Henry David Thoreau*

Much of the 25,000-acre Groton State Forest, which was once blanketed with great quilts of conifers, is today covered with fine groves of yellow birch, red maple, and white birch, a change caused in large part by intense fires that seared these uplands in the early 1900s. The sheer size of this reserve (the second largest state landholding in Vermont), sustains a rich variety of wildlife, including black bear, fisher, mink, moose, and deer.

The charm of this place hardly stops at the boundaries of the state forest. Nearby are delightful braids of twisted country roads, leading to some of the most idyllic Vermont villages imaginable. A couple of these, including nearby Peacham (sometimes called the most photographed town in Vermont) rest atop hills that afford fine views of the surrounding countryside. Such elevated sites were chosen not for the scenery (heaven forbid such frivolousness!), but to eke a few more frost-free days out of the growing season by planting crops above the colder air of the valley bottoms.

Before heading down the trail, notice the fringe of tamaracks, their lacy branches rimming the parking area like a plantation of feather dusters. Tamarack needles turn gold and drop off each

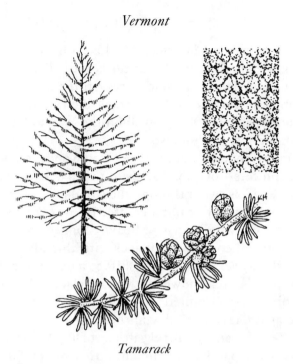

Tamarack

autumn, leaving a huddle of ragged gray skeletons. (On occasion, though, what you'll see is in fact a dead stand of trees, killed by infestations of the larch sawfly.) For early northern New England Indian tribes, tamaracks had a special relationship to the white birch, which is also visible along the path to Peacham Bog. The bark of the white birch provided shell material for constructing canoes; the sinewy roots of the tamarack were then turned into the thread with which that bark was sewn together.

Once you top the small hill beside the parking area and enter the forest, watch the ground for mats of both bunchberry and wintergreen. The damp, cold New England winters did much to aggravate rheumatism in early Indian peoples, and one of their favorite remedies was wintergreen tea. Colonists discovered the benefits of the beverage rather by accident, when they were searching for substitutes to the brew supplied by the East India Company, which was no longer available during the boycott of the 1773 Tea Act. Scientists later discovered that the oil of wintergreen is composed primarily of *methyl salicylate*, a close relative to aspirin. Wintergreen oil (now synthetically produced) is still used as an ingredient in externally applied muscle ointments.

At 0.4 mile is an intersection, the path to Peacham Bog continuing straight through a beautiful weave of balsam and birch. Two-tenths mile later cross one of two strip cuts; this area, harvested during the summer of 1984, is now filled with raspberry, pin cherry, and blackberry, and is well on the way to becoming an honest to goodness birch forest.

We mentioned earlier that the birch woods replaced large stands of conifers—over 850 acres in this particular section of forest—when fires swept through the woods around the turn of the century. Whether or not a conifer forest ever returns to a severely burned, windblown, or heavily logged area depends a great deal on soil conditions. Places with thick layers of well-drained soil may see a long-term shift to a beech-maple forest. In much of this area, however, where glacial deposits have created thin, poorly drained soils, the more adaptive conifers may once again have their day in the sun.

At 1.25 miles are beautiful gardens of hay-scented fern and woodfern, with patches of bunchberries never far away. A pocket of brackish water opens up at 1.75 miles—the southwest leg of Peacham Bog. Our path plunges back into the spruce-fir forest, finally reaching a spongy slice of true peat bog 0.5 mile later, near nice clusters of snowberry. Here is a habitat unlike any other, a haunting carpet of sphagnum, sedge, leatherleaf, laurel, rhodora, and rosemary—all spiked with huddles of tamarack and black spruce. Not many plants can withstand the high levels of acidity found in a bog like this, which registers just slightly higher on the pH scale than vinegar. (Please keep in mind that the vegetative mat of a bog is extremely fragile. Do not wander off the main trail.)

These 200 acres are unique in that they form what is commonly referred to as a raised bog. This is a phenomenon whereby thicker and thicker layers of saturated peat accumulate, ultimately building a dome-shaped mass that actually rises above the level of the original cavity. This may not seem so amazing until you realize that this means the water level is also higher in the middle of the bog than at the edges—a defiance of gravity, if you will. At this point little is understood about the mechanics of such natural engineering.

WALK #39—MOOSE RIVER

DISTANCE: 1 mile
ENVIRONMENT: Fresh Water
LOCATION: Victory Basin Wildlife Management Area. From Interstate 91, exit at U.S. Highway 2 and head east. Approximately 3 miles east of St. Johnsbury, you'll come to the intersection of U.S. Highway 2 and State Highway 18. Continue east on U.S. 2 for 8.8 miles, and turn left on a road with a sign pointing to the community of Victory (now just a small scatter of buildings). Our parking area, called Mitchell's Landing, is located on the left, 4.6 miles down this road. From the parking area, walk 0.2 mile back south along the entrance road until you see a wooden snowmobile bridge on the left crossing the Moose River. This is our walking path.

This short stroll along the beautiful Moose River can be easily combined with our other stroll at Victory Bog (see Walk #40), which also leaves from the same parking area. Taken together these two treks offer a fine introduction to one of the richest, quietest wildlife habitats in the state of Vermont.

The view from the snowmobile bridge at 0.2 mile (an old railroad route) is definitely one worth savoring. Upstream to the northeast is a wild patchwork of mountains and wetlands, the fruits of the watershed making a fast dance to the Connecticut River via the Passumpsic. (The Connecticut River drains more than a third of the land in the state of Vermont.) Pine and spruce trees were cut from these banks 150 years ago and then floated down the Moose River to downstream sawmills; this industry got a major shot in the arm when the Victory Branch Railroad was punched up the valley in the 1880s. To say that logging had a profound impact on the New England landscape is a tremendous understatement. The old Bog Pond Mill alone, which from 1892 to 1900 was the commercial center of the village of Victory, ran more than five million board feet a year through its steam and water-driven saws. Scarcely 25 years after those blades first started turning, the old growth virgin spruce forest of the Moose River drainage had disappeared.

From the bridge our path takes a sharp right turn, following the Moose River downstream for the remainder of the walk. Watch here for clubmosses, whorled wood asters, foamflower, strawberry, meadow rue, and meadowsweet. While the hillside on your left is thick with spruce, nearer the path is a more deciduous mix of maples, birch, and alder. At 0.3 mile, on the far side of the river, are the remains of an old sawmill foundation, a remnant of the lumbering days discussed earlier. From this point the pathway is a bit overgrown, but if you follow it for another 0.1 mile you'll come to a still, peaceful pool of water—a last pause for the Moose before it begins a rocky tumble southward to the sleepy village of Concord.

This river is well named. Walking down these paths in early morning or late evening offers a better than average chance of spotting moose. Those long, gangly legs that allow these animals to maneuver so efficiently when dining in the muck of swamps, also help them traverse deep snows. Unlike deer, which in winter will travel in lines to trample paths through the snow, the moose has no need for such team efforts.

WALK #40—VICTORY BOG

DISTANCE: 0.8 mile

ENVIRONMENT: Fresh Water

LOCATION: Victory Basin Wildlife Management Area. From Interstate 91, exit at U.S. Highway 2 and head east. Approximately 3 miles east of St. Johnsbury, you'll come to the intersection of U.S. Highway 2 and State Highway 18. Continue east on Highway 2 for 8.8 miles, and turn left on a road with a sign pointing to the community of Victory (now just a small scatter of buildings). Our parking area, called Mitchell's Landing, is located on the left, 4.6 miles down this road. The trail takes off across the road from, and slightly to the right of, the parking area, and is marked by number 2.

Great Blue Heron

The trails at Victory Basin Wildlife Management Area have almost no markings on them, tend to quickly end up in the middle of nowhere, and, in more than a few places, are half overgrown with a shaggy tangle of grasses, weeds, and shrubs. In other words, this is as perfect a wild getaway as you'll find anywhere in Vermont. If you're the kind of nature enthusiast who doesn't mind donning long pants and picking your way through a tumble of untrammeled nature, this is clearly the place for you. Literary historian Walter Bagehot once made a statement that applies well to the enjoyment of places like Victory Bog: "To a great experience one thing is essential—an experiencing nature."

The Moose River traces a silent, twisted path through a rich freshwater marsh and bog. A great sweep of mountains fills the eastern horizon, each autumn set afire by the fluttering reds, oranges, and golds of millions of maple and birch leaves. Moose tracks can be found in almost every lowland patch of mud, as can those of mink, weasel, otter, beaver, and muskrat; under the cover of the surrounding hardwoods are fisher, bear, and bobcat. Birds absolutely abound, with more than a dozen species of warblers and sparrows alone. Bitterns, and green and great blue herons stalk the lowland marshes; osprey, marsh, broad-winged, and red-tailed hawks hug the skies overhead.

Across the road and slightly to the south is a grassy pathway descending through the woods to the edge of Moose River. From the bank turn left, and wind your way northward along what is really an old railroad bed. By 0.1 mile the world is framed by sprawling mountain vistas on the right and a wonderful cattail marsh on the left, the latter a favorite hangout of red-winged blackbirds, swamp swallows, wrens, and muskrats. If you've read many nature books you may already be aware of the extensive list of uses people have come up with for cattails, but a few of them are worth repeating. For starters, practically all of this plant is edible (not to mention highly nutritious), from its starchy root stalks to its fuzzy brown flower head. The roots taste like potatoes, the young stalks like celery or cucumber, and the developing flowers a bit like corn. Furthermore, the pollen is a wonderful addition to breads and pancakes. Native peoples used cattail leaves extensively in weaving, soaked the flower heads in animal fat to make torches, and employed the downy seeds as both diapers and padding for cradle boards.

Continue through clumps of spruce, alder, tamarack, honeysuckle, blueberry, currant, meadowsweet, and shadbush, taking plenty of time to explore the wild edges of Moose River. Watch for sudden eruptions of wings along the banks, which likely as not will belong to the robin-sized spotted sandpiper. This is a very reclusive bird, one that you'd likely never catch sight of were you walking in a more heavily visited area. In a fascinating reversal of typical mating rituals, it's the female spotted sandpiper that attracts the male with a strutting courtship display. Once eggs are laid the male may well get left behind to incubate and raise the young, while the female goes off in search of another mate. In fall the sandpipers don't cluster, but rather slip quietly away, a few at a time in the dark of night, many bound for wintering grounds in South America and the Caribbean.

WALK #41—LAKE WILLOUGHBY OVERLOOKS

DISTANCE: 3.4 miles
ENVIRONMENT: Mountain
LOCATION: Vermont State Lands. From the intersection of state highways 16 and 5A, head south on Highway 5A to the beach at the south end of Lake Willoughby. From this point continue south on Highway 5A for 0.6 mile. Turn right onto a dirt road, and continue west for 1.8 miles to a small parking area on the right. (Stay right at the fork in the road at 0.5 mile.) The trail begins 10 yards up the road past the parking area, on the right. A small sign identifies this path as the Mount Hor Trail.

Resting in a crescent-shaped basin beneath massive glacial-scoured bluffs, Lake Willoughby is as enticing as any place in New England. The scale here is overwhelming—a fact that tends to amplify the general sense of wildness. Cliffs on the western and eastern flanks of mounts Hor and Pisgah rise to dizzying heights, while their feet lie anchored in more than 300 feet of cold, steely water. From the southernmost Willoughby Overlook you can see an endless cascade of high ridges to the southeast, flowing all the way to the great White Mountains of New Hampshire.

The path for our walk to the Willougby Overlooks begins a few yards west of the parking area, on the right (north) side of the road. Before you hit the trail, notice the beautiful purple-flowering raspberries along the road, a thornless member of the rose family which in summer sports lovely pink or lavender flowers. Your route through much of this mountain country will

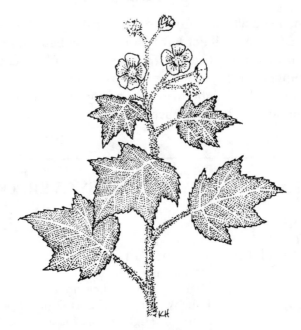

Purple-flowering Raspberry

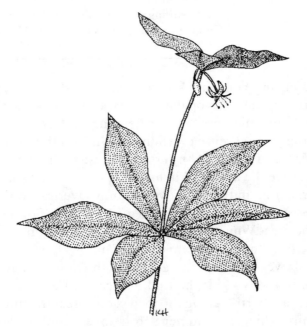

Indian Cucumber

wind through a young forest of sugar maple, birch, and beech. Equally engaging, however, are the ground plants that thrive in this moist, protected environment. During the first 0.25 mile of the walk keep your eyes to the ground for Canada mayflower, lily of the valley, horsetail, and the long, whorled leaves of Indian cucumber. This latter plant is fairly uncommon today, although Indians of the area once harvested the root—which does indeed smell and taste somewhat like a cucumber—in significant quantities as a source of both food and medicine. Indian cucumber's genus name—*Medeola*—is in fact a reference to the great sorceress and herbal healer Medea.

As you walk through the forest, notice how in some places the ground plants grow rather sparsely, while in others they form thick, lush mats. While soil composition and moisture play a big part in determining the exact nature of this weave, another important factor is sunlight. This is why you'll often see the greatest profusion of plants right along the trail; the clearing of trees for the pathway has left openings in the canopy, thus giving rise to a greater variety, and density, of vegetation.

At 0.75 mile you'll reach a "T" junction. We'll take a right here; those with some climb left in them, however, can take a left and, in 0.2 mile, be on top of Mount Hor. Near this intersection watch for the creamy white flowers of wild leek, as well as the beautiful wood sorrel, a plant with cloverlike leaves and delicate white or pink blossoms, one to a stalk. Although common in New England, wood sorrel is actually a native of the British Isles, where many claim it to be the true shamrock. It was the plant's three-lobed leaves, so the story goes, that Saint Patrick used to explain the concept of Christian Trinity to the pagan Celts.

Just under 1.4 miles the trail splits. Both forks go to very different overlooks of Lake Willougby. Begin on the right branch, gaining tremendous views across the lake to the sheer walls of Mount Pisgah, and then move on to the other overlook, which offers glimpses of the rolling landscape to the north. Each place is steeped in what seems almost regal beauty—perfect testimonies to the appropriateness of this lonely corner of Vermont having been nicknamed the "Northeast Kingdom."

WALK #42—SOUTH SHORE TRAIL

DISTANCE:	2.4 miles
ENVIRONMENT:	Forest
LOCATION:	Willoughby State Forest. From the junction of state highways 16 and 5A, head south on Highway 5A to the south end of Lake Willoughby. Forty yards past the beach, turn right into a small parking area. The trail begins on the north side of the parking lot.

This gentle meander, ideal for younger children, carries walkers through the mixed deciduous forest that blankets the steep southwest flanks of Lake Willoughby. Here are small streams dancing down dimly lit, boulder-choked ravines, and the lilting chanties of warblers. This is a relatively young forest, thick and healthy, well-nourished by the rich beds of lime that were laid down 500 million years ago. In many places along the trail the leaf canopy is woven so tightly that the lake below is all but hidden, offering little more than an occasional shimmer through the slender branches of the sugar maples. This is a trail for slow, deliberate walkers—those who revel in bright splashes of wildflowers, who enjoy the soft, cool brush of ferns against their bare legs.

Once the domain of the St. Francis Indians, by the middle 1700s the shores of Lake Willoughby were feeling the restless feet of Europeans. At first they came in trickles, arriving through the upper drainages of the Connecticut River looking for furs and fish. But by the 1780s they were coming in force, determined to wrest settlements from lands recently made available by the "Independent State of Vermont."

Unfortunately, after working their proverbial fingers to the bone to farm (under grant laws at least 5 acres had to be cultivated), tensions with the British again began to rise, culminating in the War of 1812. The people of the village of Westmore, located on the northeast side of the lake, were well aware of the dangers of this isolated location, especially given the close proximity of British troops to the north. Almost to a person the residents packed up their belongings and headed for larger population centers to the south.

The shores of Willoughby grew quiet again, becoming a perfect haven for the smugglers who hid in these twisted ravines. These particular smugglers, mind you, were hardly wild-eyed pirates with evil, toothless grins—rogues who defined a bad day as one without murder and pillage. Because of the remote location— only a few bad roads connected this part of Vermont to cities of the south—the early settlers were bound economically to Canadian population centers like Montreal. When President Jefferson issued the Embargo Act, which forbade trade with England and any of her colonies, it was a terrible blow to the people of this region. Not willing to abandon their homes, some residents took to smuggling cattle across the Canadian line, where they brought fat prices from the British. The major route for these operations was located just west of here, in the Barton Valley. The Lake Willoughby area is thought to have been a popular place for these renegade cowboys to catch their breath during dogged pursuits by federal marshals.

One-tenth mile from the parking area is an open campsite. Our walk continues down a gentle slope, and, in about 40 yards, takes off to the right on a small footpath. In June along this stretch you'll see the blooms of purple-flowering raspberry, as well as the last blossoms of purple trillium. This latter plant is as foul in odor

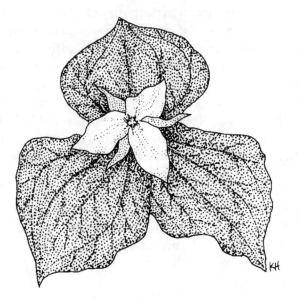

Purple Trillium

as it is beautiful in blossom. The smell, in fact, is so reminiscent of decaying flesh that early herbal medicine doctrine, which said that a plant's characteristics defined its appropriate use in humans, prescribed an ointment made from the roots as a treatment for gangrene. You may hear various nicknames for purple trillium, including stinking Benjamin, wake-robin, and birthroot. The reason for stinking Benjamin is obvious, and wake-robin refers to the fact that this is one of spring's first wildflowers. Birthroot, on the other hand, comes from the days when women were given tea made from the roots to ease childbirth.

The trail continues through stands of sugar maple, hobblebush, and striped maple. Striped maple, incidentally, especially when young, is easily recognized by bright green bark striped with white lines. As the tree matures, the bark will turn reddish-brown, with light vertical lines. Deer and moose relish this bark, a fact that gave rise to the common New England nickname of "moosewood."

Between 0.4 and 0.5 mile you'll pass several ravines, some of which are lined with clear, cold braids of water. One of these, located at 0.45 mile, is choked with giant boulders, or "glacial erratics," carried here on the great sheets of ice that flowed south out of Canada thousands of years ago. Over many, many years, the action of ice and rain, as well as the patient fingers of mosses, have broken down the upper surfaces of these rocks into layers of soil. On the tops of many boulders you'll find beautiful ferns and even young striped maples—island gardens that appear to be squeezing life out of solid stone.

At 0.9 mile you'll pass a large jumble of boulders cloaked in a thick quilt of ferns. Notice the small protected hollows lying along the base of some of these stones. On a hot summer day these wet, earthen pockets remain remarkably cool, like outlet ducts to some great subterranean air-conditioning system. Shortly afterward are the great, ice-scoured cliffs of Mount Hor rising high above the trail. Just before our turnaround point in a rocky ravine at 1.2 miles are fine views of Lake Willoughby, framed to the east by the soaring bluffs of Mount Pisgah.

Peregrine Falcon

WALK #43—MOUNT PISGAH

DISTANCE: 2.4 miles

ENVIRONMENT: Mountain

LOCATION: Vermont State Lands. From the intersection of state highways 16 and 5A at the north end of Lake Willoughby, head south on Highway 5A for 1.5 miles to Mill Brook Road, and turn left. Follow this road for 1.7 miles, at which point you'll make a right turn onto a logging access road. In 1.3 miles you'll reach our walking trail, which takes off along another access road heading to the west. (You should see a small white sign marking the route.)

It would be hard to imagine a more dramatic vista than the one offered from this small, rocky roost on the north edge of old man Pisgah. Perhaps nowhere in Vermont does the world drop away with such sheer abandon—a toss of wooded mountains and deep green valleys, ending in the steely blue waters of Lake Willoughby, 1,500 feet below. During October and November this is also an excellent perch for watching hawks beating southward on migration journeys. And if all that isn't enough, this pocket of high country is also home to some extremely rare plants, including sweet broom and mountain saxifrage—Arctic remnants of the cold, icy days that once prevailed here.

Though this trek includes roughly 0.3 mile of steep climbing, it's by far the easiest of three possible routes to Pisgah. (One note of decorum here. If you happen to meet a line of exhausted people plodding up the main north trail on a hot summer day, chests heaving, mouths sucking air, you may want to time your comments about this shorter, far more gentle path carefully.)

Fifty yards after leaving the parking area the road forks, at which point you'll take the left branch. One-tenth mile after this is a small white sign and a series of white tree blazes on the left marking the trail to Pisgah. From here you'll be rounding the northern flank of the mountain, along a lightly forested slope offering tantalizing views of Willoughby off to the northwest. Along the way look for hobblebush, raspberry, wood aster, shinleaf, bracken, baneberry, false Solomon's seal, and sarsaparilla. In time the hardwood forest thickens, becoming dominated by white and yellow birch as well as red, sugar, and mountain maples.

As you intersect the main trail from the highway at 0.6 mile, take a left, beginning a short, steep trudge toward the sky. Notice how the forest changes as you reach higher, more exposed portions of the mountain. The fact that the land here tilts to the north means even cooler, moister conditions—factors that help spruce, balsam fir, and northern white cedar to thrive. On the other hand, this isn't entirely a game of conifers. The cold-tolerant white birch has also established a firm toehold, as it continues to do all the way to the chilly reaches of Labrador.

By 0.75 mile the climb has lessened considerably, and, at about 1 mile, you'll intersect a path taking off to the right to North Overlook. There's one fork near the end of this 0.2-mile spur trail, where you'll want to keep to the left. Just a few yards past this junction the path stops abruptly on a ledge overhanging the edge of oblivion—a sensational, breathtaking place. If you love soaring, tumbling views, the name Pisgah, namesake of the biblical mountain from which Moses first glimpsed the promised land, seems an appropriate title. It's fun to watch patterns of ripples swelling and melting away on the blue waters far below. These liquid dances, which even from shore can seem independent of any discernible wind, were once thought to be the handiwork of spirits.

Long ago, instead of the cobalt-colored waters of Lake Willoughby there was a rather modest river here; all that changed, however, when ice sheets thousands of feet thick began pushing out of Canada. Like a spoon pushing through ice cream, the glacier created a rounded, "U"-shaped valley where the earlier river had sculpted a "V." Much of the bottomland gouged out by the tip of this icy finger, along with plenty of other gravelly debris carried by the glacier, was deposited to form the height of land you see at the south end of the lake. By the time the various flowages finally stopped filling against this natural dam they had reached a depth of more than 300 feet, making Willoughby the deepest lake in Vermont.

WALK #44—MOOSE BOG

DISTANCE: 1.2 miles
ENVIRONMENT: Fresh Water
LOCATION: Vermont State Lands. From the junction of state highways 114 North and 105 East in downtown Island Pond, head east on Highway 105 for 8.8 miles, and park at a large turnout on the left (north) side of the road. (This turnout is 0.8 mile east of a railroad crossing.) From the parking area, walk east along Highway 105 for 0.2 mile to our walking road, which is a small, two-track road taking off to the right (south).

Lying in the heart of the Wenlock Wildlife Management Area, Moose Bog is as wild, untrammeled a place as any walker could hope to find. Its blanket of spruce-fir forest, its sandy, two-track roads riddled with moose tracks, its forests and clearings alive with nearly a dozen kinds of birds now listed on Vermont's rare and endangered species list, seem more what one would expect to find in the far reaches of Maine or southern Canada.

As noted, leave your car at the large parking area on the north side of Highway 105 and head east for 0.2 mile to our walking road, an old logging route on the right. A few yards up this road is a fork. Stay left, on the branch blocked from vehicle traffic by a large boulder. Near this junction is a nice garden of Canada mayflower, as well as beautiful clusters of bunchberry—a member of the dogwood family that in June sends up creamy white flower bracts above its whorl of smooth green leaves. Just past this junction the road is wrapped in a curtain of conifers, and the air is thick with the delicious scent of balsam.

It's in this area that the fortunate walker might get a glimpse of the elusive spruce grouse. (You may have seen a notice posted near the highway, requesting that you report spruce grouse sightings to the Department of Fish and Wildlife, which is trying to track their dwindling populations.) Though approachable to the point of being downright tame—it has long been referred to as "fool hen"—the spruce grouse, with its white-spotted sides and rust-tipped tail feathers, is so few in numbers and so good at hiding beneath conifer branches that to see one in this area is a rare treat. In summer spruce grouse will eat a wide variety of nuts, berries, and shoots of young plants, but in winter its diet is reduced to one long helping of evergreen needles and buds. Like many birds that have adapted to the long, frigid winters of the north country, the spruce grouse dons a fine cloak of feathers, including thick leggings that extend all the way down to its feet. Even if you don't spot spruce grouse, you'll probably spot other feathered residents of this forest, including black-backed woodpeckers, gray jays, and boreal chickadees.

In approximately 0.2 mile you'll turn right onto a footpath taking off opposite a small, crescent-shaped clearing. This trail begins on a bench blanketed with spruce, and then drops gently through tufts of orange hawkweed and bristly dewberry, as well as thick mats of bog laurel, which in summer flies clusters of pink, saucer-shaped flowers. Also here is Labrador tea, the name of the plant derived from the fact that 17th-century frontiersmen of the Northeast prepared a fragrant, rose-colored beverage from the leaves.

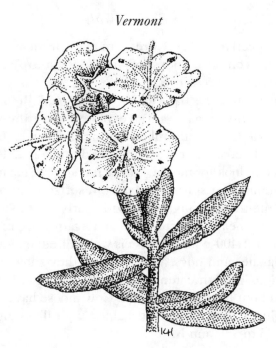

Bog Laurel

Soon the path exits the weave of spruce and laurel, arriving on the spongy peat shores of Moose Bog. The reach of open water is surrounded first by a fringe of leatherleaf, sphagnum, and pitcher plants, and then by somber huddles of black spruce. As you make your way toward the edge of the pond (please stay on the existing path) you'll notice that the ground is springy; each step squeezes water out, as though you were walking on a saturated sponge. The surface of this bog, known as the mat, rests on top of a layer of partially decomposed dead plants (and, to a much lesser extent, animals) commonly referred to as peat.

Despite their beauty and unique blend of life, bogs are one of the least understood and fastest disappearing ecosystems in the world. Thus far people have tended to view bogs only by what can be taken from them. People vacuum them with giant suction machines to produce bags of "peat moss" for gardeners, treats raw sewage in them, farms fruits and vegetables on them, and is currently looking to mine them on a grand scale both for home heating fuel as well as to produce electricity. One would hope that we'd also come to see bogs as ecosystems worth saving for their own sake. Vermont State Naturalist Charles Johnson makes the point eloquently: "Reasons there are enough for us to watch over the

Northeast's peatlands," he writes, "to cherish them as gifts and fellow travelers on earth's odyssey—to allow some to exist on their own, to go where they will."

Retrace your steps back to the logging road. Before heading back to your car, you may want to explore a bit farther down this two-track road. One-tenth mile from the trail junction are some fine stands of cedar, speckled alder, and tamarack. This is also a good place to look for moose. These remarkable creatures were once common as far south as Massachusetts; here in Vermont they were plentiful enough to provide early settlers with much of their daily meat. Despite a rather ungainly appearance, the typical 900- to 1,400-pound moose is well-suited to moving easily through marshes and bogs. What's more, they show remarkable get-up-and-go when threatened, having been clocked at speeds of 35 miles an hour for short distances. Cow moose have one or two young in June; these bouncing babies typically weigh in at a whopping 25 to 35 pounds.

■ NEW HAMPSHIRE ■

NEW HAMPSHIRE
• • •

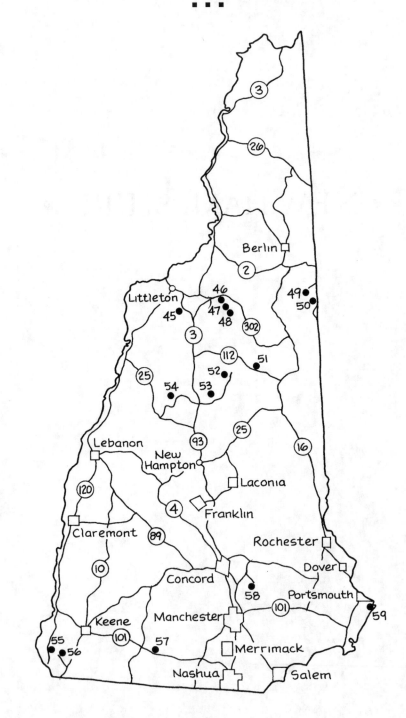

Littleton

Berlin

45

46
47
48

49
50

3

302

112

51

52

54   53

25

93

25

16

Lebanon

New
Hampton

Laconia

120

4

Franklin

Claremont

89

Rochester

10

Dover

Concord

58

Portsmouth

Keene

Manchester

101

59

55
56

101

57

Merrimack

Nashua

Salem

New Hampshire

```
WALK #45—POETRY–NATURE TRAIL

        DISTANCE:    0.5 mile
     ENVIRONMENT:    Forest
        LOCATION:    The Frost Place. From the intersection of
                     New Hampshire routes 18 and 116 in the
                     town of Franconia, follow Route 116 south
                     for just under 1 mile. Turn right, following
              ▪      the signs to The Frost Place. Note: The Frost
              ▪      Place is open limited hours from Memorial
              ▪      Day to Columbus Day. To find out the
                     current schedule, write to The Frost Place,
                     Box F, Franconia, NH 03580, or call the
                     director at 603-823-5510 or 802-763-8720.
```

> Everybody should be free to go very slow. ... What you want, what
> you're hanging around in the world waiting for, is for something to occur
> to you.
>
> —*Robert Frost*
> March 21, 1954

A great many things "occurred" to Robert Frost during his 5 full years and 18 summers spent at this idyllic Franconia country home. It was here, perched before the long, lovely swell of the Franconia Mountains, that this Pulitzer prizewinning poet would write some of his most beautiful collections of verse: *A Boy's Will, North of Boston, Mountain Interval,* and *New Hampshire.* "A poem," he once said in a letter to Louis Untermeyer, "begins as a lump in the throat, a sense of wrong, a homesickness, a lovesickness. It finds the thought and the thought finds the words."

Along this 0.5-mile trail you'll have an opportunity not only to read some of Frost's poetry, which is displayed beside the trail, but also to observe some of the same plants and bird life that kept him company during his years at Franconia. Before setting out, be sure to pick up one of the trail guides.

Our first pathway poem, "The Tuft of Flowers," is a verse about Frost's encounter with a butterfly and a streamside cluster of, appropriately enough, butterfly weed. Butterfly weed is a brilliantly colored relative of the common milkweed, and each summer without fail its orange blooms manage to attract countless butterflies, from monarchs to swallowtails. Indians and European settlers alike frequently used this plant to treat serious ailments of the respiratory system. Native peoples also crushed the long, fleshy taproot of the butterfly weed and applied it to burns and lesions of the skin.

As you enter the woodland near the beginning of the walk, keep your eyes out for Jack-in-the-pulpits, tall meadow rue, and purple trillium; this latter plant was also once known as birthroot, since a tea prepared from the plant was given to women in order to ease childbirth. Also here are balsam fir and sugar maples, both of which are doing an admirable job of reclaiming the old highway cut that can still be seen coursing through the woods behind Frost's poem "The Road Not Taken."

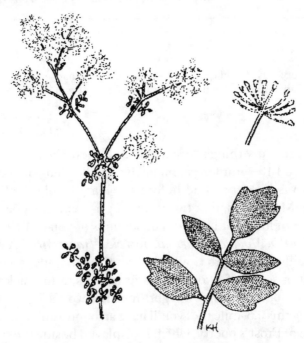

Tall Meadow Rue

More often than not this wooded stretch is wrapped in blankets of birdsong, including the melodies of one of Frost's favorite songsters, the hermit thrush. This little bird, which has the unique habit of flicking its tail up and down several times a minute, makes its nest on the floor of the forest or in a low bush. Curiously, Frost wasn't the only one to delight in the song of the thrush, which for this species consists of a single flutey tone followed by a series of rising and falling notes. Across the Atlantic, English poet Robert Browning was similarly enchanted:

> That's the wise thrush; he sings each song twice over,
> Lest you should think he could never recapture
> The first fine careless rapture!

A short distance into the forest is one of Frost's most memorable works, "Stopping by Woods on a Snowy Evening." The poet is thought to have stopped his horse that snowy night approximately 6 miles west of here, near a pocket of water known as Pearl Lake. For such a small pond, Pearl Lake has most certainly had its share of attention. First it was known as Bear Pond, for the large population of bear in the area; this was later changed to Mink Lake for all the mink. Then, in the middle 1800s, a fisherman supposedly found clam shells in the lake that contained sizable pearls. When a man named True Page was reported to have found one gem worth over $30 (and how can you doubt a man named True Page?), the "event" resulted in the name being changed to Pearl Lake. Before long people were coming by the dozens, spending sunup to sundown knee deep in lukewarm pond water, certain that a big find was just another clam away.

On the back side of the Poetry Trail is Frost's "The Quest of the Purple-Fringed." The verse refers to the purple-fringed orchid, a plant sporting a fragrant cluster of feathery lavender flowers. This particular orchid holds its pollen in a mass below the anther, to which a sticky disk is attached. Moths sticking their tongues down the bloom catch the pollen ball and inadvertently remove it, taking it with them to the next flower, which is thereby pollinated.

In the next poem, "Hyla Brook," Frost mentions jewelweed. Jewelweed is common throughout much of New England, and has for centuries provided relief from the painful itching of both stinging nettle and poison ivy. Scientists have documented that the plant also has significant fungicidal qualities, which explains one of its other common uses—a treatment for athlete's foot.

Finish the trail past runs of milkweed, selfheal, yarrow, orange hawkweed, and lupine. As you come off the path, take a moment to drink in the sweeping view of the Franconia Mountains, a portion of the White Mountains named for their resemblance to the Franconian Alps of Germany. It is a range beautiful winter to fall, an inspiration never lost to Robert Frost. It's easy to understand his ambition to end up on the front porch of this particular house, a desire he relates rather matter-of-factly in a stanza from the poem "New Hampshire":

> I had to take by force rather than buy.
> I caught the owner outdoors by himself
> Raking up after winter, and I said
> "I'm going to put you off this farm: I want it."
> "Where are you going to put me? In the road?"
> "I'm going to put you on the farm next to it."
> "Why won't the farm next to it do for you?"
> "I like this better." It was really better.

That is exactly what happened. And if the poetry he created here is any indication, then this place must have really been the better place, after all.

WALK #46—TRESTLE TRAIL

DISTANCE:	1.1 miles
ENVIRONMENT:	Forest
LOCATION:	White Mountain National Forest. From the town of Twin Mountain, head east for 3 miles on New Hampshire Route 302 to Zealand Road. Turn right (south), and proceed for 0.6 mile to a trailhead parking area on the right. Both the Trestle Trail and the Sugarloaf Trail leave a short distance south of this parking area, on the other side of a bridge crossing the Zealand River.

The cool, shaded twists and turns of the Trestle Trail make it the perfect time-out for weary highway potatoes. This path traverses dozens of quiet nooks and crannies, any of which will delight those who simply slow down enough to take notice. In the best tradition of nature rambling, it makes little difference if you do the entire 1.1-mile loop, or simply park yourself on a flat rock by the river for a soak in the sunshine.

Our walk begins in a mix of maple, birch, and fir, with smatterings of wild sarsaparilla, bunchberry, bracken, bluebead lily, and Canada mayflower. If you spend much time at all in the woods, you might enjoy selecting a few common plants, and then watch the kinds of changes that each goes through from spring to fall. In time you'll come to see the forest as a kind of timepiece, whose ever-changing face can reflect with surprising precision the slow, deliberate roll of the seasons.

For example, there's the Canada mayflower, whose shiny, pointed leaves are visible throughout much of this walk. The leaves of this ground cover appear in middle spring, pushing their way up from the forest floor in tightly rolled, inch-long projections. These will slowly uncurl to reveal plants with one, two, or three leaves. Only those with two or three, however, actually produce flowers in May— clusters of ivory-colored, star-shaped blooms that exude a rich fragrance not unlike that of lily of the valley. Four to six weeks after the

Canada Mayflower

blooms appear, toward the end of June, you'll be able to see the beginnings of fruits on the lower portions of the flower stalks. At first these appear as a speckled whitish-green, but later, nearer to autumn, they turn a beautiful ruby red. These berries may remain on the plants well into winter, providing side dishes for many a hungry grouse.

In 0.2 mile is an intersection with Middle Sugarloaf Trail, which takes off to the left. Stay right, continuing along the froth and spray of the Zealand River. In another 0.3 mile you'll cross a north-south trail, and shortly afterward, come to an enormous boulder. This is a glacial erratic, so named because 15,000 to 20,000 years ago a glacier delivered this monster here after having carried it from the uplands, inch by inch, on a thick tongue of ice.

A few yards past this erratic the trail veers to the left. Look to your left here and you'll see a small clump of young quaking aspen, their leaves dancing in the slightest puff of breeze. Aspen are the most widespread deciduous tree on the continent, and are especially good at being the first to get growing on areas that have been disturbed by fire or logging. They achieve this temporary dominance both by growing very quickly—most aspen will already be 2 feet tall by the time they reach their second year of growth—and also by being able to sprout young trees from existing root systems.

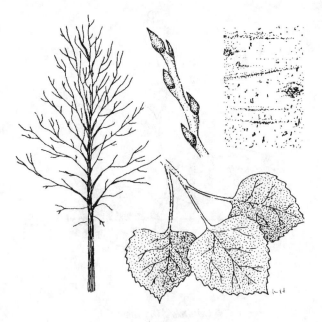

Aspen

(Bigtooth aspen can also sprout new trees from stumps.) A single root system may create a forest of thousands of trees covering more than 100 acres, though most clone groups are much smaller.

Three-quarters of a century ago, when this entire valley stood bare and ravaged from the saws and fires of timber mogul J. E. Henry's logging operations, aspen sprouts would have been a common sight. Like other "pioneer" species, however, most of these groves eventually yielded their ground to more shade-tolerant trees.

Speaking of J. E. Henry, at 0.7 mile is a footbridge over the Zealand River, sitting in almost the exact spot where one of Henry's railroad trestle bridges was located. The Zealand Valley Railroad, sometimes called the crookedest road in New England, began hauling logging cars past this point in 1884. Before long there were five trains a day snaking their way down this valley, most hauling at least eight cars of logs. (Interestingly, this valley was originally called New Zealand. Just why the "New" was dropped no one can say for sure, but the most accepted explanation is that the railroad and post office simply found it more convenient to use the edited version.)

On the other side of the bridge stay left, following the yellow-blazed trail up to the campground loop road. Take a right on this road, past fine stands of red maple, shadbush, balsam, and aspen. In 0.2 mile you'll see the Trestle Trail taking off to the right. Follow it through blueberries, raspberries, bracken fern, and false violet, reaching the parking area again in 0.1 mile.

WALK #47—MIDDLE SUGARLOAF

DISTANCE:	2.8 miles
ENVIRONMENT:	Mountain
LOCATION:	White Mountain National Forest. From the town of Twin Mountain, head east for approximately 3 miles on New Hampshire Route 302 to Zealand Road. Proceed south on Zealand Road for 0.6 mile to a parking area on the right (west) side of the road. Both this trail and the Trestle Trail are located just south of this parking area, on the other side of a bridge crossing the Zealand River.

The three Sugarloaf mountains, so named for their resemblance to the cakes of sugar that were sold in colonial times, offer up their windblown summits for far less effort than do most high perches in the White Mountains. From the top of Middle Sugarloaf you can gaze on a virtual symphony of peaks, from the awesome Presidentials exploding out of the forest to the east, to the softer, more distant highline of Vermont's Green Mountains in the west.

Our walk begins in a lovely forest canopy of balsam, maple, and yellow birch, with mats of Canada mayflower, bluebead lily, bracken fern, and bunchberry hugging the ground below. Singing a rocky song immediately to your right is the Zealand River, which twists northward toward the Ammonoosuc (literally, "fish place"), the combined waters then running across the neck of New Hampshire to the Connecticut River. Take some time to enjoy this river, since at 0.2 mile we will leave all such valley things behind to begin our climb into the highlands.

The forest on this east side of the Sugarloafs, although young, is quite beautiful. Having not yet established the full, thick canopy of a mature mixed deciduous woods, there are yet some lengthy views to be had both across the slopes, as well as into the twists and turns of a braid of moist, quiet ravines. Sarsaparilla, clubmosses, sheep laurel, blueberry, Canada mayflower, and hobblebush weave a myriad of textures onto the forest floor, and, beginning in May and lasting well into autumn, set off tiny fireworks of colored blooms and berries.

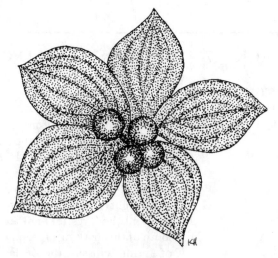

Bunchberry

Although this trail will not take you up far enough to see a full-blown high altitude forest (the summit of Middle Sugarloaf is about where such changes begin in earnest), you can still spot differences between this high ridge and walks you've taken at lower elevations. In the upper reaches of the walk beech and hemlock will not be as prevalent as down lower, and you'll find more white birch growing in among the yellow birch. At the very summit of Middle Sugarloaf spruce and fir are common, with a few mountain ash dotting the landscape where there were none before. Were this climb to continue its upward course another 1,000 feet you'd see little in the way of trees except for the conifers. It's at such higher altitudes, where cold temperatures create poorer soils and reduce a tree's ability to create new plant tissue, that evergreens, which can conduct photosynthesis all year long, become the masters of the mountain.

After a healthy huff and puff of about 0.4 mile, at 0.9 mile you'll reach the saddle between North Sugarloaf and Middle Sugarloaf mountains. Turn left here, toward Middle Sugarloaf. Just before you reach the summit a trail will fork to the right, leading to the north face of the mountain. We'll stay left here, making the final quick ascent to the summit. The top of Middle Sugarloaf is a rocky perch peppered with spruce, balsam fir, aspen, blueberry, tamarack, and shadbush.

Besides long vistas—Mount Washington to the east, Mount Hale, North Twin Mountain, and Noble Peak to the south, and Vermont's Green Mountains to the west—note the lovely blanket of forest to the southeast covering the gentle twists and turns of the Zealand Valley. What makes this scene especially appealing is the fact that three-quarters of a century ago almost every inch of this valley lay rutted and barren of trees, robbed even of the river that again dances wet and wild between these mountain shoulders.

Timber baron J. E. Henry was born in 1831, into a New Hampshire household that offered little but poverty and hard work. Often the butt of bullying and jokes about his lower-class status, Henry swore early on that one day things would be very different. And different they were. Graduating from a job he began at 15 driving freight wagons through northern New England, in the 1880s Henry began to acquire the first of the timberlands that he would ultimately parley into more than 10,000 acres—the largest single tract of New Hampshire forest ever controlled by one man.

For 40 years Henry's lumberjacks laid their steel into the trees that covered the landscape before you, wiping out in the blink of an eye what was arguably the most prime virgin forest to be found anywhere in the White Mountains.

Between Henry's timbering practices (he seldom disposed of his slash debris, and eventually fell into a kind of clear-cutting mania) and two devastating fires, both of which may have been started by his locomotives, by 1903 Zealand Valley was a veritable wasteland. "It is as if," wrote Ernest Russell in a 1908 issue of *Collier's*, "the contents of some vast cemetery had been unearthed in that little valley." In the same feature Russell relates this comment from Henry, which hardly eased his reputation as master plunderer. "I never seen the tree yet," Henry told Russell, "that didn't mean a damned sight more to me goin' under the saw than it did standin' on a mountain."

The forests of the northern White Mountains were good to J. E. Henry. Upon his death in 1912, he left an estate worth more than $10 million. Fortunately, as C. Francis Belcher points out in his excellent book *Logging Railroads of the White Mountains*, he also left a groundswell of public outrage that ultimately led to the creation of the White Mountain National Forest.

It's hard not to wonder why today we still seem capable of learning such lessons only in the midst of ecological crises. When is the right time to react to acid rain? When will critical wildlife habitat diminish past the point of no return? Unlike the remarkable return of the Zealand Valley forest, what will happen when our tinkering pushes nature beyond her ability to heal?

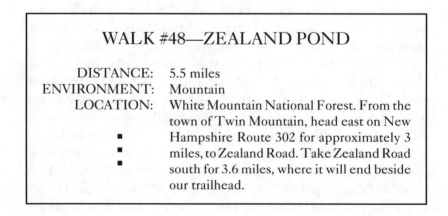

WALK #48—ZEALAND POND

DISTANCE: 5.5 miles
ENVIRONMENT: Mountain
LOCATION: White Mountain National Forest. From the town of Twin Mountain, head east on New Hampshire Route 302 for approximately 3 miles, to Zealand Road. Take Zealand Road south for 3.6 miles, where it will end beside our trailhead.

The trip to Zealand Pond is a heartening trek. Less than a single lifetime ago this walk would have been through a scarred, barren wasteland—a shattered cathedral laid to waste by as ruthless a timber harvest as any in the state of New Hampshire. The fact that this woods has come so far in healing itself, that in such a short time it could again bloom so rich and full of promise, is staggering testimony to the potential of the earth to reweave intricate webs of life that have been shredded by human hands.

Our walk begins in a wonderful forest of red maple, spruce, balsam fir, striped maple, and gray and white birch—a fairly young, well-spaced woodland that affords an endless variety of views through long, cool galleries of sunlight and shadow. Black-and-white warblers and white-breasted nuthatches scour the branches of the trees looking for spiders and wood-boring insects; ovenbirds pick at the leaf litter for caterpillars, crickets, and worms. The friendly buzz of the black-capped chickadee can be heard ringing through the trees, and on occasion, the flutey, cascading melodies of the wood thrush.

This is also a good forest in which to check wet areas for wildlife tracks. Besides black bear, moose, beaver, deer, and woodchuck, you're walking through the heart of the region's lynx population. To actually see one of these lean cats, with their thick, luxurious coats of fur and long, silky cheek ruffs, is considered one of New England's rarest and greatest wildlife experiences. Personally, considering the long centuries of dogged trapping for lynx pelts, I find it a thrill just to know these magnificent creatures are still around. The lynx is an extremely shy creature that rarely enters large open areas, and prefers to den in secluded logs or rock crevices far from human feet. Numbers of lynx fluctuate substantially with the population of its favorite prey, the snowshoe hare. When snowshoe hare are scarce, lynx tend to reproduce at a much slower rate.

At 0.5 mile is a footbridge. Immediately after crossing this bridge you'll see a trail taking off to the right; stay straight, though, on the blue-blazed path. Climb gently along a twisted mat of roots jutting up from the trail, keeping your eyes open for spatters of whorled wood aster, wild oats, twisted stalk, and hobblebush. The braid of streams, rivulets, and ponds increases in density the farther into the forest you go. In fact, by the time you reach the 1.5-mile mark you'll never be more than

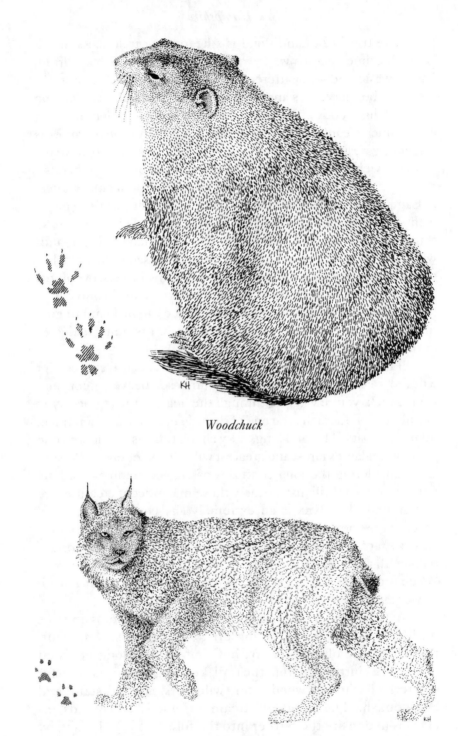

Woodchuck

Lynx

a stone's throw from either the sight or sound of mountain water, not to mention the lush mats of shrubs and wildflowers nurtured by such environments.

A particularly nice upland channel can be found at 1.75 miles, where clear, cold water gushes from pool to pool, slip-sliding through earthen bottlenecks choked with speckled alder, mountain holly, and meadowsweet. Shortly after this you'll reach a chain of flooded lowlands fringed with tamarack, alder, tall meadow rue, and wild raisin. This is the handiwork of the local beaver's union, which has managed this section of the valley with various water projects for the past several decades. If you look carefully from here to our turnaround point, you'll spot several lodges built by these crafty engineers.

Beaver will often construct lodges at the northern edges of a pond, thereby exposing them to the greatest possible amount of sunlight; this assures that the surrounding ice will melt away quickly in the spring. These are incredibly strong structures, usually built as mounds of sticks and mud from which chambers are then excavated from underneath. Typically, there is only one chamber in a lodge, the size of which varies according to the number of animals in the family. (Very large families will have two chambers, each with its own entrance tunnel.) Most chambers are crafted on a split-level design—a lower dining platform and an upper sleeping shelf covered with wood chips. (Placing the sleeping area higher than the rest of the lodge helps keep it dry.) If the location of the lodge proves to be satisfactory, with plenty of food nearby, beavers may stay there for many years, adding reinforcements each fall. In less than a decade a lodge can end up looking like a regular apartment building, measuring more than 10 feet high and 40 feet across!

At 2.4 miles, just before intersecting with the A-Z Trail, you'll meander through exquisite, leafy arches formed by white birch leaning out from either side of the path. Birch often lean into areas cut by trails, roadways, or streams, straining their necks for an extra splash of sunlight. When set ablaze by fall colors, such stretches of trail are among the most beautiful places on earth. Robert Frost also loved the lean of birch trees, and in one of his poems is moved to remember days of climbing to their upper stories and then swinging down to the ground on their supple trunks. "One could do worse," he wrote, "than be a swinger of birches."

As you near the Zealand Pond look for lovely gardens of sumac, wild sarsaparilla, bracken fern, shadbush, and silky dogwood. At 2.75 miles, roughly 0.25 mile past the intersection with the A-Z Trail, a small spur trail descends to the edge of Zealand Pond. Across the water, against a sheer rock face, you'll see the white veil of Zealand Falls—a dramatic exclamation point for a stream that has made its way here via a dizzying plunge from the high forests south of Mount Hale.

Birches, ponds, birds, waterfalls, wildlife—what an idyllic spot! Slow down. Take in as much of it as you possibly can.

WALK #49—WILD RIVER

DISTANCE:	6 miles
ENVIRONMENT:	Forest
LOCATION:	White Mountain National Forest. From U.S. Highway 2 in extreme southwestern Maine, head south on Maine Highway 113 for 2 miles to a signed turnoff on the right leading to Wild River Campground, 5.7 miles to the southwest (in New Hampshire). Continue a few yards past the campground entrance station to a small parking area on the left, where both the Basin and Wild River trails meet.

This easy path rubs elbows with the beautiful Wild River, a clear, swift stream doing a sprightly hopscotch on its journey from Black Mountain to the Androscoggin. (Androscoggin, by the way, is a word that first showed up in the journals of Captain John Smith in 1616, and literally means "fish curing place." This name is testimony to the great runs of migratory ocean fish, including shad, alewives, and salmon, that once ran up the cool waters of the Androscoggin to breed.)

This is an enjoyable walk during much of the year, though it takes on a special appeal when the land is cloaked in the colors of autumn. Leaves, cut off from nutrients and water, begin to lose the green chlorophyll masks they've worn since spring, revealing colors we could never have guessed were there had we not seen this all before. On this trail carpets of birch leaves pad your steps, shimmering in the October sun like weathered chips of gold on a roadway to kingdom come. Even Shakespeare was at his best when it came to writing about the melancholy beauty of autumn:

> That time of year thou mayest in me behold
> When yellow leaves, or none, or few do hang
> Upon these boughs which shake against the cold,
> Bare ruined choirs, where late the sweet birds sang.

Looking at this forest today, it's hard to believe that from 1860 to 1917 it was laid bare by heavy logging. The tracks of a lumbering railroad twisted not only along the path you're walking, but up most of the side stream ravines as well, hauling out enormous amounts of softwood, and tons of hemlock bark for tanning shoe leather. The place where Maine Highway 113 meets the road to our trailhead was the site of the boisterous logging town of Hastings, a hodgepodge of boarding house, general store, post office, school, engine house, and mills serving more than a thousand people.

It's difficult to imagine the rate at which our early forefathers went through wood—for firewood, fences, building materials, and quite often, simply because it was a nagging impediment to the spread of agriculture. Construction of items from shingles to barrel staves was completed using only the choicest cuts of wood, while much of the timber was, as described in one 1800 Maine diary, "piled and burned on the spot." Seventy-five percent of the forest in eastern Massachusetts was gone by 1825. From then on building projects depended on wood being sent by ship from forests like this one in the far north. Yet even these didn't last long. It's been estimated that the vast stands of commercial softwoods in the great White Mountain forests to the west were gone by 1890.

With the trees, of course, went the animals that made their homes there—white-tailed deer, beaver, elk, bear, and various species of game birds. (Again, wildlife was far worse off in southern New England. Massachusetts closed lands to deer hunting for the first time in 1694. By the end of the 18th century the abundance of game animals that so impressed early colonists had vanished. "Hunting with us," wrote Timothy Dwight in the late 1700s, "exists chiefly in the tales of other times.")

For the first 1.1 miles of trail you'll wind through groves of white and yellow birch, hemlock, sugar and striped maple, oak, alder, and mountain ash, with a few bigtooth aspen thrown in for good measure. At the point where the road ends, however, the Wild River is clearly the star of the show. Take the opportunity during this next 0.5 mile to find a granite perch from which you can bask in this churning, watery world. Especially beautiful are the jumbles of giant boulders choking the stream, pushing the water into chutes, splitting it into forks, flinging it headlong over high slabs into deep, smooth basins. You may notice in places piles of sticks, grass, and even tree trunks lying in rock crannies 6 or 7 feet above the stream. This is testimony to the high water levels that occur on the Wild River during spring floods, when rain and snowmelt roar down out of the White Mountains like a runaway freight train.

The path continues to flirt with the river, arriving at its edge and then disappearing again into the forest, which by now is peppered with spruce and balsam fir. At 3 miles you'll intersect the Black Angel Trail. Turn right, and proceed to our turnaround point on a footbridge crossing the Wild River. The upstream view from this bridge is especially beautiful, a toss of river framed on either

Marten

side by birch and conifers, and in back by the high, sweet swell of 3,303-foot Black Mountain.

On the upper flanks of Black Mountain, where the Wild River first begins its long run to the northeast, coniferous woods provide excellent habitat for pine martens. Members of the weasel family, martens are covered with thick coats of rich, silky fur. It was this fur that led to the animal's demise at the hands of trappers in the White Mountains—a situation that wasn't helped by the fact that martens seem totally unwary of traps. Even in the remote wilds of Maine, these animals required full protection for 35 years before their numbers stabilized again. The marten is a tremendous tree climber, and sustains himself on generous helpings of everything from red squirrels and chipmunks to insects, small birds, and fruits.

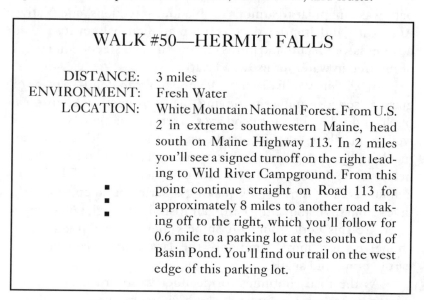

WALK #50—HERMIT FALLS

DISTANCE: 3 miles
ENVIRONMENT: Fresh Water
LOCATION: White Mountain National Forest. From U.S. 2 in extreme southwestern Maine, head south on Maine Highway 113. In 2 miles you'll see a signed turnoff on the right leading to Wild River Campground. From this point continue straight on Road 113 for approximately 8 miles to another road taking off to the right, which you'll follow for 0.6 mile to a parking lot at the south end of Basin Pond. You'll find our trail on the west edge of this parking lot.

It would be hard to think of a more beautiful beginning to a walk than a slow saunter beside the still waters of Basin Pond. This magnificent, 1,500-foot amphitheater was carved 15,000 years ago by the head of a massive glacier that flowed into Cold River Valley to the east. Today the basin is cradled by a striking mosaic of timbered slopes and ridges, and sheer, vertical walls of granite. On a calm day Basin Pond turns into a glassy reflecting pool, providing a double dose of not only mountainscape, but of lovely clumps of shoreline birches, their slender frames looking like ballet dancers frozen in the middle of a pirouette.

Our path first enters a woodland community comprised primarily of birch and maple, with a few dark dashes of balsam fir and hemlock. On the ground are hobblebush, blueberry, bracken, ground cedar, meadow rue, and partridgeberry, as well as nice gardens of wintergreen and bunchberry, the latter especially beautiful when bedecked with red fruits.

For centuries the plants of the northern forests have had a reputation as both grocery store and pharmacy. From the hobblebush, blueberry, and even bunchberry came edible fruits. Wintergreen contained an aspirinlike substance that proved effective in treating the discomforts of colds, flu, and muscle aches. Some Indians wiped their bodies with bracken fern fronds in order to mask their scent during hunting expeditions. Tea from hemlock bark was a popular treatment for bladder infections, and Native Americans and frontier doctors alike applied balsam resin as a healing salve for cuts and burns of the skin, and steeped the twigs of the tree in water for use as a laxative.

In 0.4 mile you'll reach the far end of Basin Pond—a place of grasses, sedges, and water-loving plants fringed with maples, birch, and alder. This is a good spot to see an occasional moose, as well as marsh wrens, tree swallows, and snipes. It's the snipe, incidentally, that gives off that strange whistling you may have heard while hiking around wet areas such as this. The birds announce their territory by making a series of steep, dramatic dives from high above the earth, air rushing through tail feathers to create this eerie sound. A snipe's diet consists primarily of animal matter, most commonly the larvae of aquatic insects, earthworms, and snails.

As the road continues to meander westward it offers fine glimpses through the forest of the high, rocky rim of the glacial cirque. It wasn't until 150 years ago that scientists began to realize the extent to which glaciers have at various times covered much of North America. Some landscapes were covered in sheets of ice thousands of feet thick, each carrying rocks and debris that would scour and polish the earth like belts of sandpaper.

At 1.3 miles, just after crossing Basin Brook, the light-colored forest of beech and birch trunks is suddenly flushed with dark green wisps of young hemlock. Much of this area was at one time thick with mighty hemlock, but these were harvested in great quantities during the 19th century for their tannin-rich bark, used

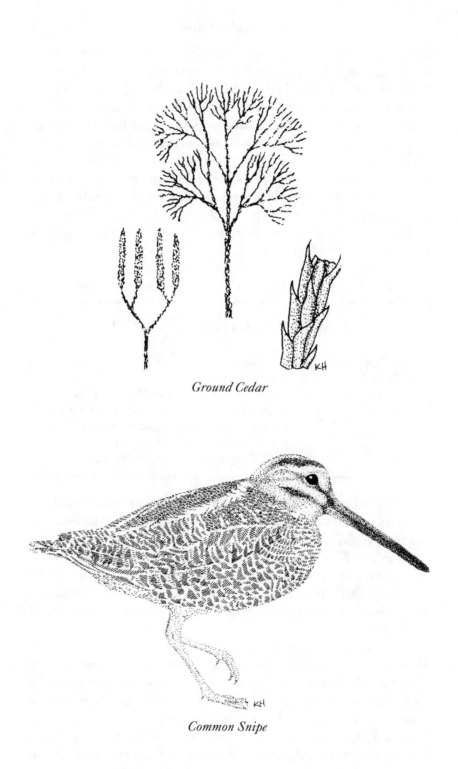

Ground Cedar

Common Snipe

in the tanning of leather. Approximately 0.1 mile, just past this last stream crossing, is a small side path marked by a sign that reads "Hermit Falls Loop Trail." We'll climb along this route for another 0.1 mile to our turnaround point at the base of Hermit Falls. Along the way keep your eyes open for fine clusters of polypody fern. The roots of polypody contain a licorice-flavored substance many times sweeter than sugar; even before Roman times it was valued as a remedy for coughs and chest congestion. Don't be alarmed if you hear strange noises in the woods around these plants—footsteps, twigs crackling, even voices; some cultures believed that people carrying the ripe spores of polypody would be rendered invisible.

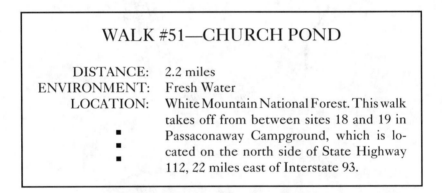

WALK #51—CHURCH POND

DISTANCE:	2.2 miles
ENVIRONMENT:	Fresh Water
LOCATION:	White Mountain National Forest. This walk takes off from between sites 18 and 19 in Passaconaway Campground, which is located on the north side of State Highway 112, 22 miles east of Interstate 93.

If you happen to be among those rare souls who are able to enjoy (or at least tolerate) sloshing through roughly 0.3 mile of wet bog trail, you'll find Church Pond to be among the more engaging walks in the White Mountains. Besides getting a close-up look at a true peat bog, sprouting rich mats of laurel, black spruce, small cranberry, leatherleaf, and Labrador tea, Church Pond itself is a true beauty—a wild-looking pool of water fringed by regal stands of red pines.

Our walk begins in Passaconaway Campground, which takes its name from the great Penacook Indian Chief Papisse-conwa ("bear cub"). In the early 1600s Papisse-conwa ruled a powerful federation of tribes spread across much of northern New Hampshire; over the years he bravely led his people through thick and thin, including a long, bitter period of disease and death that descended on the tribes after the arrival of the colonists. When

Papisse-conwa died, legend says he rose into heaven from the summit of Mount Washington, ascending in a great sled drawn by a pack of wolves.

The Church Pond Loop Trail takes off between campsites 18 and 19. The first order of business on this walk is to ford the Swift River, which the Penacooks called Chataguay, or "the main stream." On the far side you'll find a nice thicket of speckled alders waiting for you, a tree that provides valuable browse for both deer and moose. The water-loving alder is remarkably resistant to rot; a cousin of this tree—the European alder—was used by Hollanders to create the piles on which they raised the city of Amsterdam. From the north shore of the Swift the path follows a gravelly channel for a few yards, and then takes a right into a forest of maple, birch, and mixed conifers. Soon you'll come to yet another water channel, although this one can be crossed easily with no more than a bit of light-footed rock hopping.

In 0.3 mile is a place where the loop trail splits; stay left. For the next 0.3 mile you'll be in a tranquil forest of spruce, balsam, and white pine, the path in places covered with a carpet of needles so thick that your footsteps will make not a whisper. Look here for clumps of blueberry, Canada mayflower, shinleaf, trillium, bunchberry, and bluebead lily. At 0.5 mile there are also nice clusters of bracken, interrupted and hay-scented ferns, and, a short distance later, small mats of wintergreen and snowberry.

By the time you reach the 0.8-mile mark you'll be in an honest to goodness bog, the open, spongy vegetation mats peppered with tamarack and black spruce, huddled like ragged old men against the wet and cold. As you make your way along this soggy path (as peat bogs are very fragile, try your best to stay on the existing trail), you'll be surrounded by lovely bunches of bog laurel—in June bedecked with striking pink and white flowers—as well as leatherleaf and Labrador tea. Keep eyes and ears open for both the boreal chickadee and the white-winged crossbill, the latter of which uses its hooked, crossed beak to retrieve seeds from the cones of black spruce.

There is a wild, remote feeling to this place—the quiet of the bog, the crumpled quilt of conifers rising westward toward Sugar Hill and Greens Cliff. Standing here toe deep in brackish brown water, it's interesting to consider the slow rate at which such ecosystems are created. It may take more than a century to make

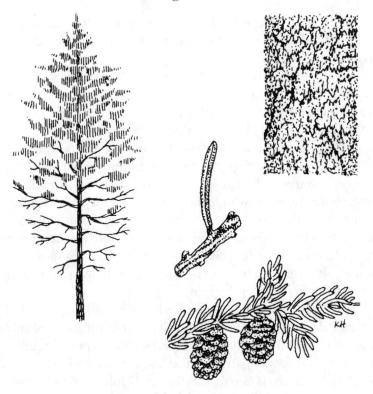

Black Spruce

a single inch of peat; in the lower reaches of the bog, cut off from oxygen, the process is even slower. Eighteen inches of peat bog may take more than 2,000 years to form.

Nearly half of this peat consists of *humic acids*, substances that tend to act as preservatives for organic materials. Pull a 200-year-old cedar log from the depths of a peat bog, for example, and it's likely to have an amazing amount of its original structural integrity. Particularly common in this brew is a waxy, resinous substance known as *bitumen*, a word which you may recognize from the type of soft coal we call "bituminous." This bog you're now walking on may one day be a coal deposit, in the same way that today we mine coal from what were, millions of years ago, vast peatlands.

Interestingly, core samples taken from peat bogs such as this provide remarkable windows for looking into events of the past. The eruption of an ancient volcano, for instance, will show up in the bog as a thin layer of ash. We can trace the sudden influx of Europeans on the continent by noticing the increase of ragweed pollen. But there are also more recent, much more troubling developments to be found in the upper layers of bogs: the sudden surges of lead that have accompanied the spread of automobiles, and higher and higher levels of poisons such as DDT and PCBs. In 1 mile you'll come to the end of the bog, and at 1.1 miles, find yourself in a beautiful grove of red pine. Here you'll have your first view of beautiful Church Pond. This is definitely a place to linger—to explore the quiet inlets, to soak in the sun and piney air. Rather than follow the loop around, which will take you through longer, even more severe sections of bog, it's best to return to the campground the same way you came.

WALK #52—GREELEY PONDS

DISTANCE: 6.8 miles
ENVIRONMENT: Mountain
LOCATION: White Mountain National Forest. From Interstate 93, head east on State Highway 49 for approximately 15 miles, to the town of Waterville Valley. Just before this highway dead-ends in the town, turn left next to the library onto West Branch Road. (You'll see a large tennis complex on the right just before this intersection.) This road crosses the Mad River over a one-lane bridge, then turns sharply to the right. Just before you reach a second bridge, 0.8 mile from the intersection with Highway 49, you'll see a road taking off to the right, beside which is a large parking area. (This parking area has a large trail information board beside it.) Park here, and begin your walk down this road. You'll find the Greeley Ponds Trail taking off to your left in 0.3 mile.

It's hard to refute the appropriateness of the name "Waterville Valley" since, besides the Mad River, which we'll follow to its source, there's also an extensive braid of smaller mountain streams tumbling out of the high country from every direction. Background to this grand dance of water and mountain is the striking beauty of the forests. Here are rich stands of spruce, fir, beech, and birch—a tapestry stitched to the side of every swell, as far as the eye can see. In the mid-1920s this land, including all of the upper Mad River drainage from here to Greeley Ponds, was owned by the Parker-Young Company, which was making plans to clear-cut it. At the time the region included the largest remaining old growth forest in the entire state.

While there was considerable objection to this scheme, much of it thanks to the dogged efforts of the Society to Protect New Hampshire Forests, saving these woods required some fancy footwork. In 1911, Massachusetts Congressman (and New Hampshire native) John Weeks spearheaded the passage of a law that took Gifford Pinchot's notion of creating national forests out of publicly owned lands, and modified it to allow Congress to appropriate funds to purchase private holdings, as well. This law opened the door to establishing federal forest reserves in the east, which was certainly no small feat. For years Weeks' plan had been met with strong opposition from conservative legislators—in particular, Speaker of the House Joseph Cannon, who's credited with uttering the now-famous cry "not one cent for scenery!"

But there was a catch. At the time Parker-Young planned to strip Waterville Valley, the only eastern lands that had ever been acquired for national forest designation were those already logged. An able group of New Hampshire citizens went to work, making strong arguments to legislators about the importance of scenic lands. In an unprecedented move Congress did finally appropriate the funds to buy the Waterville Valley forests. (The fact that then-President Calvin Coolidge was from neighboring Vermont probably didn't hurt.) The battle of Waterville Valley did, in no small measure, help mark the beginning of a more enlightened American land ethic.

Although at 6.8 miles the walk to Greeley Ponds is fairly long, it is extremely gentle. What's more, you can turn around at virtually any point before reaching the ponds and still be awfully glad you came. A quarter-mile from the parking lot you'll see a large open area on the right. This is a good place to look for summer color, including the purple-tipped staffs of fireweed and the puckered yellow blossoms of the birdsfoot trefoil—a plant, like so many here, introduced from Europe. At 0.3 mile you'll see our path—the Greeley Ponds Trail—taking off to the left onto a smaller two-track road. Growing along this road, on the edges of a forest of birch and maple, is a nice variety of common New Hampshire plants, including hay-scented fern, partridgeberry, cutleaf and red-banded sedge, bunchberry, bluebead lily, purple trillium, flat-topped white aster, and selfheal. Selfheal, incidentally, a member of the mint family, has been used medicinally for more than 400 years. Some of its popularity as a healing herb occurred in the 16th century, when it was given to members of the German Imperial Army to treat a contagious illness called "the browns," which was marked by fever, sore throat, and a brown coating of the tongue. The Latin name of this illness later became the plant's genus name.

By 1 mile the Mad River will be close by your side. Other trails leave both right and left from our roadway at 1 and 1.2 miles, but we'll keep walking straight. At 1.45 miles, past tufts of strawberry and sweet-scented bedstraw, is a bridge across the Mad River. This is a good spot for a bit of tree identification. Looking upstream next to the bridge is a fine white (or paper) birch. Many native tribes of the northeast used paper birch in making canoes; the thin bark was stretched over frames of Atlantic white cedar, and then sewn together with hemlock root. Finally, the seams were made waterproof by caulking them with resin taken from balsam fir.

Also visible from this bridge, a short distance upstream on the right, is a beautiful white pine—the largest of the eastern pines. To colonists this tree was one of the most important in the forest, its light weight and remarkable strength making it ideal for building. Finally, if you turn around, on your left and slightly overhanging the bridge is a beautiful yellow birch.

The trail continues to wind pleasantly past woods and clearings, past orchids, trillium, and false violet. Fresh out of Greeley Ponds, the Mad River has so far gained only a hint of the pluck and spirit it musters farther downstream, when water from countless other sources join it on its run down the mountains. The Mad doesn't really live up to its name until well down the valley, and even there, some would argue, only when sufficiently prodded by heavy rains or melting snow.

Bluebead Lily

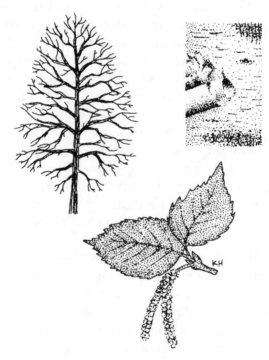

White Birch

WALK #53—WELCH MOUNTAIN LEDGES

DISTANCE: 2.8 miles
ENVIRONMENT: Mountain
LOCATION: White Mountain National Forest. From Interstate 93, head east from exit 28 on State Highway 49. About 5 miles east of the town of Campton the highway will cross the Mad River, after which you'll see a parking area on the right for the Smarts Brook Trail. Our turn is a short distance past this Smarts Brook parking area—the first bridge crossing the river on your left. Once across the river, follow the signs for the national forest access, which is located 1.35 miles from Highway 49, past a large condominium complex. Once past the condominiums take the road on the right, which leads to the trail parking lot.

Though the majority of walkers on this trail make the steep, bare-rock climb to the summit of Welch Mountain, our much easier trek to the high, blueberry-laden ledges lying to the south will offer you no shortage of opportunity to bask in a true New Hampshire mountainscape.

The long, wonderful swell of high country stretching from here northward, which for centuries has been known as the White Mountains, has captured the imagination of countless wanderers. Like magnets of the human spirit they drew writers, poets, and adventurers of the 19th century—people like Nathaniel Hawthorne, Henry David Thoreau, Ralph Waldo Emerson, Henry Wadsworth Longfellow, and William Cullen Bryant. These peaks were equally full of magic to Native Americans, who of course knew them long before Samuel de Champlain first set eyes on them in 1605 from 10 miles out in the Atlantic. "Ask them whither they go when they die," wrote one visitor of the local Indians in 1672, "they will tell you, pointing with their finger, to heaven beyond the White Mountains."

After crossing a stream tumbling southward to a meeting with the Mad River, the trail winds through a fairly young forest of yellow birch, maple, beech, and hemlock. The hearty

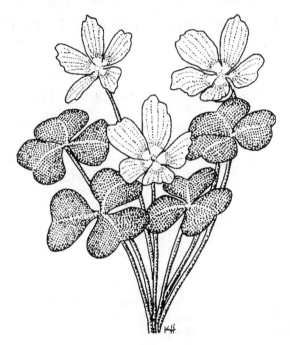

Common Wood Sorrel

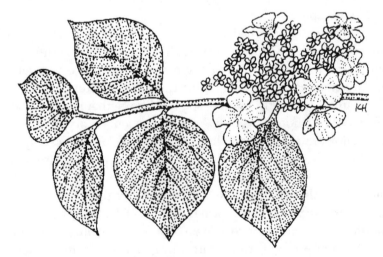

Hobblebush

hobblebush has cast its round-leaved branches across much of the forest floor, with bracken fern, bluebead lily, wood sorrel, wild sarsaparilla, and an occasional purple trillium also close at hand. Our path gets down to more serious climbing at about 0.4 mile, but this lasts less than a mile before reaching the face of an open, windswept table of granite.

Take your time along this bare shoulder, stopping for close-up looks at plants you may not have seen in the forest below. Blueberries appear from nearly every earthen pocket, as do occasional smatterings of sheep laurel. You'll also find the small, shrublike tree known as shadbush. The common name of this plant alludes to the fact that its clusters of beautiful white blossoms occur at the same time that silvery shad make their way upriver to spawn. This particular combination of bloom and spawn never went unnoticed by the early Puritans, who were convinced that the simultaneous events were a special blessing for the faithful. (Shad were at one time pulled from New England's ocean rivers in incredible quantities, filling nets so full that teams of horses had to be employed to drag them out. Though some colonists snubbed the shad as a source of food, the fish did have its share of devotees, including General George Washington and the troops at Valley Forge. It was an early run of shad in late February of 1778 that literally saved the lives of Washington and his cold, hungry men.)

Follow the blaze marks along the rocks to a point where you can head south a short distance to the edge of the ledges. Here are clusters of red oak, bigtooth aspen, red spruce, and mountain maple, with patches of deer moss forming a shaggy carpet across the stone. At the end of the ledges is a yawning view of the Sandwich Range Wilderness to the southeast, and the Mad River below, hurtling itself toward the Atlantic via the Pemigewasset and the Merrimack. Longfellow had a few words to say about the temperament of this river, which changes dramatically from its humble beginnings in the placid waters of Greeley Ponds:

> Men call me Mad, and well they may,
> When, full of rage and trouble,
> I burst my banks of sand and clay,
> And sweep their towns away
> Like withered reeds or stubble.

WALK #54—THREE PONDS

DISTANCE:	4.4 miles
ENVIRONMENT:	Fresh Water
LOCATION:	White Mountain National Forest. From State Highway 25, approximately 3 miles east of West Plymouth, head north on the road to Rumney and Stinson Lake. The trailhead for our walk is on the left (west) side of this road, about 0.6 mile past the north end of Stinson Lake.

The weave of forest and ponds northwest of Stinson Lake makes this area a perfect place to ramble on foot—a land of nooks and crannies, each filled with the remarkable doings of nature. The sense of calm here is a far cry from what awaited southern New Hampshire resident John Stinson, whose name marks both this lake and a mountain just to the southeast. Surprised by a band of St. Francis Indians during a trapping expedition in the spring of 1752, Stinson and one of his companions lost their scalps on these peaceful shores, while a third man, 24-year-old John Stark, was spirited off to Canada. (Despite the attack, Stark, who remained with his Indian captors for five weeks before being exchanged for a pony, would later say that he was treated far better than were prisoners of war in any civilized country. Stark went on to become a respected soldier in both the French and Indian and Revolutionary wars.)

This is a wonderful trail for getting a sense of how not only soil type but moisture levels determine what plants will be found in any given area. Some plants, such as hobblebush, can exist across a fairly wide range of conditions, while others, like marsh fern, are quite particular about their surroundings. This also speaks to the fact that when beaver come in and flood the land, as they have in places along this trail, the entire plant community is changed in the process. Not coincidentally, as the water level increases, so do many of the plants that beaver relish, including iris, water lilies, rushes, and spatterdock.

At 0.1 mile is a trail junction; stay left, following the path marked with yellow blazes. This is a pleasant forest, filled with the flutter of

Wild Sarsaparilla

maple leaves, the golden, shredded bark of yellow birch, and the aromatic boughs of balsam fir. On the ground you'll spot horsetail, whorled wood aster, sensitive fern, selfheal, and bluebead lilies. At about 0.3 mile into the walk the path passes through large mats of wild sarsaparilla. The root of this plant was once used as both a flavoring for root beer, as well as for a drink known as sarsaparilla. The berries, however, which usually ripen in July, are not edible.

The trail continues through several open areas and a small marsh, and at 0.9 mile, after passing a garden of hobblebush, arrives at Sucker Brook. Cross this stream on the bridge, and turn right. From this point on water in some form, either stream or pond, will be your constant companion. As you make your way along Sucker Brook, keep your eyes on the ground for violet, Indian cucumber, round-leafed orchid, shinleaf, and partridgeberry. This latter plant, incidentally, was used often by New England colonial women, who made a tea from the leaves as a remedy for menstrual cramps. The berries, which have a faint taste of apple, are sometimes added to jellies and jams.

Just before reaching the first of several stream crossings at 1.5 miles, there's a large flooded area on your right. If you comb the fringes of this pond you'll find the stumps of several trees cut down

Beaver

by beaver, their incisor marks still visible in the wood. Though on occasion beavers are killed by the trees they fell, far more often they perceive the event in time to dash away, usually into the safety of a nearby pond. There they'll stay for a while, watching for predators, finally emerging with the rest of the family to begin cutting the branches. Armed with his ever-sharp incisors, it takes a beaver only about 10 minutes to drop a 6-inch birch. There are records of beaver cutting down mammoth trees; one in British Columbia measured more than 3 feet in diameter and was 110 feet tall!

Still more beaver signs can be found on the left at 2 miles. This is also a good place to look for both blueberry and huckleberry. Besides being good to eat, herbalists have long prescribed a tea made of either young blueberry or huckleberry leaves to prevent kidney stones. If you're here in summer, look for the delicate ivory blooms of false violet.

In 2.1 miles is a relatively large pond, actually the middle member of the "Three Ponds." Just past this, at 2.2 miles, the trail will fork. The right branch heads uphill, and eventually makes its way north to another pond a short distance away. We'll stay on the left branch, which leads to a pleasant opening along the shore. There's a remote look and feel to this land. It's the kind of place that seems like it should have required more huffing and puffing to reach. Then again, maybe that guy who said "good things never come easy" wasn't entirely on the mark. (He was probably the same one who thought up those workaholic sayings about beaver, like "eager beaver" and "busy as a beaver" when, in fact, this little engineer labors very little during the warm months.) Sitting on this sunny shore at Three Ponds, I much prefer Gershwin's thinking:

Summertime
And the livin' is easy.

WALK #55—KILBURN POND

DISTANCE: 1.5 miles
ENVIRONMENT: Forest
LOCATION: Pisgah State Park. The Kilburn Road access to Pisgah State Park is located on the east side of State Highway 63, 4.5 miles south of the intersection of state highways 63 and 9. There's a gravel turnoff immediately adjacent to the highway, with a metal gate across Kilburn Road. Park outside the gate and begin your walk on this roadway.

There's a beautiful lay to the lands in this northwest corner of Pisgah State Park. A twisted braid of ravines tumbles sharply from the surrounding highlands—Porter Hill to the south, Bear Mountain to the west, Davis Hill to the north, and to the east, 1,303-foot Mount Pisgah. Though like most of New England this area has been logged many times, the earth has yet again produced a splendid blanket of trees, providing critical habitat for a myriad of ground plants, animals, and birds.

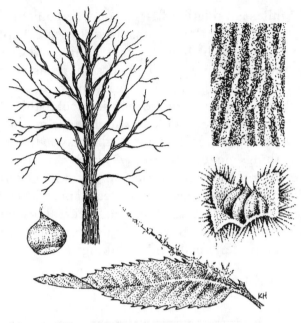

American Chestnut

Along this 0.7-mile stretch of Kilburn Road are stands of birch and beech, as well as striped maple, hemlock, mountain maple, and red oak. If you look carefully you may also see young sprouts of American chestnut, that formerly grand resident that has all but disappeared from the American forest. There was a time in much of New England when gathering chestnuts was a wonderful tradition. After the husks had been split by heavy frosts, many a youngster would bundle up and head into the forest on chilly fall mornings to gather nuts by the basketful. As a crooning Nat King Cole suggests, "chestnuts roasting on an open fire" was indeed a common way of preparing these harvests, since heat made it easier to peel away the outer shell and bitter inner husk, revealing the sweet, mealy chestnut inside. These nuts could be eaten on the spot, made into pudding, or even added to vegetables. New England's native peoples, besides enjoying the nuts, also made a tea out of the leaves that was reportedly effective in treating whooping cough.

From the time the chestnut blight first arrived in New York from Asia in 1903, not 20 years passed before virtually every tree in New England had been infected. The young trees you see here are growing from sprouts, and will only reach heights of 10 to 20 feet before they too will feel the sting of blight in their upper branches, after which the fungus will slowly work its way down until the tree is destroyed. Naturalist John Kieran once called American chestnut saplings the "Peter Pans of the tree world," since they, like that fictional character, can never grow up.

At 0.2 mile are some fine stands of mountain laurel. In winter these evergreen leaves stand out in sharp relief against the blankets of snow, and in late spring and early summer the plants produce delicate pink and white flowers. Mountain laurel can grow to heights of more than 15 feet under ideal conditions, and will occasionally live for more than 100 years. The genus name of this plant, *Kalmia*, is in honor of Peter Kalm, a European who traveled America collecting specimens for the famous Swedish botanist Carolus Linnaeus. It was Linnaeus who, in the first half of the 18th century, set a goal for himself of naming every item in the three kingdoms of the natural world—minerals, plants, and animals. Though of course he fell far short of his mark, he nonetheless had a tremendous influence on modern botony. His two-part system for labeling plants—one name for genus and one for species—is still used today.

Continue walking down the Kilburn Road. At 0.7 mile, near the bottom of a small hill, turn right onto the Kilburn Loop Trail. This is a 4.3-mile loop walk that heads well south of Kilburn Pond and then returns on the east side. For our walk, however, we'll simply make our way along Kilburn Pond for a few hundred yards, looking for any good cutoff through the trees that will bring us to the edge of the water for a better look. In this area you'll see hobblebush, and in mid-to late summer after a good rain, the almost translucent white stalks of Indian pipe. Indians crushed the juice from this plant and mixed it with water as a wash for irritated eyes. There are even reports of Indian pipe being used to treat epilepsy, hence one of its other common names, "convulsion-root."

The edge of Kilburn Pond is a shaggy place, with a shoreline so convoluted that it provides little opportunity to glimpse the entire body of water. A thick blanket of both deciduous and coniferous trees crowd the water's edge, with pond lilies and islands of sedge and rush lining the bays and open channels. Much of Pisgah State Park has this kind of wild, soothing flush to it, a welcome respite from the civilization that continues to sprout like summer weeds across the breadth of southern New Hampshire.

WALK #56—FULLAM POND

DISTANCE: 2 miles
ENVIRONMENT: Fresh Water
LOCATION: Pisgah State Park. From Keene, head south on New Hampshire Route 10 to the town of Winchester. In the center of town, turn right at the traffic light onto Elm Street, which immediately crosses the Ashuclot River on a steel bridge. Continue on Elm Street to a five-way stop intersection. From here take Old Chesterfield Road 2.4 miles to the park boundary, and then continue on it for approximately 2.4 miles farther until you reach the Nash Trailhead on the right. Park outside the Nash Trail gate.

Encompassing 13,000 acres, Pisgah State Park is the largest tract of undeveloped land in southern New Hampshire, offering sweeps of nature that one would expect to find only on lands lying far to the north. Each twist of the trail carries you deeper and deeper into the wilds, until, at the north edge of Fullam Pond itself, you'll be in the middle of a marvelous woodland thick with beaver, deer, heron, and hawk. A quiet afternoon spent in a place like this can foster new appreciation for the wisdom of land preservation. "One looks from outside at works of art and architecture, listens from outside to music or poetry," wrote conservationist Bob Marshall more than half a century ago. "But when one looks at and listens to the wilderness he is encompassed by his experiences of beauty, lives in the midst of his esthetic universe."

Our forest is a fine mix of soft and hard woods, with yellow and gray birch adding slivers of light to the somber huddles of hemlock. Clusters of witch hazel also dot the route, while the edges of the road are lined with the nodding, supple trunks of striped maples. On the ground are shinleaf, Canada mayflower, bunchberry, bracken and interrupted fern, as well as purple trillium and false Solomon's seal.

Take special note of the hemlock—not only a beautiful tree, but one of the easiest to recognize. Its branches are long and slender, often drooping to give the tree a rather shaggy appearance. (Pioneer women often used these branches as brooms.) The needles are spread in two rows, and have two white lines on the underneath. If you have a good hand lens, take time for a close-up inspection of the many small pores—*stomata*—that dot the underside of each hemlock needle. These tiny holes—more easily seen on the hemlock than on most other trees—are what regulate the flow of air and water in and out of the leaf. Hemlock bark contains high levels of tannin. In the early part of the 19th century this bark was stripped from trees throughout New England for use in tanning shoe leather.

On the branches of these trees you're likely to see, or at least hear, the incessant chatter of red squirrels gathering seeds. During winter months the porcupine also makes regular rounds of the hemlock woods, chewing away on both branches and bark. Large groves produce such dense blankets of shade that none but hemlock seedlings, which are very tolerant of low light conditions, can manage to get a foothold. Thus until fire, disease, or logging disturbs them, there will be no contenders to threaten their position in the forest.

The road continues its gentle meander through the woods, passing small patches of ground cedar and wood nettle along the way. At 1 mile notice the white pine needles and cones visible along the road; at times these are the only clues this stately tree is even present, so high do its bristly canopies fly above the rest of the forest. The inner bark of white pine was used first by Indians and then by settlers as a remedy for coughs and sore throats, while some herbalists used the gum of the tree to produce a medicine for rheumatism. So strong and useful in building was the white pine that colonists chose it as their emblem on the first flag of the Revolutionary War.

Another plant to watch for is the Indian pipe—a short, ghostly white plant that, through a partnership with root fungus, takes its nourishment from decayed organic material. At just under 1.2 miles, on either side of a small stream running through a culvert beneath the road, make a sharp left off Nash Trail onto the Fullam Pond Trail. (Because of the thickness of the vegetation, you may hear the stream rather than actually see it.) This path is faint at first, but becomes quite clear once you've made your way a few yards along it.

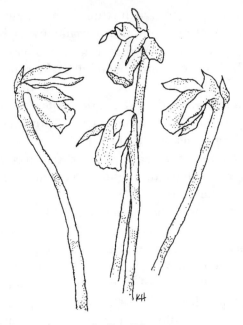

Indian Pipe

A short distance down this road are quiet pools on the right side of the trail, where beaver have backed up the stream flow. Look closely, and you'll see tree stumps with the beaver's tooth marks plainly visible. The chewing teeth of the beaver, like those of many rodents, are remarkable in that they become sharper with use. The back of the incisor is made up of a soft dentine, while the front is composed of a hard enamel. When a beaver chews on trees, those rear layers wear down at a much faster rate, giving the teeth an angled shape. What's more, because the lower pair of incisors rubs against the upper pair, they tend to sharpen themselves with use.

Nudged against clumps of blueberry and clubmoss is the north channel of Fullam Pond, 0.3 mile from where you turned off Nash Trail. Although this is hardly the most encompassing view of Fullum, it's certainly one of the wildest. The shaggy runs of trees pushing their way to the very edges of the pond, dead trunks rising up from the water with arms frozen gray against the sky, give this place a delicious feeling of seclusion. Breathe it in, and then take it with you wherever you go.

Continue along Fullam Pond Trail to its intersection with Nash Trail; turn right to retrace your steps back to your car.

WALK #57—CIRCLE TRAIL

DISTANCE: 0.4 mile
ENVIRONMENT: Mountain
LOCATION: Miller State Park. This park is located on the north side of State Highway 101, 3.8 miles east of the intersection of State Highway 101 and U.S. Highway 202 East. Turn into the park, and follow the entrance road 1.3 miles up to the summit. *Note:* The road to the summit is narrow and winding, not suitable for large vehicles or vehicles pulling trailers.

Miller State Park, crowned by 2,290-foot South Pack Monadnock Mountain, is the oldest park in New Hampshire, donated in 1891 as a memorial to War of 1812 hero General James Miller. It provides a wonderful opportunity for walkers to experience a southern New Hampshire summit with no more effort than a series of rather hard twists on the steering wheel. (Those who feel guilty about reaching the top of a mountain without breaking a sweat can walk up from the base on either the Blue or Marion Davis trails.) On clear days the views from this peak are remarkable, stretching southeastward all the way across Massachusetts into the concrete peaks of Boston.

Once you've parked on top of the mountain, if you walk around the loop road in a counterclockwise direction, the Circle Trail—marked by a series of red dots—will be found next to the last picnic table on your right. Though the trail can be bit of a challenge to follow at times, rest assured that the red marking dots are indeed there, either on the bark of trees or the faces of rocks.

At the beginning of the walk you'll be afforded fine views of Monadnock Mountain, 12 miles to the west. This 3,165-foot peak, whose name is now a geological term for uplifts that have resisted the forces of erosion, is the highest point in southern New Hampshire. Like the mountain you're standing on, Monadnock is a residual of the Littleton Formation—a towering upswell of rock that remained unbroken by the great tongues of glaciers that once scoured this landscape. Much of the bare areas visible along the upper 400 to 500 feet of Monadnock are not the result of harsh alpine conditions, which occur only at much higher elevations, but are the work of early settlers who set countless fires on the mountain to drive wolves away from their sheep. (At one time Spanish merino sheep were extremely common in this part of New England; in Vermont, they outnumbered people five to one!)

Monadnock is one of the most visited mountains in the world, having claimed such visitors as Ralph Waldo Emerson, Henry David Thoreau, Rudyard Kipling, and even Mark Twain. Twain, waxing especially poetic about the autumn vistas near the base of the peak, said that "the sight affects the spectator physically, it stirs his blood like military music." Nor for that matter did the appeal of this area die with the 19th century. Just to the west, near Peterborough, is McDowell Colony, a retreat that has attracted people from Thornton Wilder to Aaron Copland.

But enough of Monadnock. Let's take a closer look at this, her smaller sister. Our trail drops gently past tufts of meadowsweet, and then takes a right into the hush of a red spruce grove, the path peppered here and there with clusters of hay-scented fern. As you come out of this forest into a clearing, watch for nice mats of blueberry, which can be seen growing in abundance throughout

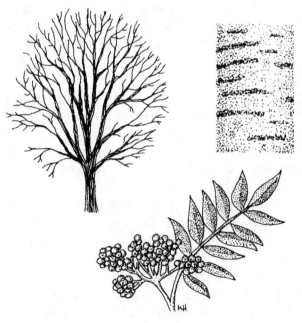

Mountain Ash

much of this trek. In 0.1 mile you'll cross an open area paved with flat rocks, and, shortly afterward, begin a short descent into a mixed forest of gray birch, spruce, mountain ash, maple, and sumac. (The hollow stems of this sumac were once used as taps for sugar maples.) At the bottom of the ravine the path grows cool and shady, framed by ferns, bluebead lily, Canada mayflower, and bunchberry.

Shortly after leaving the woods there is an open, rocky area with a bench on the right—the perfect perch from which to survey views of the tumbling swell of land to the north. When you've had your fill of scenery, continue around the summit toward the east, passing into a broken forest of yellow birch and maple, their feet wrapped in tight clusters of hobblebush. In spring you'll see splashes of purple trillium, or "birthroot," the latter name alluding to the fact that a tea from the plant was once given to women who had just given birth in order to help control bleeding. Certain Indian tribes also crushed the leaves of the purple trillium and applied the juice to burns and insect bites.

All too soon, at a mere 0.4 mile, to be exact, you'll again reach the parking area. Perhaps you'll want to make this loop again, in the other direction. The views only get more enjoyable, the rush of wind through the rips in the tree canopy more refreshing.

WALK #58—BEAR BROOK STATE PARK

DISTANCE: 3 miles

ENVIRONMENT: Forest

LOCATION: From the intersection of U.S. Highway 3 and State Highway 28, proceed north on Highway 28 for 3 miles to the park entrance road, and turn right. Continue east for 3.2 miles, staying to the right at the one "Y" fork in the road, to a camping area entrance on the right. Turn here and, again keeping to the right, continue for 1.4 miles to our trailhead, which is on the right marked by a letter "D."

These 3 miles of pathway pass remarkably easily—a flat, wooded meander through stands of conifers and hardwoods of varying ages, with plenty of chances to rub elbows with fine slices

Hay-scented Fern

Interrupted Fern

of marsh and meadow. Do keep in mind that from spring to midsummer the second leg of the trek can have a few muddy spots; make sure your feet are ready.

Our walk takes off on a grassy two-track road, passing nice gardens of interrupted, sensitive, and hay-scented ferns. There's something special about ferns. Braided into a feathery quilt at the feet of the forest, they seem to bring a delicate hush to the land—a reminder to lighten your step, to cock an ear now and then for a chance to hear the sound of honest to goodness quiet.

All ferns reproduce by means of spores, which in some species are held in cases that appear as tiny dots or rust-colored lines on the underside of the fronds. Most of these spore cases are covered by thin shields, designed to protect them until the time is right for their release. Some ferns produce millions of spores, so light and durable that some researchers suggest that they may be transported from continent to continent in the jet stream; recently this idea gained support when a fern that grows only in Asia and Europe suddenly showed up on the east slope of the Colorado Rockies.

When one of these spores germinates, it first grows into what looks like a very thin thread. If conditions are right this thread expands into a tiny heart-shaped object known as a *prothallium*. (Those willing to put their nose to the ground in a suitable habitat, such as a carpet of moss, can often spot dozens of these.) Prothallia are independent, self-contained plants, sporting both male and female organs of microscopic proportions. Sliding on a thin film of water, male sperm wriggle into the funnel-shaped female organ and fertilize the egg. Though nursed for a while by nutrients contained in the prothallium case, eventually the plant sends a root into the soil and begins making its own food. The parent prothallium withers away while the young fern continues to grow, unrolling its fronds from "fiddleheads"—the only plants, incidentally, to uncoil their leaves in such a manner. The time required for a ripe spore to become a new fern plant can vary according to species and growing conditions; sometimes the process takes only a few weeks, and at other times it may span 20 years.

Even though ferns are outnumbered by seed-bearing plants 30 to 1, there are few places in the world where they cannot be found—from the Arctic to the Antarctic, and a million mountain ledges, lakes, ponds, fields, and forests in between. The lore surrounding ferns is long and complex, ranging from an old Irish belief that they were a sign of fertility, to their having been viewed by some religions—including Christianity—as being in a strange relationship with evil serpents. Ferns also had plenty of medicinal applications. Sweet brake was used from early Greek days to modern times as a remedy for tapeworm. Polypody has long been used as a laxative, and a tea made from maidenhair fern has for 2,000 years been favored by herbalists as a means of treating coughs.

Continue through a forest of oak, hemlock, white pine, yellow birch, and witch hazel, and trailside patches of Canada mayflower, wintergreen, sedges, and clubmoss, as well as the lovely spotted orange petals of the wood lily. At 0.9 mile, just after crossing a small stream and a fine huddle of hemlocks, is marker "B." Turn right here and follow the path through a moist forest laced with fern, blueberry, Indian pipe, ground cedar, and bunchberry.

At 1.5 miles is marker "A," where you'll once again turn to the right, picking up gray birch and sugar maple, as well as a towering stand of white pine at 1.75 miles. The marsh mentioned earlier—a humanmade water project to encourage wildlife—will be found at marker "4." Follow the road along the north side of the marsh, and then, 50 yards past it, turn right onto a small trail taking off through the woods. This will soon join another road, where you'll take yet another right. Just after this turn you'll be cradled by a nice sedge and wildflower meadow on the right, and by bracken fern, oak, white pine, gray birch, aspen, mountain maple, pin cherry, and milkweed on the left. Take a right when you reach the entrance road at the far end of this clearing, and walk 0.3 mile back to your car.

WALK #59—ODIORNE POINT

DISTANCE:	0.3 mile
ENVIRONMENT:	Coast
LOCATION:	Odiorne Point State Park. Located south-east of Portsmouth, near the village of Rye. From the intersection of U.S. Highway 1 and State Highway 1A, follow Highway 1A south for approximately 4 miles to the entrance of Odiorne Point State Park. Our footpath takes off to the north from a paved road connecting the parking area to the Russell B. Tobey Visitors' Center. The trailhead is just west of the visitors' center.

Much has happened since Scotsman David Thomson dropped anchor at the mouth of the Piscataqua River in the spring of 1623, and proceeded to discharge his hopeful settlers (along with their miscellany of cooking kettles, tools, seeds, gunpowder, rope, and fishing nets), thereby beginning the first European settlement in what is now the state of New Hampshire.

This preserve—the last significant stretch of undeveloped shoreline in the state—takes its name from settler John Odiorne, who began farming and fishing on this point in 1660. Fully 10 generations of Odiorne's descendants lived and worked on this rocky seacoast, their legacy broken only by the onset of World War II, when the U.S. government purchased the land and turned it into a coastal defense installation to protect the naval shipyard at Portsmouth Harbor. Almost overnight, a lazy mosaic of woods and gardens yielded to 16-inch guns and 155-millimeter anti-aircraft cannon. Today, the remains of concrete bunkers stand alongside the faint remnants of pathways, gates, and fountains of the former residents—odd bedfellows indeed.

Our walk, which is really a free-form ramble up the coast, begins on a trail located just west of the Russell Tobey Visitors' Center. (Be sure to visit this fine center either before or after your walk.) A short distance after leaving the pavement, heading north, you'll arrive at the edge of the coast. Stay right, passing rocky bluffs fringed by rose, sumac, alder, Scotch pine, tansy, and St. Johnswort, soon arriving at an intriguing collection of tidal pools. From here you can continue farther up the coast, past a pebble beach to the tip of Frost Point. For this particular outing, however, let's concentrate on some of the more remarkable mysteries held in these salty pools.

Besides the obvious need to watch where you walk in a tidal area, please remember that everything you handle should be returned to the exact place you found it. Living on the edge, so to speak, is a precarious business. Simply turning over a rock can expose tide pool residents to predators, as well as to the drying effects of the sun—conditions that will almost surely lead to their demise.

Many of the creatures living at the edge of the sea are so good at camouflage that you can look them right in the oyster and not realize they're there. One of the best things about tidal pool watching, in fact, is that it forces you to slow down, to focus on tiny things, slices of the world far smaller and more delicate than the broad brush strokes that paint our everyday lives. Let's begin by looking at a few of the more common, easy-to-spot residents of Odiorne Point.

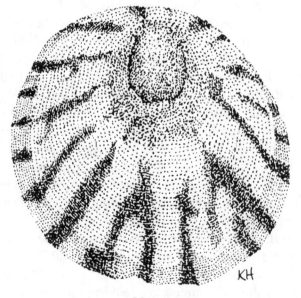

Limpet

Of course there are barnacles here—ivory-colored, volcano-shaped buttons, glued fast to seaside rocks. This relative of the shrimp was in its larval stage a swimmer, though it soon traded in the life of a drifter for that of a homebody, constructing its rigid house by secreting calcium carbonate plates and cementing them to rocks, ships, lobster traps, piers, etc. (This barnacle "cement" has as much holding power per square inch as any substance known to humans, a fact that shipowners, who spend thousands of dollars scraping barnacles off their hulls each year, are painfully aware of.) A barnacle essentially stands on its head in this bomb-proof home, and, when covered with seawater at high tide, sticks out a set of feathery appendages every few seconds to gather in plankton and various other particles of food.

Two other common residents in these pools are the chiton and the limpet. The chiton lives in an oval shell divided into plates, while the limpet resides in a symmetrical, cone-shaped shell that looks rather like a Chinese hat. Unlike barnacles, which are fixed in one place, limpets and chitons move slowly across rocks or the shells of other creatures, scraping off bits of edible organic material as they go.

You're also likely to see a particularly bold, active crab here, a mottled green color with ten scallops on the front of its dorsal shield. This is the green crab, and as many a barefoot beachcomber has found out, it has a particularly strong pincer; proportionally, a green crab can latch onto your big toe with 20 times the force that most people can muster in their hands. The green crab is a carnivore, and he is often spotted at high tide scurrying from side to side in a tireless, fearless hunt for food.

Other creatures you're likely to see at Odiorne include dog whelks, rock crabs, spiral worms, periwinkles, mussels, sea urchins, starfish, and hermit crabs. The daily activities of these creatures have changed little since ancient times. On the other hand, the stories told in these pools are never exactly the same; both the actors, as well as the stage itself, can change dramatically with each new wash of seawater.

▪ MAINE ▪

MAINE

■ ■ ■

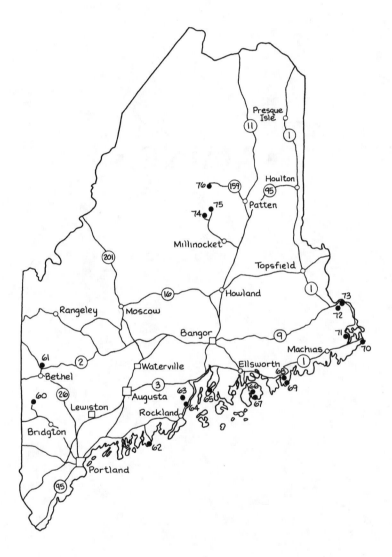

Presque Isle

⑪   ①

76●─⑲   Houlton
    75   ⑨⑤
74●   Patten

        Millinocket

            Topsfield

②⓪①
        ⑯   Howland   ①   73●
    Rangeley   Moscow   72●
        Bangor   ⑨   71●
61●   Machias   70●
②   Waterville   Ellsworth   ①
    Bethel   ③   63●   68●
60●   ②⑥   Augusta   65●   66●   69●
    Lewiston   Rockland   64●   67●
Bridgton

        62●

⑨⑤   Portland

Maine

WALK #60—SABATTUS MOUNTAIN

DISTANCE:	1.6 miles
ENVIRONMENT:	Mountain
LOCATION:	Kezar Sportsmen's Club. The village of Center Lovell is located approximately 22.5 miles south of the town of Bethel, on State Highway 5. From Center Lovell, 0.8 mile north of where state highways 5 and 5A intersect, turn right (east) onto Sabattus Road. Follow this for 1.5 miles, and veer to the right on Sabattus Mountain Road. In 0.3 mile you'll reach a small parking area on the left side of the road. Our trail takes off across from this parking lot.

... In such places standing alone on the mountaintop it is easy to realize that whatever special nests we make—leaves and moss like the marmots and birds, or tents or piled stone—we all dwell in a house of one room—the world with the firmament for its roof—and are sailing the celestial spaces without leaving any track.

—John Muir

The twisted path up the north side of Sabattus Mountain gives no indication of the magnificent views southward across the Oxford Hills that await you at the end of the trail. These vast drifts of untrammeled highlands, each blanketed with thick runs of deciduous and coniferous forest, are striking enough to send the imagination spinning.

Our walk begins in a logged area in the early stages of forest succession. The stars of the show at this point in time are birch and aspen, but these will eventually yield the stage to more shade-tolerant species. You'll actually be passing through several stages of forest growth along this walk, ranging from young saplings like these, to small groves of mature white pines. This latter tree, identified by its shiny bundles of five needles, was a dominant resident in much of Maine for 5,000 years, succumbing not to the forces of nature, but to 200 years of saws and axes.

As you reach a more mature woodland at just over 0.1 mile, keep your eyes open for gardens of bracken and woodfern, as well as clusters of Indian cucumber, wintergreen, white and whorled wood asters, blueberries, Canada mayflower, star-flower, hobblebush, trailing arbutus, and pipsissewa. The rather lyrical name of this latter plant is a Cree Indian word meaning "breaks into pieces." This refers to a belief that prolonged consumption of a tea made from pipsissewa leaves could break down bladder and kidney stones. The plant was widely used as a diuretic throughout much of the American frontier, and some people also made compresses with it for the relief of pains in the joints. Even today pipsissewa isn't without practical uses; an extract of the leaves, for example, is a common ingredient in the flavoring of root beer.

The trail continues to climb steadily on its route to the top of Sabattus, passing at 0.75 mile nice clumps of sheep laurel, growing at the feet of several towering white pines. The journey comes to an end rather abruptly at a wide opening beside the remains of an old fire tower. Here you'll find several rocky outcroppings from which to drink in the view, most cradled by beautiful red oaks, with a few tenacious gray birch hanging by their toes from the sheer south side of the mountain. (Like many of its relatives, the branches of the gray birch are so supple that heavy snows may pin them to the ground for several months without doing serious damage to them.)

Looking across this roll of timber, it's easy to believe that 87 percent of Maine (the "Pine Tree State") is forested—a fact that accounts for it producing enormous quantities of lumber, pulp paper, and, not that anyone is counting, 25 million toothpicks every year. But even completely untouched, the trees of Maine serve an invaluable role in the well-being of those who would simply pause long enough to take notice of them. "Keep a green tree in your heart," says an ancient Chinese proverb, "and perhaps the singing bird will come."

WALK #61—STEP FALLS

DISTANCE: 1.2 miles

ENVIRONMENT: Fresh Water

LOCATION: The Nature Conservancy. Follow combined routes U.S. Highway 2 East and State Highway 26 north out of Bethel, to the point where these routes split. Follow Highway 26 for 8 miles, to a small grassy parking area on the right side of the road, just before a bridge crossing Wight Brook. The path leaves from the north side of the parking area.

This stream is more than just another pretty face tumbling down from the high country, bound for the Gulf of Maine. Working against a carefully sculpted flow of granite laced with glimmering intrusions of quartz, mica, and feldspar, Wight Brook has transformed the upper reaches of this ravine into one of the most comely marriages of rock and water I have ever seen. If it's true, as Richard Franck claimed three centuries ago, that art imitates nature, then surely there could be no finer source of inspiration than this.

Established in 1961 as the first preserve of the Maine Chapter of the Nature Conservancy, the lower reaches of Step Falls is cradled by groves of spruce, fir, and hemlock, with the higher, more open areas containing a lovely blend of beech, white and yellow birch, and sugar and striped maple. Wildflowers and ground covers abound as well, including Canada mayflower, partridgeberry, trillium, blueberry, wood sorrel, bunchberry, Indian cucumber, hobblebush, and goldthread. This latter plant of the cool woods—sporting shiny, strawberrylike leaves and delicate white flowers—was named for its shallow braid of yellow, threadlike roots. Many a colonist used this bitter rhizome as a treatment for fever blisters and canker sores, and also made a mouthwash to soothe sore throats. The active substance in the roots of goldthread is a gentle alkaloid pain killer known as berberine.

Shortly after reaching a grove of white birch at 0.5 mile, you may want to work your way up and across the granite rock flows that form the bed of Step Falls. (Be very careful, however, as these can be slippery.) The cooling of this granite from its molten state caused parallel fractures to develop in the rock. The waters of Wight Brook found these weak joints, along with splits that occurred from later upthrusts, and generally probed, gouged, and polished the gorge into the striking collage of falls and plunge pools you see today.

When you reach the center portion of the rock flow, brace yourself, and turn around for a dizzying, breathtaking view of the high, forested peaks on the south side of Bear River. Standing on this perch, it's easy to believe John Muir's claim that "the great poets, philosophers, prophets, able men whose thought and deeds have moved the world, have come down from the mountains." If greatness was indeed within them, what better incentive for its flowering than these soaring, rocky realms of the gods?

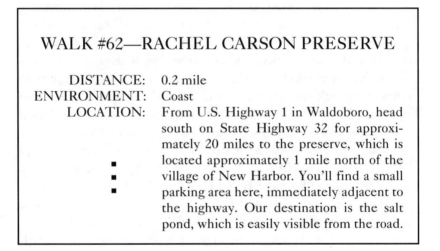

WALK #62—RACHEL CARSON PRESERVE

DISTANCE:	0.2 mile
ENVIRONMENT:	Coast
LOCATION:	From U.S. Highway 1 in Waldoboro, head south on State Highway 32 for approximately 20 miles to the preserve, which is located approximately 1 mile north of the village of New Harbor. You'll find a small parking area here, immediately adjacent to the highway. Our destination is the salt pond, which is easily visible from the road.

Managed by the Maine Chapter of the Nature Conservancy, the Rachel Carson Preserve is a place well-suited to those willing to drop to their knees in front of a tidal pool or press their noses to a rock plastered with barnacles. The patient, curious visitor will find mysteries unfolding in a hundred nooks and crannies—tiny strands of the complex weave of life that wraps this bridge between land and sea.

Descending past a thin roadside fringe of gray birch, meadowsweet, strawberry, rose, and goldenrod, you'll quickly reach the upper edge of the tidal zone. Here you'll find thick, slippery carpets of blue-green algae—the organism that many scientists

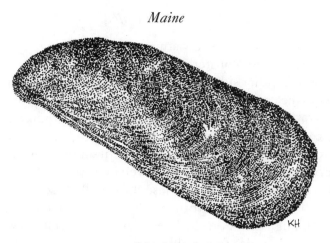

Blue Mussel

consider to have been the first life form ever to leave its saltwater home and colonize the land.

This line is also marked by an abundance of rockweeds and knotted wrack, their air sacks tangled and tossed together like plates of pregnant pasta. The tiny air chambers you see on some of these plants allow them to float high in the water, maximizing their exposure to the sun. Here you'll also find an abundance of Irish moss, as well as rough periwinkles, blue mussels, and tortoiseshell limpets. Beneath this level blue mussels continue to be abundant, as are common periwinkles, sea stars, and hermit and Jonah crabs. Finally, farther down is a submerged garden of rubbery kelp, some of which may weigh in at a whopping 25 pounds. Kelp survives the force and fury of breaking waves not by fighting them, but by "going with the flow," engaging in a loose, sinewy dance. In addition, kelp stalks are extremely well anchored to their rock underpinnings; most of these fastenings can withstand forces of nearly 800 pounds per square inch before breaking.

The Salt Pool, sitting center stage in the preserve, is a wonderful spot to see green crabs, smooth periwinkles, dogwinkles, and, if you're lucky, an occasional green sea urchin. True to its name, this subtidal resident is covered by a bright green pincushion of protective spines. Urchins feed on kelp, as well as by scraping algae off rocks, using a circle of five teeth that grind back and forth, powered by a strange weave of cartilage and muscle. Adjacent to this "mouth" is the digestive tract, and, in season, the gonads, which gourmet chefs around the world consider to be true delicacies. Despite their spiny armor, sea urchins are preyed upon by seagulls, cod, and lobster.

Framing either side of the preserve are folded gray layers of *granulate*, a rock created from sediments that were deposited on the ocean floor hundreds of millions of years ago, and then folded by violent collisions of the continental plates. The heat that accompanied such movements was sufficient to turn some of the granulate into fiery hot magma, which then flowed like warm honey through cracks in the more solid rock. These flows, called *dikes*, are visible along much of the shore north of the salt pool, seen as colored braids running through the bedrock. These patterns, as well as a wonderful collage of boulder fields, sills, and warped strata, make this a geological wonderland.

Phenomena such as drifting continents, rocks being laid down particle by particle on the bed of ancient seas, and the slow grind of glaciers prod us to transcend our normal perception of time—to consider, as Rachel Carson did, a world that lies far beyond one comprised of years and centuries and even millennia.

> Once this rocky coast beneath me was a plain of sand; then the sea rose and found a new shore line. And again in some shadowy future the surf will have ground these rocks to sand and will have returned the coast to its earlier state. And so in my mind's eye these coastal forms merge and blend in a shifting, kaleidoscopic pattern in which there is no finality, no ultimate and fixed reality—earth becoming fluid as the sea itself.
>
> —The Edge of the Sea

WALK #63—FERNALD'S NECK PRESERVE

DISTANCE: 2.75 miles
ENVIRONMENT: Fresh Water
LOCATION: The Nature Conservancy. From U.S. Highway 1, turn north onto State Highway 52. Just past the village of Youngtown Corner, you'll see the Fernald's Neck Road taking off to the left. Follow this for 1 mile, keeping to the left at the one fork. The parking area is in a field on the left side of the road, adjacent to a small opening in the forest.

Viewed from any of several high perches nearby, Fernald's Neck, located at the northeast corner of Lake Megunticook, appears as a patchwork of green forest and cool, blue water. This is a quiet, rather subdued place, a spot where upland streams gather and pause before tossing themselves headlong into the waiting arms of the Atlantic. Though not spectacular, this Nature Conservancy Preserve is most certainly an engaging place. The laughing of loons still rolls across the lake into the thick of balsam and birch. Feathery fern gardens can be found here, as well as huddles of red pine, hemlock, and northern red oak. Slow down when walking these trails. You may see moose, white-tailed deer, or any of nearly six dozen species of nesting birds.

Our trail begins at the edge of an open, grassy swell, but soon thereafter plunges into a woodland filled with the sweet, spicy smell of balsam. In less than 0.2 mile is the official entrance point for the 315-acre preserve, where you'll find a blue trail taking off to the right, and our path—an orange-blazed route—taking off to the left. Along the first few hundred yards are mats of huckleberry, whorled wood aster, clubmoss, ground cedar, and bracken and hay-scented fern, as well as some nice stands of red pine.

Shortly after a fork in the trail, our orange route taking off to the left, you'll arrive at the edge of Great Bog. Look for pitcher plants, busy garnering nitrogen for themselves by breaking down the bodies of unlucky insects that have drowned in pools of water held by the plant's tight weave of leaves.

You'll also find nice clumps of blue flag iris here. True to their name—taken from Iris, the Greek goddess of the rainbow—these blossoms are extremely rich in color, made all the more striking when held against the dull greens and browns of the bog. It was the regal yellow flag iris, incidentally, that once adorned the staffs of French kings, the three-part bloom representing courage, faith, and wisdom. The reason you usually see iris growing in clusters is because the flowers sprout directly out of the root rhizome, which, growing just beneath the surface of the soil, each year thickens and splits into branches. Though toxic, these rhizomes were for centuries used by Indians of the Northeast as a diuretic, a blood purifier, and as a poultice for treating bruises.

There's an ethereal quality to this bog, especially if coastal fog has tiptoed in during the night. Watch for clumps of beech, witch hazel, red maple, and oak mixed in among the conifers, and listen for

Red Squirrel

Common Loon

the chatter of red squirrels as they furiously announce their squatter's rights from the shaggy canopies overhead. Go right at a split in the trail at 0.7 mile, which in another 0.15 mile will deliver you to the shore of Lake Megunticook. This Indian name is thought to have meant "big mountain harbor," and originally referred only to the quiet waters of Camden Harbor. As often happened, though, European settlers either didn't care or were too confused to understand what the boundaries of the highly descriptive native names really were, so today Megunticook also labels a river, a mountain, and a lake.

Lake Megunticook is where you may spot the common loon, in summer wearing a black and white checkerboard jacket with a striking zebra-striped necklace around its black-feathered head. The large webbed feet of the loon are set well back on the body, an arrangement that provides a great deal of kicking power in the water, but proves more than a little cumbersome when it comes time to navigate on land (which these birds seldom do). Loons are tremendous divers; some have been caught in fishermen's nets at depths of over 200 feet.

Even if you never actually see a loon, just hearing its call is an unforgettable experience. Besides the unbridled laughing that loons are so famous for, the birds also emit a rather mournful yodel—a sound that some Maine Indian tribes believed foretold the coming of the wind. Henry David Thoreau wrote of the pleasures of listening to loons, especially after having been serenaded by them on the shores of Maine's Chamberlain Lake. "I could lie awake for hours listening to it, it is so thrilling," he said. In *The Maine Woods*, published two years after his death in 1862, Thoreau tells how he used to lie quietly in the middle of the night and try to decipher the sounds of the woodland's inhabitants. "I had listened to hear some words or syllables of their language," he recalled, "but it chanced that I listened in vain until I heard the cry of the loon."

The trail continues around the deeply scalloped edges of Lake Megunticook, past northern red oaks, balsam, spruce, birch, and red maple, with pond lilies, arrowhead, and bur reed growing in the quieter stretches of the lake. At just over 2 miles you'll complete the loop portion of the path, after which you'll retrace your steps for 0.7 mile back to the parking area.

An old political saying that originated in the late 1800s claims that "As Maine goes, so goes the nation." Oh, but that the rest of the nation could have ended up with more wild slices of nature like this.

WALK #64—OCEAN LOOKOUT

DISTANCE:	3 miles
ENVIRONMENT:	Mountain
LOCATION:	Camden Hills State Park. This park is located along U.S. Highway 1, 1.75 miles north of Camden. Park at the lot located just to the left of the entrance station and just south of Mount Battie Road. Our path, which follows the Mount Battie Nature Trail, leaves from Mount Battie Road, just a few yards from the campground entrance road.

This forested hill country, perched above the shimmering waters of Penobscot Bay, has long been a favorite of those looking for the ultimate in seaside living. Seekers of the good life started coming here 100 years ago in magnificent 250-foot yachts, their white sails billowed against the blue waters of Camden Harbor. In time they brought art and music, and for years it could be heard rising from white clapboard cottages on Rockport's Mechanic Street—Josef Hofmann's piano, Felix Salmond's cello, the harp of Carlos Salzedo.

Today some would say that the delicate balance between humans and nature has been upset by a rush of people bound and determined to have their share of this earthly paradise. And, when seen from inside a car gridlocked in downtown Camden on a July afternoon, one might be hard-pressed not to agree. But all is not lost. Climb up to either Mount Battie, or to our destination at Ocean Lookout, and you'll find the land still rich and full of enchantment, a tapestry of steeples and seashore, spruce and sky.

Our walk begins in a rather young mixed deciduous forest of red oak, beech, white and gray birch, beaked hazelnut, and striped and red maple. Closer to the ground are splashes of Canada mayflower, interrupted, sensitive, and Christmas ferns, and clumps of arrowwood. This latter plant takes its common name from the fact that Indians once used the young shoots in making arrow shafts. Another resident you'll see during the first mile of this walk is wild oats, a member of the lily family

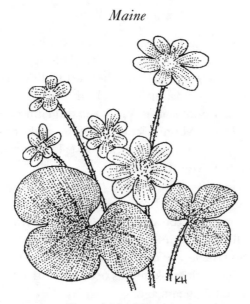

Round-lobed Hepatica

bearing beautiful, creamy yellow, bell-shaped flowers from late April through June. Because these drooping blooms look rather like the soft lobe that hangs down from the rear palate of a person's mouth, the plant was once thought valuable for treating disorders of the throat.

The practice of using plants as healing agents based on their similarity to some human characteristic is known as the *Doctrine of Signatures*—so-named because each species offers a "signature" of the organ it's meant to treat. Thus, round-lobed hepatica, which resembled the liver, was used in treating liver disorders; Chinese lantern, with its bladder-shaped calyx, was used for disorders of the urinary tract. This view of medicinal plants is thought to have been pioneered during the Renaissance by Swiss physician Bombastus von Honenheim, or, as he was often called, Paracelsus. While today it may appear that Paracelsus was doing overtime in the wishful thinking department, his contributions to medicine were in fact rather substantial. It was he, for example, who first realized the importance of chemistry in the preparation of medicines.

In 1.1 miles, after passing nice patches of wintergreen, fern, and bluebead lily, is the Tablelands Trail. Turn right, and proceed for approximately 0.8 mile to Ocean Lookout. The last part of this trail is fairly steep, along a rocky path traversing a forest thick with young beech, as well as smatterings of northern red oak, birch, fir, and spruce. Those who trudge on will find plenty of reward. From this windswept, 1,300-foot summit the world falls away in a cascade of glacier-carved uplands, and the shining waters of both Lake Megunticook and Penobscot Bay. Up the ridge immediately to the northwest is Mount Megunticook, which, at 1,385 feet, is the second highest peak on the Atlantic coast. Directly to the west is the rugged knob of Mount Battie.

Both Battie and Megunticook peaks are made of extremely hard rock, a metamorphose fired from the ancient sand and gravel beds that were once located at the edges of the continental shelves. During the collision of the continents, tremendous pressure and heat transformed these gravelly beds into the rock you see today—a rock so hard that little erosion has occurred since the last ice age retreated over 10,000 years ago.

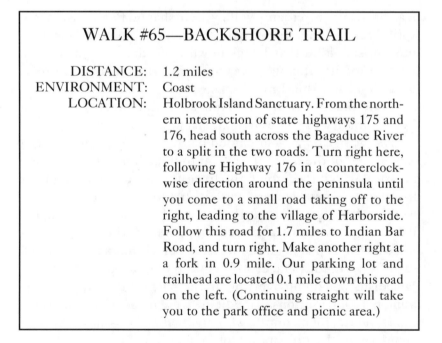

WALK #65—BACKSHORE TRAIL

DISTANCE: 1.2 miles
ENVIRONMENT: Coast
LOCATION: Holbrook Island Sanctuary. From the northern intersection of state highways 175 and 176, head south across the Bagaduce River to a split in the two roads. Turn right here, following Highway 176 in a counterclockwise direction around the peninsula until you come to a small road taking off to the right, leading to the village of Harborside. Follow this road for 1.7 miles to Indian Bar Road, and turn right. Make another right at a fork in 0.9 mile. Our parking lot and trailhead are located 0.1 mile down this road on the left. (Continuing straight will take you to the park office and picnic area.)

It would be hard to imagine a more beguiling blend of natural beauty than the mainland portion of Holbrook Island Sanctuary. Here old volcanic hills wear patchwork robes stitched with wildflowers and mixed hardwood forest. There are fresh-water marshes

and ponds, estuaries, mudflats, and beaches, each providing critical habitat for a variety of birds and mammals. You can sit atop any
of a dozen windswept grassy knolls and pull daydreams out of the
blue waters of Penobscot Bay, then send them soaring on the
outstretched wings of bald eagles and ospreys.

For much of this you can thank Anita Harris—the feisty
matron saint of nature on these 1,200 acres, as well as on her private
estate on Holbrook Island, both of which she bequeathed to the
state of Maine for the protection of the wild creatures that brought
so much joy to her 92 years.

On more than a few occasions, Ms. Harris chose the good
of nature over good relations with her neighbors. Shortly after
she and her sister acquired this mainland sanctuary in the early
1960s, they closed it to hunting and trapping. In response, a
gang of incensed, trigger-happy hunters proceeded to slaughter
an entire herd of deer. Nor was she particularly popular when
she fought efforts to create a copper mine on the edge of the
preserve. But perhaps at no time was she less appreciated than
when she created a private nature preserve out of this property
and then claimed that, as such, the parcel should be given tax-
exempt status. When the courts disagreed, she promptly donated the land lock, stock, and barrel to the state of Maine.
"The villagers call me an old bitch," she informed Governor
Ken Curtis before signing over the deed to this property in
1971. "Since the female of the canine species is loyal and
intelligent," she added, "I take that as a compliment." In truth,
were it not for the generosity and devotion to principle of this
fiercely independent woman, the people of Maine—indeed, all
of New England—would be far poorer.

Our walk begins in clusters of white pine, alder, cherry,
and apple trees underlain by fallow meadows. Here is a wonderful glimpse of how wild nature quickly and methodically reclaims the land. (At her own estate on Holbrook Island, Ms.
Harris helped things along considerably by requiring that, upon
her death, all but one of the buildings there be demolished.)
Here on the mainland the old fields are already well seasoned
with clover, meadowsweet, curly dock, goldenrod, thistle, milkweed, and Queen Anne's lace, while each year the sun-loving
members of the hardwood forest march a little farther across the
open ground.

Most of the above-mentioned meadow plants are considered weeds, a term Emerson once said we carelessly applied to any plant whose virtues have not yet been discovered. In the case of several of these species uses were indeed found, but ultimately forgotten. Consider, for example, Queen Anne's lace. The legend behind the naming of this plant says that Queen Anne pricked her finger while making lace, thus producing the single tiny red flower you see at the center of the bloom. (For centuries people believed that eating these red flowers would prevent epileptic seizures.) Queen Anne's lace is actually the mother of our garden carrot, set free when the carrots of the colonists escaped cultivation and began roaming the countryside.

Likewise, the "spring greens" of curly dock were a common table vegetable during the Depression, while a tea made from the root of the plant has long been an effective treatment for constipation. The fluffy seeds of milkweed, on the other hand, came to America's rescue just a half-century ago. In 1942, the Japanese captured a group of East Indian islands containing large groves of silk cotton trees, which at the time was our major source of flotation material for Navy life jackets. In the end, milkweed was found to be the perfect substitute.

We could go on and on about the links that modern life has to plants: quinine from Peruvian cinchona trees to treat malaria, heart medication from foxglove, emetine from the ipecac root to treat amebic dysentery, the secretions of barnacles in the development of super adhesives. If we need a pragmatic argument for slowing down today's high rate of plant extinction, the potential of unexplored species as healing agents, or even food sources, is a pretty convincing one.

At 0.2 mile is a "T" junction, where you'll make a right turn along the edge of a forest of sugar maple, red spruce, and white birch. At 0.4 mile, beside nice clusters of sweet fern, the path enters the hush of a woodland—the domain of wood sorrel and Canada mayflower, along with beautiful gardens of hay-scented, sensitive, and northern beech ferns.

In 0.5 mile the path reaches the rocky shore of Penobscot Bay. (Penobscot, incidentally, is an Indian word meaning "rocky place" or "descending ledge place." The native people originally used the term in reference to a rough, rocky section of the Penobscot River between Treat's Falls and Old Town Great Falls.) This shore is an excellent place to see cormorants, gulls, bay ducks, bald eagles, and ospreys. During low tide look for sand dollars, sea urchins, blue mussels, and horseshoe crabs.

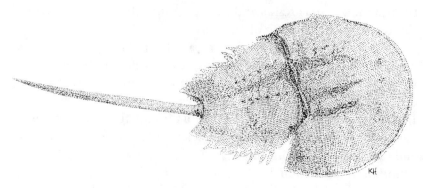

Horseshoe Crab

WALK #66—WATERFALL BRIDGE

DISTANCE: 1.8 miles
ENVIRONMENT: Coast
LOCATION: Acadia National Park. From the Bar Harbor–Hancock County Airport, south of the town of Ellsworth on State Highway 3, head south, following signs for state highways 102 and 198. At a traffic light 6 miles south of the airport these latter two routes will split. Continue to follow Highway 198 for 4 miles from this traffic light, to a parking area located on the east side of the road, just north of Upper Hadlock Pond. A small footpath takes off through the forest from the north edge of the parking area, meeting a carriage road in about 20 yards. Turn right here, and in less than 0.1 mile you'll reach another carriage road, where you'll turn left.

If you doubt the magic that unfurls when land meets sea, then Acadia will surely convince you otherwise. An astonishing 500 species of plants have been identified on this largest of the Atlantic rock islands, as well as 300 species of birds, including nearly 20 species of nesting warblers alone. Geological features abound: enormous boulders carried to the tops of high granite peaks in the icy arms of glaciers; a beach where more than half the sand grains are fragments from broken shells of sea creatures; fanciful sea arches and caves cut into the volcanic tuff by the relentless battering of the waves.

Once you've splashed your face with sea spray, once you've explored the headlands and the clear, rich tidal pools, then step back into the mountainous interior of this island for an entirely different perspective. This walk along one of John D. Rockefeller, Jr.'s famous carriage roads will lead you through fine spruce forests, past sweeping views of Upper Hadlock Pond and the coast beyond, and finally, to a hanging veil of cool, tumbling water—the highest waterfall in the national park.

Turning left onto a carriage road at just under 0.1 mile (see directions above), you'll find yourself in the thick of a beautiful spruce forest. Much of the eastern portion of Mount Desert Island was once covered with dense runs of spruce and fir, but this was consumed in 1947 by a tremendous 17,000-acre fire. Today that area of the park is quilted with a mix of birch and aspen, both of which are quick to reclaim any land suddenly

Bayberry

opened to the sun. Eventually, though, conifers will again reign supreme. As you continue to climb you'll pass rocky areas where only a few plants have managed to take hold on the thick slabs of granite. Some of these rockscapes have the charm of a Japanese garden—a clean, spare patchwork of huckleberry, blueberry, white cedar, and spruce, each clinging tenaciously to the scattered pockets of soil.

Turn right at a "T" junction at about 0.4 mile, beside nice bouquets of sweet fern and bayberry. It's the waxy, aromatic fruits of this latter plant that are used to make bayberry candles. After this last turn is a good view straight ahead of the granite dome of 1,373-foot Sargent Mountain, framed by spruce, maple, and white cedar. Shortly afterward the road turns briefly to the southeast and rounds an open corner, with views of Upper Hadlock Pond and the ocean beyond.

The trail climbs steadily past long mats of sweet fern and sheep laurel, with maples, spruce, and white pines close behind. At 0.8 mile is Hemlock Bridge, which, true to its name, offers glimpses of a rather spry mountain stream dancing through a lacy curtain of hemlock branches. The next bridge, and our turnaround point, is another 0.1 mile up the road. Built in 1925 and appropriately named Waterfall Bridge, this beautiful span of stone lies in front of an airy veil of water, making a dizzy tumble from the flanks of Sargent Mountain.

It's a sobering thought to consider the amount of time needed for these ribbons of water to work their erosional magic, for them to sculpt the land into fissures hundreds of feet deep, as if this were a world made not of granite, but clay. The slow, patient peeling of mighty rocks is an image man has long held as an analogy for forever—a point beyond which it seems the imagination will stretch no further. As Shakespeare wrote in Troilus and Cressida:

When time is old and hath forgot itself,
When waterdrops have worn the stones of Troy ...

WALK #67—AMPHITHEATER LOOP

DISTANCE: 5.5 miles
ENVIRONMENT: Coast
LOCATION: Acadia National Park. From the Bar Harbor–
Hancock County Airport, south of the town
of Ellsworth on State Highway 3, head south,
following signs for state highways 102 and
198. At a traffic light 6 miles south of the
airport these latter two routes will split.
Continue to follow Highway 198 for 5.3
miles from this traffic light, to a parking area
located on the east side of the road, a short
distance south of Upper Hadlock Pond. A
small footpath takes off from the east side
of the parking area. Follow this for just
under 0.1 mile to a carriage road, where
you'll turn left.

Like most ecosystems, the delicate weave of life on Acadia is
easily unraveled in careless hands. And yet there seems to be a
certain strength, a tenacious permanence to this island paradise. It
has already survived the aggressive advance of the land-hungry
Virginia Company which, by the hand of King James I in 1601, was
"given" not only the Maine seaside, but the entire Atlantic coast.
Later, Frenchmen launched many a ship from these protected
coves to attack English shipping vessels, while English soldiers
raided Yankee settlers from the time of the American Revolution
all the way to the War of 1812.

By the 1880s Mount Desert Island was well on its way to
becoming a playground for the rich—a place of spas and orchestras
and full-dress balls; of polo matches, lawn parties, theater, and
croquet. Then in late October 1947, a fire began to rage across the
island, fueled by 85-mile-per-hour winds. Before the flames finally
came to rest on November 14, more than 17,000 acres had burned.
Gone were timber, meadows, and more than 225 residences,
including dozens of stately summer mansions of the rich.

It was an owner of one of these mansions, John D. Rockefeller,
Jr., who was responsible for the system of carriage roads—all of which
remain closed to automobiles—that you'll be walking along during

our two Acadia treks. Although you might wonder about the appropriateness of building any kind of roads on lands set aside for preservation, a good portion of these routes was constructed while the land was still in private hands. (Rockefeller donated nearly one-third of the lands in this national park—more than 10,000 acres in all.)

Follow the small footpath at the rear center of the parking lot to a "T" intersection with a dirt carriage road, and turn left. This route climbs gently through a lovely forest of spruce, striped maple, birch, white pine, bracken, and clubmoss. At an intersection at 0.1 mile, marked by number 18, stay to the right. Notice the long carpets of sweet fern along this section of road, a deciduous shrub that grows on drier sites from Nova Scotia to North Carolina. The leaves of sweet fern make a good tea, and some eastern Indian peoples made a wet compress to relieve the itch of poison ivy and poison oak. Also here are sheep laurel, wintergreen, blueberry, and meadowsweet, as well as thick mats of huckleberry.

Pause at a clearing at 1.1 miles for a magnificent view over your right shoulder of the Atlantic Ocean and the lovely Cranberry Isles. The assorted tales of intrigue and misadventures along these waters would fill a bookcase. Few, however, have the sting of the ill-fated voyage of the *Grand Design*. The *Grand*

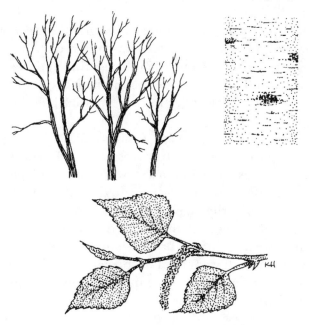

Gray Birch

Design was a large sailing ship that set sail in 1739 with more than 200 wealthy Irish men, women, and a host of bonded servants bound for Pennsylvania. Raging autumn storms pushed the ship far off course, and then dashed it to splinters against a peninsula of granite framing the entrance to Ship Harbor, at the southwestern corner of Mount Desert Island.

It would be hard to imagine a more remote, difficult location to be stranded. (The first settlers on Mount Desert would not arrive for 23 years.) With winter on their heels and no hope of rescue, the captain of the *Grand Design* and 100 single men made the decision in early December to cross the island and look for help. Not a single one was ever heard from again. By the time rescuers finally did arrive, brought in by a note the castaways had persuaded an Indian to deliver for them, only a handful of survivors were left—all starving, wrapped against winter in the fine Irish linen they had carried across the Atlantic.

Two-tenths mile from this overview a road enters from the right. Keep to the left here, and in 0.5 mile you'll reach Amphitheater Bridge, the longest of Rockefeller's 16 magnificent stone bridges. Beneath the bridge runs lovely Little Harbor Brook, gingerly dancing down a rock staircase framed by spruce, hemlock, maple, and birch.

From this point the road heads south, offering wonderful views into and across the forested canyon carved by the patient fingers of Little Harbor Brook. You'll pass fine huddles of white pine here, as well as gray birch, mountain ash, bigtooth aspen, and maple. Along the fringes look for hardhack and mountain holly.

At the forks in the road at 2.5 miles and 2.9 miles (posts 21 and 22), keep to the right. After crossing Little Harbor Brook Bridge at 3.3 miles you'll begin a slow, steady climb back out of the valley through thick spruce groves, laced with striped maple. In autumn the leaves of these striped maples lend mellow splashes of gold to the dark green of the conifers. Join the entrance road again in 4.1 miles, at marker post 20, and turn left. Tree lovers will want to take special note of this junction, as it contains several fine specimens of sugar maple, birch, white pine, spruce, and hemlock.

WALK #68—BIRCH POINT

DISTANCE: 4 miles
ENVIRONMENT: Coast
LOCATION: Petit Manan National Wildlife Refuge. From the intersection of U.S. highways 1 and 1A in Millbridge, head south on Highway 1 for 2.7 miles to Pigeon Hill Road, and turn left. Follow this road south for 6 miles to the trailhead parking area, located on the right side of the road. Our path heads west from the parking area through a large cleared field. *Note:* The road past the parking area is private. Please do not drive vehicles beyond the designated trailhead parking site.

Your first steps along this pathway will be through a large open field, kept clear by regular burning to produce "edge habitat" for a variety of birds and mammals. In most summers this means something wonderful for humans, as well—blueberries! "As big as the end of your thumb, real sky blue and heavy," as Robert Frost would say. Although Maine's inland blueberry barons, who produce nearly half the total North American crop of these juicy fruits, wouldn't consider this a particularly productive field, for about six weeks during most summers it seems a blueberry lover's dream.

On the far side of this clearing, just before entering a young woodland guarded by a feathery clump of tamaracks, there are also cranberries growing on the left side of the trail. Once inside this woodland look for clusters of wild raisin backed by speckled alder, gray birch, and the slow-growing northern white cedar. Since the middle of the 16th century this latter tree has also been known as arborvitae—"tree of life." And so it was for explorer Jacques Cartier and his crew, who in 1535 were saved from scurvy by drinking vitamin C–charged tea made from white cedar bark and foliage.

Since we seem to be on a roll with food, take note of the bracken fern at just over 0.1 mile. For centuries people from around the world have relished the young, curled spring shoots, known as *fiddleheads*. (While young curled shoots of bracken are edible, as they age the plants become poisonous.) There is evidence to suggest

Bracken Fern

that certain native hunters feasted on fiddleheads during their spring deer hunt, believing that the plants helped mask their scent.

The path winds past additional clearings (with yet more blueberries!), as well as past fine stands of balsam fir, white and black spruce, and aspen. By the 1-mile mark, however, young white birch have stolen the show. They form a shimmering, delicate arch, their milky white trunks leaning over the roadway for better access to the sky. Woven in between these light-skinned youngsters are the beautiful dark green branches of balsam fir; together they form the loveliest of contrasts, the kind of patterns that make the forests of the northeast among the most beautiful on earth.

At 1.5 miles is a side trail to Lobster Point; stay left. Just 0.1 mile later the trail splits into a loop that circles Birch Point. On my visit the left branch was impossible to follow. If this is still the case, work your way around the head of the peninsula counterclockwise, and then retrace your steps back the way you came. When you reach the west side of the head you'll find fine views of Dyer Harbor, with Sheep and Sally islands clearly visible offshore. The high tide mark is defined by a crooked, matted line of bladder rockweed; above this the land is covered with blankets of grasses and wildflowers, including the beautiful lavender blooms of the beach pea. Visitors from the west coast will recognize this lovely trailing vine, as it's quite common on the Pacific coast from California all the way to Alaska.

WALK #69—SHORE TRAIL

DISTANCE: 2.2 miles
ENVIRONMENT: Coast
LOCATION: Petit Manan National Wildlife Refuge. From the intersection of U.S. highways 1 and 1A in Millbridge, head south on Highway 1 for 2.7 miles to Pigeon Hill Road, and turn left. Follow this road south for 6 miles to the trailhead parking area, located on the right side of the road. *Note:* The road past the parking area is private. Please do not drive vehicles beyond the designated trailhead parking site.

Make no mistake about it: there is magic on this granite isle. Its interior is a toss of spruce, alder, birch, and pine, woven around fields flushed with bushels and bushels of blueberries. Deer, bear, porcupine, raccoon, and even fisher steal through the forests. Dozens of bird species, from woodcocks to warblers, crisscross the spring and summer skies, while in autumn, the rocky shores erupt in flurries of migration—eiders, laughing gulls, black ducks, cormorants, scoters, scaups, and Arctic terns. It would be difficult indeed to find a richer, more enticing place to walk.

From the trailhead parking area, follow the roadway southward for about 0.6 mile, where you'll see Shore Trail taking off to the east through a field of blueberries. What stage of succession this field will be in when you visit depends on when it was last burned. Refuge managers fire these clearings every three years in order to provide edge habitat for a wider variety of birds and mammals; you can tell roughly how long it's been since the last fire by noting the size and number of speckled alder growing here. Given the right conditions, alder wastes no time in making a serious bid for control of any available clearing. In return, root nodules of the alder offer homes for organisms that take nitrogen from the air and change it into a form plants can use, thereby enriching the soil. The leaves of speckled alder also provide good browse for both moose and deer.

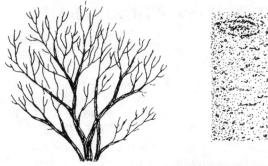

Speckled Alder

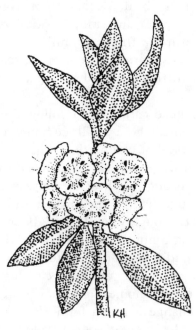

Sheep Laurel

The next 0.5 mile of walking is through a patchwork of forest and clearing. Graceful spruce, birch, and red maple dominate the woods, with bunchberry and wintergreen building bright red berries at their feet. In open areas look for the lovely pink blossoms of sheep laurel, a plant once used by native peoples for treating headaches and back aches. You'll also see Jack pine here, a fire-dependent tree that quickly colonizes burned or logged areas. Jack pine does especially well in poor, sandy soils; large groves are often referred to as "pine barrens."

An idyllic seashore cove is 1.1 miles from the parking lot, a gentle nook lined with cinnamon fern, cranberry, wintergreen, and baked-apple berry, the shoreline itself paved with a carpet of granite pebbles. From here you can make a fairly arduous hike south along the coast for another 2.5 miles, past a tangle of coves and bluffs, and, depending on the time of year, enough birds to satisfy the most feather-happy. The waters off Petit Manan offer a unique mix of bird life, primarily because of an overlapping of what for many species is their most northern breeding range, while for others it is their most southern.

Of all the winged visitors here, sea ducks are especially numerous. This is an excellent place, for example, to watch common eiders, which at Petit Manan are along the southernmost fringe of a breeding range that extends all the way to Greenland. If you've ever come across the phrase "soft as a bed of eider down," this is the eider they're talking about. The breast feathers of the female common eider are remarkably full and soft, and have been used in Europe for centuries to stuff blankets and pillows.

Arctic Tern

The female common eider lays her eggs in nests constructed on offshore islands, then faithfully sits with them almost without rest for nearly a month, during which time she will take no food. Soon after hatching the chicks are ready for travel, and loose groups of mothers and young head across the waters toward shallow, sheltered waters along the mainland. It's along such shorelines where they find the shellfish—mussels, clams, crabs, etc.—that make up the majority of their diet. Not ones for fancy dinner rituals, eiders simply gobble up mussels and clams whole, eventually crushing the shells with a powerful set of stomach muscles. If you're here in the fall after the young are reared you'll see males and females back together in great floating masses called *rafts*, the numbers sometimes reaching the hundreds or even thousands.

Also here are laughing gulls, which are at this point near the northernmost point of their breeding range, as well as beautiful wood and goldeneye ducks, scaups, sleek-looking black guillemots, surf scoters, black scoters, and Arctic terns, to name but a very few. It's the feisty Arctic tern, incidentally, that holds the record among all birds for the most distance covered during migration. When an Arctic tern leaves here in the fall it will fly east along the Maine coast, cross the Atlantic, continue down the coast of Europe and Africa, finally—perhaps 10,000 miles later—arriving at its wintering grounds along the coast of Antarctica.

The full exploration of the east side of the peninsula deserves an entire day. On the other hand, don't feel bad if you set off for the

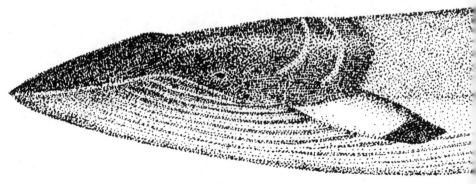

Minke Whale

point and never reach it. Along the way are an almost endless number of wonderful distractions, each quite capable of undermining the need to end up anywhere else at all.

WALK #70—WEST QUODDY HEAD

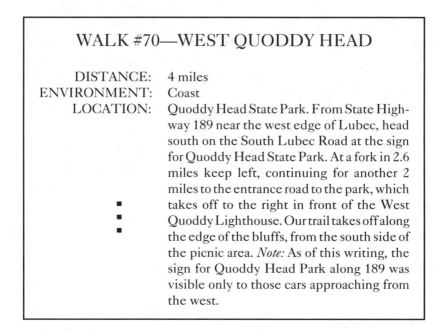

DISTANCE: 4 miles

ENVIRONMENT: Coast

LOCATION: Quoddy Head State Park. From State Highway 189 near the west edge of Lubec, head south on the South Lubec Road at the sign for Quoddy Head State Park. At a fork in 2.6 miles keep left, continuing for another 2 miles to the entrance road to the park, which takes off to the right in front of the West Quoddy Lighthouse. Our trail takes off along the edge of the bluffs, from the south side of the picnic area. *Note:* As of this writing, the sign for Quoddy Head Park along 189 was visible only to those cars approaching from the west.

By the time you reach West Quoddy Head, the easternmost point in the United States, you will have left the hustle and bustle of the southern Maine coast far behind. There are no miniature golf

KH

courses here, no go-carts or petting zoos or T-shirt shops, no stores laden with "Maine" pen and pencil sets and piggy banks and lobster pot lamps. This is a place where, for the most part, the wild sea is still the only attraction. Waves batter against mammoth volcanic and gabbro cliffs, and southern breezes pull thick coverlets of fog across the bays. A bald eagle soars overhead. Rafts of eiders and surf scoters bob on the ocean swells, each making dive after dive to hunt for shellfish. In the distance, a lone minke whale rises to blow, and is gone.

Our walk begins on a trail that takes off along the shore from the far side of the picnic area. If you're a fan of tidal pools you may be interested to know that those below the picnic area contain rich populations of green and Jonah crabs, periwinkles, dog whelks, blue mussels, and nudibranches. As you may have noticed on the interpretive sign located at the picnic area, this region has very high tides—nearly 16 vertical feet. A reason for this is that ocean waters flow from the south into inlets that become narrower and narrower;

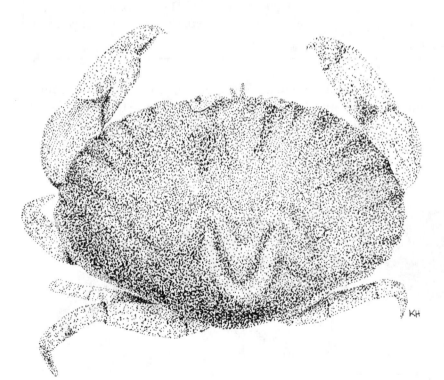

Jonah Crab

as the water is compressed into a smaller and smaller space, it causes a greater rise and fall than what which occurs at the mouth. At the head of nearby Bay of Fundy, located between Nova Scotia and New Brunswick, spring and neap tides may rise and fall as much as 50 feet!

Although most of us tend to take tides for granted, the phenomenon is really quite remarkable, a visible connection between our planet and that silent, glowing moon riding with us through space. The gravity of the earth holds things in place on our planet, not the least of which are the oceans. Yet the moon (and to a lesser extent the sun), effects its own gravitational draw, actually pulling the waters up and then releasing them again each time it circles the earth. We can predict the timing of this pulling (high tide) and releasing (low tide) based on the length of time it takes for the moon to make its journey. Generally speaking, there will be two low tides and two high tides every 24 hours, each advancing at a rate of approximately 50 minutes a day. If on the afternoon of your visit to Quoddy Head the low tide occurs at 2:00, for example, tomorrow that same tide will occur at 2:50, the following day at 3:40, etc.

But if the moon orbits the earth only once in a 24-hour period, you may ask, why are there two high and low tides each day? When the moon is tugging at the earth, the ocean waters lying on the side farthest away from the moon are not pulled as much as the land in between. These waters actually bulge away from the earth, causing a high tide to occur. Low tides simply mark the halfway point between the two simultaneously occurring high tides. (The sun is not without its own effects. Extreme high tides, known as spring tides, occur twice each month as the sun, moon, and earth line up with each other. Extreme low tides, on the other hand, known as neap tides, also occur twice a month, when the sun and moon are at right angles to each other. It's the moon's changing orientation to the sun, then, that causes the heights of tides to fluctuate.) If all this seems much too colorless an explanation, you may prefer to stick with a more ancient notion, which said that tides were caused by the breath of a giant monster that lived at the bottom of the sea.

This is truly a spectacular coast. Tattered blankets of spruce and fir top volcanic cliffs rising 150 feet above the rush and roil of the surf. Clusters of bluebead lilies, bunchberries, raspberries, and meadowsweet add splashes of color to the trail, while mats of cinnamon fern lend feathery relief to the bristle of the conifers. At about 0.5 mile is a trail on the right; follow this for about 600 feet to a wonderful peat bog, nicely interpreted by a set of descriptive panels. Back on the main trail again, in 200 to 300 feet is another path, this one on the left, leading to High Ledge. From this perch, sprinkled with patches of blue flag iris, you'll have a commanding view of the ocean to the east. It's an excellent place to watch for some of the more intriguing mammals that spend time along this coast, including harbor seals and minke and finback whales.

The shy but curious harbor seal can often be seen leaping, rolling, and swimming in circles. These remarkable mammals are able to dive to depths of 300 feet, can stay under water for almost 30 minutes, and can swim for short distances at speeds of over 12 knots. You may have difficulty seeing them if you're here during low tide, especially in warm weather, since that's when they haul out for a bit of shut-eye. The staff at West Quoddy Biological Research Station, which you'll pass if you elect to return to the parking area by way of the road, has nursed many an injured harbor seal back to health so that they could be returned to their ocean homes. Unfortunately, the most common ailment plaguing seals that end up here is gunshot wounds. Some fishermen consider the harbor seal to be a major nuisance, and at least in nearby Canada, it's still legal to handle the problem with bullets.

Harbor Seal

At just under 2 miles you'll reach Carrying Place Cove, an inlet fringed with meadowsweet, clover, bluets, asters, and alders. In the fall this cove is a particularly good place to watch migrating seabirds. At 2.2 miles is a neck of land crossed by South Lubec Road; the trailhead parking area is approximately 1.8 miles down this road to the right. A portion of this neck is part of a 43-acre peat bog, the north side of which has been exposed to a height of 10 to 15 feet by both rain and the cutting action of waves. This kind of cross-sectional view of a bog is extremely uncommon, so much so that the site has been declared a National Natural Landmark. It's a beautiful place to explore, offering fine opportunities to see spatulate-leafed sundew, cranberries, Labrador tea, cotton grass, baked-apple berry, and pitcher plants. Those with an eye for birds should watch for both Lincoln sparrows and palm warblers in the brushy thickets; in most years the light, trilly song of this latter bird is the first warbler music of spring.

WALK #71—TROUT BROOK FLOWAGE

DISTANCE: 1.6 miles
ENVIRONMENT: Forest
LOCATION: South unit of Moosehorn National Wildlife Refuge, near Cobscook Bay State Park. From the intersection of State Highway 86 and U.S. Highway 1, head south on Highway 1 for 3 miles, to Weir Road, a small, gated dirt road on the west side of the highway. Park here and begin walking southwest on Weir Road. *Note:* Refuge managers use this road on a regular basis. Do not block the gate.

Moosehorn is notable for its gentle roadway walks through coniferous and mixed deciduous forests, many of them flushed with deer, black bear, raccoon, coyote, fisher, and moose; furthermore, there's no shortage of ponds peppered with ducks, geese, osprey, and beaver. The 0.8-mile walk along Weir Road to Trout Brook Flowage provides a quick, easy breath of fresh air for pavement-weary travelers on Highway 1. Those wanting more of Moosehorn can continue walking another 0.5 mile to Maple

Black Bear

Flowage, then another 0.25 mile to Alder flowage, then another 0.4 mile to Middle Brook Flowage, then … well, you get the idea.

Surrounding the gate next to the highway are a few clumps of bigtooth aspen and alder, but these give way quickly to blankets of white and black spruce, and balsam fir. Bunchberry makes a good showing along the early stretches of the walk, as does sweet fern, wintergreen, sheep laurel, and that common, unfairly maligned summer weed—goldenrod. It was long assumed that goldenrod released clouds of pollen into the air which then found their way into people's sinus tracts, where they caused some rather amazing sneezing fits. In fact, goldenrod pollen isn't released into the air, but is instead carried by insects. It's actually ragweed, a plant that blooms at the same time as goldenrod, that deserves the blame for harassing hay fever sufferers.

Goldenrod flowers produce a beautiful yellow dye, and tea made from the plant's leaves not only tastes good, but is a proven remedy for gas. It's been suggested that when colonists rebelled against unfair taxes by dumping a shipload of British tea into Boston Harbor, it was goldenrod that came to the rescue, offering a substitute beverage dubbed "Liberty Tea."

As you proceed southward along this road, watch for black spruce draped with spindly tufts of "old man's beard," a grizzled green lichen that, given sufficient sunlight, often hangs in profusion in old stands of spruce and fir. Contrary to appearances, lichens such as old man's beard aren't parasites simply sponging off their hosts for food. (The branches of these trees do, however, allow the lichen to gain access to far more sunlight than they would be able to garner were they to remain on the forest floor.) Lichens are actually two organisms—a fungus and an algae—that have gone into business together. Basically, the algae provides manufactured sugars while the fungus offers physical protection to the algae and, to a limited extent, nutrients from rootlike structures known as *hyphae*. Lichen is one of the most successful partnerships in all of nature. Together these two organisms withstand not only grueling cold and drought, but sometimes manage to eke out a living from the slimmest fare imaginable, including the bare face of solid rock.

Beneath the chatter of red squirrels—who, when not scolding intruders are busy consuming everything from conifer seeds and sap, to insects, flowers, and fruits—the road winds through lovely stands of white pine and white birch. Near the forest edge are pockets of bracken fern, blueberries, raspberries, wintergreen, and St. Johnswort. Because it tends to bloom near the time of the summer solstice, St. Johnswort was once a major part of pagan sun-worship rituals. Though the Christians that followed would have nothing to do with such rites, they did pay attention to this plant. It was promptly renamed after Saint John the Baptist, whose birthday occurred shortly after the summer solstice; later it became a favorite holy herb of priests in the Middle Ages, who used it to assist in exorcisms. In a more pragmatic vein, Native Americans long used a tea made of St. Johnswort to treat tuberculosis.

Trout Brook Flowage is reached in 0.8 mile, the water fringed by sedge and cattail, with nice mats of hop clover, orange hawkweed, and birdsfoot trefoil growing nearby. This pond has a rather lonely look to it, clusters of dead trees making frantic, frozen gestures against the evening sky. If you happen to be here as the last light of the day is fading, it's easy to imagine that a hale gang of old gray ghosts has risen from the puddles, back for a final fling among the living timber.

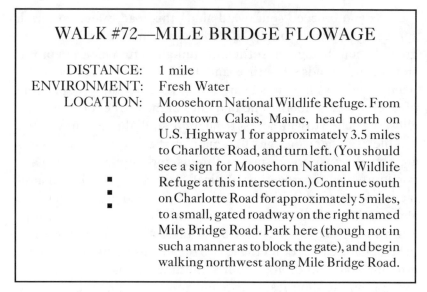

WALK #72—MILE BRIDGE FLOWAGE

DISTANCE: 1 mile
ENVIRONMENT: Fresh Water
LOCATION: Moosehorn National Wildlife Refuge. From downtown Calais, Maine, head north on U.S. Highway 1 for approximately 3.5 miles to Charlotte Road, and turn left. (You should see a sign for Moosehorn National Wildlife Refuge at this intersection.) Continue south on Charlotte Road for approximately 5 miles, to a small, gated roadway on the right named Mile Bridge Road. Park here (though not in such a manner as to block the gate), and begin walking northwest along Mile Bridge Road.

This short trek takes walkers to a fine wetland set in a woody lowland just east of the Moosehorn Wilderness. This is a land rich with waterfowl and raptors, from black ducks and Canada geese to bald eagles and osprey. Mile Bridge Flowage, located just 0.5 mile from the parking area, should be approached as quietly as possible so you have the best chance of sighting one of these feathered beauties.

Our walk begins in a forest of black and white spruce, white pine, birch, and balsam fir, with an occasional tamarack lending a light, feathery touch to the scene. The airy structure of tamarack branches allows modest amounts of sunlight to drip through to the forest floor below. This is why, if soil conditions are right, you'll often find more ground covers and wildflowers doing business at the feet of tamaracks than would otherwise be found in, say, a forest of spruce or balsam fir.

But what makes the tamarack (also known as American larch) truly different is the fact that it's deciduous. Late each autumn needles turn yellow and fall to the ground, to be replaced the following spring by an entirely new crop. Tamaracks do not do well in shade, however, and hence they are eventually replaced by conifers whose young can better survive having grown-ups continually blocking the sun. The tamaracks' trump card, if you will, is that they have a very high tolerance for acidic soils, making them—along with black spruce—almost the sole heirs to bogs and peatlands.

A short distance past a clearing on the right filled with raspberries, purple vetch, flat-topped white aster, and orange hawkweed is a sizeable stand of dead spruce. These unfortunate fellows are victims of spruce budworm, which is the larva of a small moth that feeds on the buds of both spruce and fir. Spruce budworm infestations can be devastating, and tend to run in cycles of about 60 to 80 years. The last major outbreak in the state of Maine occurred in the late 1970s and early 1980s.

At 0.5 mile is the eastern edge of Mile Bridge Flowage, a long, sinewy pocket of water fringed with cattails, sedges, and alder. Along the road here are evening primrose, orange hawkweed, goldenrod, and, that most famous of all the natural remedies for the itch of poison ivy or stinging nettle, jewelweed. Jewelweed is also known as spotted touch-me-not, and during late summer and early fall it produces fruits that explode at the slightest touch, sending off a battery of tiny seeds in every direction. On sweltering summer days you may see the leaves of the jewelweed drooped and wilted; this is a temporary condition, thought to be a means of conserving water.

Approximately 40 yards to the west of where our walking road first joins Mile Bridge Flowage is an osprey nest atop an artificial platform. One of the greatest thrills in all of nature is to watch one of these magnificent "fish hawks" hovering above a lake or pond, finally

Osprey

making a fast, silent plunge to grab a fish and carry it back to its nest or treetop feeding roost. Such hunting requires that the osprey be able to see its prey clearly; this is why so often you'll find these birds along quiet waters, where the surface remains unbroken by waves. When young osprey are in the nest during early summer, only the male will be out hunting, making dive after dive in order to supply his mate and her hungry brood with food. (Osprey eat only fish.) By mid-August the youngsters will be hanging from the skies as well, each trying to master the delicate art of aerial spearfishing.

The high ridge visible ahead in the distance and slightly to the left is the eastern boundary of the Moosehorn Wilderness. If you have binoculars, scan the skies along this high line for a glimpse of a bald eagle, which have been nesting in the area on a fairly regular basis. These great birds of prey often make use of their imposing strength and size—6-foot wingspans aren't uncommon—by stealing fish from neighboring osprey.

As you walk along Mile Bridge Flowage, you may wonder why there's a thick blanket of coniferous trees on the right, while the pond side of the road is covered predominately with aspen and a few red maple. Wildlife managers have burned the left side of the road in order to encourage the growth of hardwoods, which provide better forage for wildlife. If left alone, the more shade-tolerant members of the coniferous forest would soon begin reclaiming their lost territory.

WALK #73—VOSE POND

DISTANCE: 3 miles
ENVIRONMENT: Fresh Water
LOCATION: Moosehorn National Wildlife Refuge. From U.S. Highway 1 west of Calais, turn south at the sign for Moosehorn National Wildlife Refuge. Follow this road south for several miles. Our walk is reached by turning left (east) on a small dirt road directly opposite the road which leads to the refuge head-quarters. You'll reach a fork in the road 0.1 mile after turning off the pavement; both branches have been gated off. Park here, and begin your walk along the left fork.

Although Moosehorn isn't necessarily a dramatic place, it clearly has its own unique beauties. Contained in this north unit of the refuge is a fine collection of quiet, lush nooks filled with a myriad of waterfowl, as well as a list of wildlife ranging from bear to beaver, moose to muskrat. Most of the treks here are along gentle roadways closed to motor vehicles—perfect routes for easy ambling.

Sometimes the images Moosehorn brings to mind are gentle ones—the wake line of a muskrat swimming across a glassy pond, the waddle of a porcupine disappearing into the cover of a spruce grove. But the sights here can also be startling. If you visit in spring you may be treated to the striking aerial spirals and high-speed plummets that mark the courtship ritual of the male woodcock. On the other hand, in the fall you'll have a good chance of coming upon the rather surprising spectacle of a fat black bear dining in the high reaches of an apple tree.

Up the road on the right 0.1 mile is Tyler Flowage. This is one of more than 50 water control areas in the refuge that were built beginning in the 1950s, in order to increase habitat for waterfowl. Look for mergansers, and ring-necked and black ducks, as well as an occasional loon. Beside the culvert running beneath the road at Tyler Flowage are the remains of a beaver dam. "No matter what level we keep the water," muses refuge manger Doug Mullen, "the beaver feel obligated to alter it." Aspen and birch, both of which are in good supply around the perimeter of the pond, serve as both food and building materials for the beaver.

Continue up the road past a fairly young forest of black and white spruce, white and gray birch, red maple, and white pine. Along the fringes of the road are nice clusters of wild sarsaparilla, bunch-berry, whorled wood aster, Canada mayflower, purple vetch, and orange hawkweed. Hawkweed, by the way, takes its name from an old belief that hawks ripped apart these plants and bathed their eyes in the juices to sharpen their vision. It has long been given by herbalists for the relief of diarrhea and respiratory disorders.

In 0.4 mile the road will split; stay right. Just past this intersection, in the forest on the right, are several narrow cleared areas. These are strip cuts, harvested on a 50-year cycle in order to create the type of early successional vegetation preferred by many forms of wildlife, including the American woodcock. One mile from the trailhead, after passing collections of wintergreen, bracken, meadowsweet, and sheep laurel, you'll come to Upper and Lower

Orange Hawkweed

Raccoon

Goodall Heath Flowages—large, wild-looking waters cradling both sides of the road. This is not only a good place to see beaver, but also osprey and marsh hawks. At the next road split continue bearing to the right, and at 1.5 miles you'll reach Vose Pond.

Vose Pond is an especially lovely place in the fall, when the surrounding canopies of birch, aspen, and maple catch fire with reds, oranges, and yellows. Very soon the woodcocks will be leaving for some faraway river or stream in the forests of the Carolinas. Black bear continue to fatten themselves on apples, berries, mice, and maybe even an occasional porcupine, one day to drag their bloated bellies into some hollow log or rocky den just one step ahead of the cold slap of winter. The geese are restless now, rising and falling from the open water in a clatter of honks and a rush of wings. "Days decrease," wrote Robert Browning. "And autumn grows, autumn in everything."

WALK #74—LITTLE ABOL FALLS

DISTANCE: 2 miles
ENVIRONMENT: Forest
LOCATION: Baxter State Park. Enter Baxter through Togue Pond Gate, located at the southeast corner of the park. Once through the gate, bear to the left, following signs for Abol Campground. Park across from the campground on the south side of the road and walk in. At the first branch road in the campground, turn right. Our trail takes off between camping shelters 8 and 10.

In a region that can only be defined by superlatives, humble little Abol Falls Trail, climbing gently through a regenerating forest, doesn't exactly stand out. It has none of the glassy pockets of blue water that frame nearby Daicey and Grassy ponds, or the dizzying, breathtaking plunges that hang off the steep, rugged sides of Abol Trail. What this walk does have, though, is a long draw of forest wrapped in peace and quiet, a few teasing glimpses of Mount Katahdin's mighty south face, and in the end, one of the loveliest white-water dances you could hope to set eyes on. If you're in the mood for an easily accessible daydream spot, Little Abol Falls is hard to beat.

Barely out of Abol Campground you'll cross clear, crisp Abol Stream, making a quick dash to the southeast. Immediately afterward our path makes a sharp left turn into a young forest of white birch, balsam fir, red maple, white pine, and spruce. This is also a good place to find whorled wood and large leaf asters, bunchberry, and pearly everlasting. Farther still, at approximately 0.7 mile, are some nice examples of striped maple, which in some parts of the country is known as moosewood.

Keep your eyes peeled for occasional glimpses of Katahdin, its staggering flanks looming across the northern horizon like a fortress for some mythical kingdom. (The name Katahdin, incidentally, is derived from an Abnaki Indian phrase meaning principal or great mountain.) Any view of this magnificent peak tends to make one bless the day that Governor Percival Baxter took up the banner to protect this "grandest and most beautiful of all the natural attractions of our State" for the people of Maine. Baxter engineered the creation of the park by donating more than 200,000 acres of land; further, in his estate he provided a land acquisition

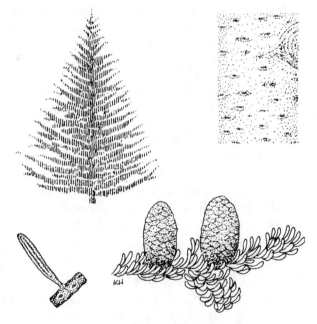

Balsam Fir

account of some $8 million, some of which was used recently to add another 1,000 acres to the preserve.

At 0.9 mile the path descends into a cool, moist hollow, and then rises again to meet the watercourse just a few yards upstream of Little Abol Falls. Notice on the far side of the cascade how clumps of white birch hang from the high, rocky ledges by their toenails—a heroic effort to grab some of the sunshine that pours into the twists and turns of this open gorge.

Two miles north of where you now stand the Appalachian Trail makes its final ascent up a steep southwest ridge of Mount Katahdin, ending a magnificent 2,000-mile run from Springer Mountain, Georgia. By the time *end-to-enders* (people walking the entire length of the trail) make it to Katahdin, they have experienced something that will remain forever chiseled into their hearts. In 1964, Chuck Ebersole and his son John became the first father and son team to traverse the entire Appalachian Trail in a single season. Chuck's recollection of a night spent at Lake-of-the-Clouds Hut in New Hampshire's White Mountains offers a look into the deep camaraderie that exists between people daring enough to live as if personal adventure really mattered:

> When suppertime came the guests sat on long benches while the hut boys served steaming dishes family style on the varnished surfaces of the wooden tables. Grace was said, and then amid laughter and chatter, everyone enjoyed the tasty meal. While the hut boys cleared things away, hiking groups recited poems or sang songs. Darkness settled in, and then the real fun began. Hiking musicians arrived with an accordion, two guitars, a banjo, and an enormous bull fiddle. When the kitchen chores were finished those instruments were tuned up and put to work. All kinds of songs were played, with everyone singing. The hut boys made another huge pot of hot chocolate and served it with cookies. The singing lasted for several hours. One song which tugged at my heart was "This Land is Your Land." A song like that always brings tears to my eyes. I love the green hills, the blue sky, the clean streams, and the good soil of Mother Earth, and that song exemplified what I was trying to find and enjoy by hiking the Appalachian Trail.

(*Author's Note:* This is taken from *Hiking the Appalachian Trail*, Volume 1, edited by James R. Hare, 2 volumes, Emmaus, PA: Rodale Press, 1975, pp. 426–427.)

WALK #75—SANDY STREAM POND

DISTANCE: 3 miles
ENVIRONMENT: Mountain
LOCATION: Baxter State Park. Enter Baxter through Togue Pond Gate, located at the park's southeast corner, and follow Roaring Brook Road for 8 miles to its end at Roaring Brook Campground. The trail leaves from the north side of a large parking area.

This loop trail requires virtually no climbing, and yet offers a generous helping of the pleasures of the high country. Plan to walk it early on a still summer morning, when Katahdin's headwalls are catching the first sunlight of the day, and moose are out in force just

Moose

ahead of you, stamping king-sized footprints in the patches of cool forest mud.

Though several trails take off near Roaring Brook Camp-ground, the Sandy Stream Pond route is well marked. After crossing Roaring Brook the path settles into a classic Maine forest of spruce, balsam fir, white and yellow birch, and striped and red maples. Watch the ground for mats of bunchberry, hobblebush, snowberry, sarsaparilla, and whorled wood aster, as well as occasional starflowers, trilliums, and bluebead lilies. As you pass through wetter, more open areas along the loop, notice how the plants change. Suddenly there are colorful threads of meadow rue, meadowsweet, rhodora, blueberry, and cotton grass.

At 0.4 mile is an open area offering beautiful views of 3,122-foot South Turner Mountain—a striking reminder that Katahdin is hardly Baxter's only resident peak. In fact, from South Turner Mountain northward is a dramatic jumble of high mountains stretching for 15 miles, broken only once by the beautiful Wassataquoik Stream valley. All in all there are 46 mountain peaks in Baxter State Park, 18 of which are more than 3,000 feet high.

The more open areas along our walk are wonderful places to spot moose. Anyone hoping to see one of these splendid creatures, however, should walk the trail as quietly as possible. While moose may not be endowed with great eyesight, they can hear voices and footsteps very well indeed. A mere half-century ago, poaching, disease, and loss of habitat through forest fire suppression reduced the Maine population of moose to perhaps no more than 2,000; today, much to the delight of Maine residents and visitors alike, there are more than 20,000 of them. As is true with most wildlife, never approach a moose too closely, especially females with calves.

These giants, by the way, provide striking testimony that your mother wasn't lying about the value of eating vegetables. A moose will eat 40 to 50 pounds of greens every day—birch, aspen, willow, pond lilies, etc. And look what it's done for them! Large bulls tower more than 6 feet tall at the shoulder, and weigh in at nearly 1,500 pounds.

At 0.4 mile make a detour onto a view trail taking off to the left; this route follows the edge of Sandy Stream Pond for a short distance, and then returns you to the main trail not far from where you left it. The views of Katahdin from this side spur are truly magnificent. The two large cirques visible high on the mountain are North and Great basins, which were carved out by huge sheets of ice that covered this land roughly 10,000 to 18,000 years ago. To the left of these cuts is 4,902-foot Pamola Peak, named for the fierce mountain god who is said to reside still in this craggy palace. There is a rich weave of folklore about the Katahdin god Pamola—more, in fact, than exists about virtually any other mountain spirit in America. One tale says that Mount Katahdin was created by a council of the highest gods for use as their sacred meeting place. When Pamola, who was somewhat lower on the supreme-being social register, was refused a seat at the council, he retreated to the peak you now see, where he has lived ever since.

A surveyor who visited this area in 1804 relayed that the Indians around Katahdin believed Pamola lives on the peak during the winter, and then "flies off in the spring with tremendous rumbling noises." Later information revealed that Pamola stole a beautiful Indian maiden whom he protects from pursuers by hurtling thunderbolts at them; in fact, anyone who climbs Katahdin runs the risk of incurring the savage wrath of this big sourpuss. Pamola is often portrayed as a blend of half-man and half-eagle. Roy Dudley, who for years lived at Chimney Pond near the foot of Great Basin, added further valuable information about what Pamola is really like by informing us that he smokes forest fires in his pipe, and is occasionally bothered by porcupines nesting in his ears.

Continue to work your way around the north side of Sandy Stream Pond. At 0.7 mile you'll reach the junction with South Turner Mountain Trail, surrounded by mats of interrupted and hay-scented ferns, Canada mayflower, cut-leaf sedge, bunchberry, sarsaparilla, and blueberry. Stay left here, working southward past occasional dead snags of spruce and fir, the victims of spruce budworm.

At the junction with Russel Pond Trail, take a left. In another 0.5 mile you'll reach a fine bog, peppered with pitcher plants, Labrador tea, elderberry, blueberry, and cotton grass. From here the trail continues through nice blankets of birch, balsam, and spruce, arriving back at the intersection with the Sandy Stream Pond Trail at 2.4 miles, 0.1 mile from the parking area.

WALK #76—SOUTH BRANCH FALLS

DISTANCE:	1.2 miles
ENVIRONMENT:	Mountain
LOCATION:	Baxter State Park. From Interstate 95 north of Bangor, take the Sherman Exit, and then follow Maine routes 11 and 159 north for 8 miles to the town of Patten. From Patten continue west on Route 159 for 27 miles to the north entrance of Baxter State Park, at Matagamon Gate. Continue west along the northern edge of the park on Perimeter Road for 9 miles, and turn left (south) on South Branch Road, toward South Branch Pond Campground. In 1.3 miles you'll come to a small parking area on the right (west) side of the road. Our walk begins here.

Standing in the quiet forest that warms the feet of Mount Katahdin, it's difficult to believe that this landscape could be the child of violent, wrenching geologic changes. Yet millions of years ago, vast inland seas covering the region shuddered and sizzled in the face of thunderous earthquakes and massive volcanic explosions. Countless millennia later, thick sheets of ice ground over the land with terrific force, gouging out and polishing cirques and valleys like a hot metal scoop in a carton of ice cream. The easy walk to South Branch Falls will present a chapter of this history through a beautiful cascading stream, sliding northward across polished gray volcanic bedrock.

Our path begins in a rather young forest containing white birch, beech, yellow birch, and red and striped maple; at 0.25 mile you'll also find a nice cluster of beaked hazelnut—a relative of the European hazel that produces the tasty filbert nut. The flowers of this small tree appear early in the spring, well before the leaves, when shafts of sunlight pour like honey over clumps of bracken and interrupted ferns, bunchberry, Canada mayflower, ground cedar, and clubmoss.

At 0.5 mile is South Branch Ponds Brook. Head downstream along slabs of tilted gray rock that frame a series of sluice channels and cool, quiet plunge pools (pools much too inviting to pass up on a hot summer day). This lovely sculpture, crafted over eons by the patient fingers of South Branch Ponds Brook, is made up of *Traveler rhyolite*, a combination of lava and volcanic ash that has a chemical composition similar to that of granite. Notice how these rocks were uplifted at some point, and now tilt decidedly toward the north.

Were you to continue downstream you'd see this gray polished rhyolite yielding to a younger bed of sedimentary rock—a mix of pebbles, sandstone, and shales laid down in an ancient sea. It's in such sedimentary rock, especially around South Branch Pond Campground, that you'll find a wealth of fossils. Fossils, incidentally, are not just actual pieces of prehistoric life, but any trace that such life forms did in fact exist. Thus the imprint of a shell or leaf or even a footprint is considered a fossil. In this particular region of Baxter Park some of the most common fossils are those of *brachiopods*, which are small, bottom-dwelling marine animals that look similar to clams. In some parts of the world these are known as lampshells, due to their resemblance to early Roman oil lamps. Brachiopods still exist today, but their heyday was in the Paleozoic era, 225 to 500 million years ago. Thus far, scientists have described nearly 30,000 different species.

It's humbling to stand beside the prints of organisms that were going about their business more than six million human lifetimes ago. Likewise, the thought of the rise and fall of entire mountains, the filling and draining of vast inland seas, the inch-by-inch advances and retreats of enormous ice sheets, can push the imagination into a dizzy spin of timelessness. Indeed, perhaps it's at places like Katahdin, where the inertia of the world seems showcased in every nook, on every horizon, that we stand the best chance of finding some kind of a window into the restless underpinnings of eternity.

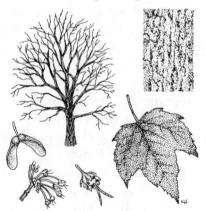

Red Maple

· Suggested Reading ·

Bell, Michael. *The Face of Connecticut*. Hartford, Conn.: Department of Environmental Protection, 1985.

Beston, Henry. *The Outermost House*. New York: Ballantine, 1985.

Cronon, William. *Changes in the Land*. New York: Hill and Wang, 1983.

Delaney, Edmund. *The Connecticut River*. Chester: The Globe Pequot Press, 1983.

Eckstorm, Fannie Hardy. *Indian Place Names of the Penobscot Valley and the Maine Coast*. Orono: The University of Maine, 1978.

Hakola, John W. *Legacy of a Lifetime: The Story of Baxter State Park*. Woolwich, Maine: TBW Books, 1981.

Johnson, Charles W. *Bogs of the Northeast*. Hanover, N.H.: University Press of New England, 1985.

Jones, L.R., and F.V. Rand. *The Handbook of Vermont Shrubs and Woody Vines*. Rutland, Vt.: Charles E. Tuttle Company, 1979.

Jorgensen, Neil. *A Guide to New England's Landscape*. Chester, Conn.: The Globe Pequot Press, 1977.

———. *A Sierra Club Naturalist's Guide: Southern New England*. San Francisco: Sierra Club Books, 1978

Hill, Ralph Nading. *Yankee Kingdom: Vermont and New Hampshire.* Woodstock, Vt.: Countryman Press, 1984.

Kendall, David L. *Glaciers and Granite: A Guide to Maine's Landscape and Geology.* Camden, Maine: Down East Books, 1987.

Marchand, Peter J. *North Woods.* Boston: Appalachian Mountain Club, 1987.

Peattie, Donald Culross. *A Natural History of Trees of Eastern and Central North America.* Boston: Houghton Mifflin, 1966.

Peterson, McKenny. *A Field Guide to Wildflowers: Northeastern/Northcentral America.* Peterson Field Guides. New York: Houghton Mifflin, 1968.

Simmons, William S. *Spirit of the New England Tribes.* Hanover, N.H.: University Press of New England, 1986.

Sutton, Ann, and Myron Sutton. *Eastern Forests.* Audubon Society Nature Guides. New York: Alfred A. Knopf, 1987.

Teal, John, and Mildred Teal. *Life and Death of the Salt Marsh.* New York: Ballantine, 1969.

Thoreau, Henry David. *The Maine Woods.* New York: Penguin Books, 1988.

Tree, Christina. *How New England Happened.* Boston: Little, Brown and Company, 1976.

Van Diver, Bradford B. *Roadside Geology of Vermont and New Hampshire.* Missoula, Mont.: Mountain Press Publishing, 1987.

· Index ·

· About the Author ·

Gary Ferguson has been a full-time freelance writer for 13 years. His natural history and travel articles have appeared in more than 100 national magazines, including *Travel-Holiday*, *Modern Maturity*, *Sierra*, *Outside*, *Ford Times*, and productions of New York's Children's Television Workshop. He is also the author of 10 books on nature, science, and medicine, including *Northwest Walks* (Fulcrum, 1995) and *Rocky Mountain Walks* (Fulcrum, 1993), and *Walking Down the Wild* (Simon &

Schuster, 1993). His 1990 coffee-table book, *Montana National Forests*, received the National Association for Interpretation Award for Excellence in Communication.

Before beginning his freelance writing career, Gary spent four years as a naturalist with the U.S. Forest Service. He lives in Red Lodge, Montana, with his wife, Jane.

· About the Illustrator ·

Kent Humphreys is a respected illustrator of both natural history and medical subjects. He has 10 books to his credit, including *Rocky Mountain Walks*, *Northwest Walks*, and *The Heart Attack Recovery Handbook*. Kent lives in Ashland, Oregon.